D0468800

RIVER DOG

Also by Mark Shand

SKULDUGGERY
TRAVELS ON MY ELEPHANT
QUEEN OF THE ELEPHANTS

RIVER DOG

A Journey Down the Brahmaputra

MARK SHAND

LITTLE, BROWN

A *Little, Brown* Book

First published in Great Britain in 2002 by Little, Brown

Copyright © Mark Shand 2002

The moral right of the author has been asserted.

The author and publishers thank The Society of Authors
as the Literary Representatives of the Estate of John Masefield
for their permission to quote from *Cargoes*.

All rights reserved.
No part of this publication may be reproduced,
stored in a retrieval system, or transmitted,
in any form or by any means, without the prior permission
in writing of the publisher, nor be otherwise circulated
in any form of binding or cover other than that in which it is published
and without a similar condition including this condition
being imposed on the subsequent purchaser.

A CIP catalogue record for this book
is available from the British Library.

Typeset in Sabon by M Rules
Printed and bound in Great Britain
by Clays Ltd, St Ives plc

Little, Brown
An imprint of
Time Warner Books UK
Brettenham House
Lancaster Place
London WC2E 7EN

www.TimeWarnerBooks.co.uk

For Ayesha and Clio
with love always

If you pick up a starving dog
and make him prosperous,
he will not bite you.
This is the principal difference
between a dog and a man.

Mark Twain

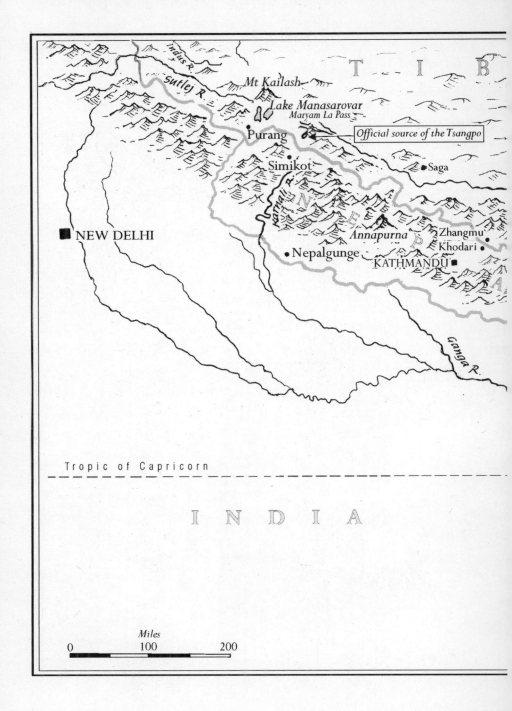

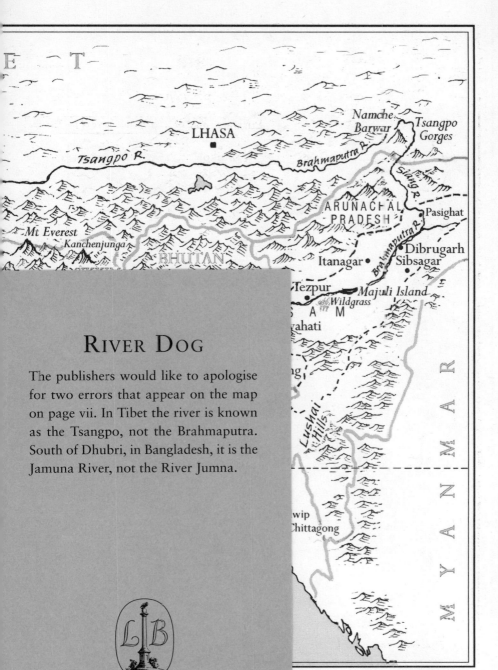

RIVER DOG

The publishers would like to apologise for two errors that appear on the map on page vii. In Tibet the river is known as the Tsangpo, not the Brahmaputra. South of Dhubri, in Bangladesh, it is the Jamuna River, not the River Jumna.

LITTLE, BROWN

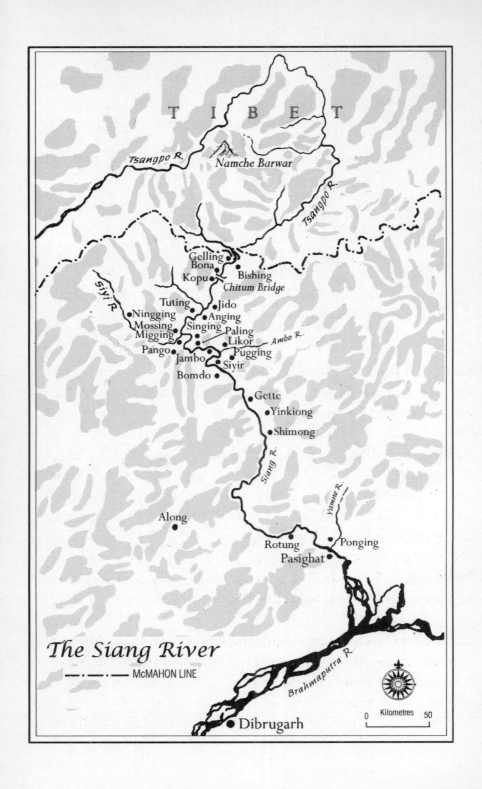

T I B E T

Tsangpo R.

Namche Barwar

Tsangpo R.

Siyir R.

Gelling
Bona
Kopu
Bishing
Chitum Bridge

Tuting
Ningging
Mossing
Migging
Singing
Jido
Anging
Paling
Likor
Ambo R.
Pango
Jambo
Pugging
Siyir
Bomdo

Gette

Yinkiong

Shimong

Siang R.

Yanne R.

Along

Rotung
Ponging
Pasighat

The Siang River

— · · — · · — McMAHON LINE

Brahmaputra R.

● Dibrugarh

0   Kilometres   50

ACKNOWLEDGEMENTS

Foremost I would like to thank Charles Allen. Not only did he give me the inspiration, he selflessly allowed me to hijack his dream. He even introduced me to the River. Salaams.

I am deeply indebted to the following people. Without their help, I would not have been able to embark on my journey: Salman Haidar; Lord Howe of Aberavon; Dr L. M. Singhvi; Mr A. H. Mahmood Ali; Sir David Gore-Booth; Smt Maneka Gandhi; HE the High Commissioner to Bangladesh, David Walker; Krupa David; Abu Subhan; Ranjit Barthakur; Manju Barua; Ambuj Sharma; John Edwards; Dinesh Kumar; John Greengrass; Geoffrey Fairhurst; Vira Mehta; and Ozing Dai.

I relied heavily on the generosity and kindness of many different people in many different countries and from all walks of life. Some have preferred to remain anonymous. Others I never knew their names. I thank you all very sincerely.

In India: the Government of India; the Ministry of Home Affairs;

the Ministry of Defence; the Government of Arunachal Pradesh; the Government of Assam; the Government of Meghalaya; GSO 1 (Intelligence) HQ Eastern Command, Fort William, Calcutta; Shri Apang Gegong; Shri Pranab K. R. Bora; Shri Naba K. R. Das; Basker Kulbe; Ranjit Choudhury; Gayatri Barua; Mr B. C. Paul; Gudu and Christina Patnaik; Arin Ghosh IFS; Bijon and Anita Dey; Bheem Dev Varma; Manjula Patankar; Mrs Kamla Devi Jadhav; Moumin Latif; Bob Wright; Shenny Italia; Alka Abrahams; Rajan Dowerah; Pratima Pandey; The Goodricke Group Ltd, Kolkata; Dr Diptimonto Baruah; Mary Gogoi; Colonel M. M. Mitra; 11 Assam Rifles; Flt Lt Shantanu Basu; Flt Officer R. V. Prakash; 127 HV AF 'First of The Ranas'; Ruplal Singh; Indra Singh; Prodeep and Rani Boruah; Yani Dai; Ajoy Brahma; Ajeet Kapoor; Dr S. S. Pandey; Dr Samar S. Mahendran; Sundip De; Prabin Tanti; Mr Raju Das; Mr and Mrs Rana Jung; Mr and Mrs N. K. Puri; Ms Sangeeta Goswami; Shri Azam Siddique; Ms Meenakshi Sharma; People for Animals, New Delhi; People for Animals, Guwahati; Dulal Saikia; Muhikanta Bora; Mr S. N. Singh; Mr S. Dutt; Mr C. B. Mitra; Shri Matilal Baraik; Ken Washington; Mr P. R. S. Oberoi and the management and staff of the Oberoi Hotel, New Delhi; Tiger Mountain India; Wild Grass Tourist Camp, Kaziranga; Mr Khan and the staff of the East End Hotel, Dibrugarh.

In Bangladesh: the Government for the People's Republic of Bangladesh; the British High Commission; Duncan Brothers (Bangladesh) Ltd; Farooq Sobhan; Mr Md F. Karim; M. Shafiqul Hasan; M. Shah Alam; A. W. Choudhury; Tamiz; Juned A. Choudhury; M. Aminul Islam Khan; Lt Col. Md. Abul Basher; The Bangladesh Rifles; Mrs Nahar; M. Yusuf Hossain; Don Bradley; Azad Shamsi; Mahavir Pati B.

In Tibet: John Bulmer; Alastair Kenneil; George Allen; and special thanks to Binod Rai and his team for keeping me alive.

In Nepal: Jagdish and Philemon Rai of Nepal Insight Trekking;

Tiger Mountain Nepal; Carolyn Syangbo; Steve Webster; and my great friend Lisa Choegyal.

In England: the Indian High Commission; the High Commission for the People's Republic of Bangladesh; Peter Leggat; Alex Grembein; Katie Garrod; Emily Cloney; Bobbie Ferguson; Nicholas Claxton; Peter Firstbrook; Caroline Casey; Patrick Mark; Dugal Muller; Teddy Goldsmith for allowing me unlimited access to his extraordinarily eclectic library; Alexander Goldsmith; Raphael Brandon; Clive Lathey; David Pritchard; Joan Falconer; Ben Elliot and the team at Quintessentially.com; Mike O'Neill; the Oriental and India Office at the British Library; Dr Rita Gardner and Nigel Winser; the Royal Geographical Society; and Cotswold Adventure Travel.

From my publishers Little, Brown, I would like to thank my editor Tim Whiting, Joanna Thurman, Rachael Ludbrook, Catherine Hill and Linda Silverman. I would also like to thank Phillippa Harrison, who originally commissioned the book, and my agent, Abner Stein.

I owe an enormous debt of gratitude to Annabel and Simon Elliot who housed, fed and generally put up with me and my moods at their house in Dorset for four long months while I wrote the book; to the Rajmata of Jaipur for her patience, kindness and hospitality while I was in Delhi; to Don McCullin for being the most dependable of friends; and, as always, to my father, Bruce Shand, and Gita Mehta, who either consoled or cracked the whip when the going got tough.

For my fellow travelling companions, no acknowledgement is enough. Very special thanks to the crews of the *Kailash*, the *Koyel*, the *Tanvir* and *Oh God*; and to Neeraj Pathania; Jaro Dai; Nawang Topgay; Yatish Bahuguna; F. H. M. Shamsuzzaman – 'Shaams'; and of course to my old friend and veteran of many journeys together and many more to come, Aditya Patankar.

Finally, whom I can never thank enough, the Assamese siblings

Reeta Dev Verma and Ranesh Roy, the former for giving me Bhaiti, the latter for giving him a home.

Oh. How could I forget. A huge hug to the most faithful of *all* companions – my Tripuri hound from the Lushai Hills of Assam – Bhaiti.

PREFACE

Aloof, mysterious and forbidding, high on the desolate plateau of western Tibet stands a 6714-metre pyramid of rock, snow and ice. Though it is not as high as many other Himalayan peaks it is infinitely more powerful. It is Asia's most sacred mountain, revered as the home of their gods by Hindus, Buddhists, Jains and Bonpos.

In its metaphysical aspect it was called Meru, the axis of the universe, the navel of the world. It stood 84,000 leagues high with four walls of crystal, gold, ruby and lapis lazuli. From its summit fell a stream that formed a lake, one of the highest and holiest bodies of water in the world. From the lake emerged four great rivers in copper pipes which circled the lake seven times before taking their respective courses to the north, to the south, to the east and to the west.

In its earthly incarnation the mountain has two names: Kailash, the 'crystal', or Kangri Rinpoche, the 'jewel of snows'. The lake is Manasarovar, the 'lake born in the mind of God', or Mapham Tso, the 'turquoise lake'. The four rivers are the Indus or Lion River flowing to the north, the Karnali or Peacock River (a main tributary of the Ganges) to the south, the Sutlej or Elephant River to the west, and the Brahmaputra, the Horse River, flowing to the east.

Like a gem of infinite value, Kailash demands the most awesome array of security. It is surrounded by some of the greatest natural barriers on earth: to the north and to the east, the vast and inhospitable deserts of the Takla Makan and the Gobi; and, to the south, the white fortress of the Himalayan range.

From the peaks of Nanga Parbat in the extreme west to Namche Barwa in the extreme east, a collection of strange, brave and eccentric individuals succeeded in infiltrating that fortress over a period of four centuries, drawn by the secrets that lay beyond, in the 'forbidden land' of Tibet. They came to find the Crystal Mountain and the Holy Lake and to locate the sources and trace the courses of the four great rivers. They came to find fame and fortune; they came to find spiritual enlightenment; and they came to spy. Many returned. Some did not.

A more diverse group is hard to imagine: Jesuit priests and Japanese monks; soldiers of fortune, swamis and shikaris; gentlemen travellers, geographers, cartographers, and botanists; pilgrims, political officers and the indomitable pundits – the Indian explorers that Her Majesty's Government employed as spies in the nineteenth century.

Their accounts of what they found were as diverse as the ways in which they sent them back – from maps drawn in blood to tiny rolls of detailed notes hidden in prayer wheels. For centuries many of their findings remained hidden from the public eye. One or two were published and became instant bestsellers, like Edward Savage Landor's *Forbidden Land*, but most, if official recognition was desired, were destined for the clinical, priggish and sometimes biased scrutiny of that bastion of Victorian exploration – the Royal Geographical Society.

Here, a distinguished frock-coated committee debated and

dissected reports from the field to establish their veracity. No stone was left unturned: fellowship of the august institution was the prized reward. A candidate's destiny lay in its hands. Brave men emerged bemedalled and lauded or else simply rejected out of hand, their claims tarnished with suspicion. In one or two extreme cases, controversy demanded that awards were declared void and they were stripped of their fellowships, never to be reinstated, their life in ruins.

The astonishing exploits of these remarkable individuals remained for many years largely unknown, except by those with a particular interest in that period of Asian exploration. Even then, it was a question of trawling the relevant libraries, sifting through the journals, papers and maps of the Royal Geographical Society and relying on the goodwill of second-hand travel-book dealers.

But in 1982 the writer, historian and explorer Charles Allen compiled their stories in his book *A Mountain in Tibet: The Search for Mount Kailash and the Sources of the Great Rivers of India*. Here, in the high adventure, colour and excitement of his pages, I found the inspiration for and makings of a journey: a journey that has haunted, fascinated and frustrated me for over twenty years. It was a journey down a river, no ordinary river but one that spans three countries, and embraces three religions. Charles Allen called the voyage I imagined the 'last great Asian adventure'. For me it was to become in many ways the last great Asian misadventure. I planned to follow the Brahmaputra River from its source to the sea. No one is known to have travelled its entire length.

ONE

A river born of legends, the Brahmaputra begins its long journey as a tiny glacial stream and sweeps eighteen hundred miles to end its journey, as wide as a sea, in the Bay of Bengal.

Brahmaputra means the 'son of Brahma', the great Hindu god of creation. And, as Jere Van Dyk, another twentieth-century explorer wrote, 'like a Hindu deity the river has many avatars, or incarnations, changing its names and nature with the myriad cultures and landscapes'. In western Tibet it is the Tamchok or Horse River, while in central and eastern Tibet it is simply the Tsangpo or The River; in Arunachal Pradesh in north-east India it becomes the Siang; in Assam it's known traditionally as the Lohit or Red River; and in Bangladesh it becomes by turns the Jamuna, the Padma and finally the Meghna.

The true source of the Brahmaputra lies some sixty miles south-east of Mount Kailash, in the ranges of the Chemayungdung mountains. The spring which spills from the glacier is known as Tamchok Khambab – 'coming out of the celestial horse's mouth'. The Tibetans say that the water is cold, the sands are composed of cats' eyes and emeralds and those who drink from the newborn stream become as strong as horses. From here the Tsangpo, the highest river in the world with an average elevation of around 4000 metres gathers breadth and volume from the melting snows and winds its way eastwards, separating the great Himalayan ranges from the vast, empty deserts of Tibet.

In eastern Tibet the snow-capped massif of Namche Bawar (7765 metres) blocks the Tsangpo's eastward progress, forcing it into a dramatic hairpin bend. From here it drops a phenomenal 3050 metres over 150 miles, twisting like an angry serpent through a series of tortuous and precipitous chasms that form what is now officially proved to be the deepest valley in the world – the 5030-metre Tsangpo Gorge.

As the Siang, the river thunders over the McMahon Line, the disputed India–China border, and through the remote and forbidden state of Arunachal Pradesh, the 'land of the dawn-lit clouds', one of the last unexplored regions on earth.

Fortified by tributaries, the river broadens majestically, sweeping westwards through Assam, from where, fuelled by further tributaries from the north and now known as the Jamuna, it races south, rising into Bangladesh like a tidal wave. Every monsoon season it engulfs around two-thirds of this densely populated country, leaving millions homeless.

Here, it meets at a major confluence another great river nearing its journey's end – the sacred Ganges. Like twins separated at birth to pursue their own destinies, the Ganga, the 'mother of all rivers', and the 'son of Brahma', the father of all rivers, join thousands of miles later in their old age and flow together as the Padma towards the sea.

To complete the trinity it finally becomes the Meghna, fragmenting into a maze of watery arteries, like the roots of some colossal, ancient tree, rushing down into the Indian Ocean as the largest river delta in the world.

By the beginning of the twentieth century exploration of Tibet was, in effect, done and dusted. The mystical legends of Mount Kailash and Lake Manasarovar had been reduced to solid geographical fact, and the sources and courses of three of the great Asian rivers located and traced. But for centuries the exact course of the Brahmaputra of India or the Tsangpo of Tibet had puzzled geographers, mapmakers and explorers. Were they two separate rivers, or one? No one knew, because no one had been able to penetrate the Tsangpo Gorges. To all intents and purposes, the Tsangpo seemed to disappear when it hit the Namche Bawar. Fanciful tales, lack of precise information and inaccurate maps had led to a popular belief that the Brahmaputra started south of the Himalayas, while the Tsangpo was thought to be an extension of the Irrawaddy in Burma. Indeed, one imaginative map of 1654 showed its source in a lake north of Burma.

But there was another body of opinion. As early as 1715, a young Jesuit priest, Ippolito Desideri from Pistóia in northern Tuscany, had gained information while travelling in western Tibet that these two rivers were one and the same: 'Flowing from west to east it [the Tsangpo] traverses the centre of Third Tibet [Tibet proper] and then turning to the south-east enters the country of Lhoba whence it descends to Rongmati [Assam], a province of Mogor [Mogul India] beyond the Ganges, into which this principal river of Tibet at last flows.'

Unfortunately this priceless information lay gathering dust for another 150 years, along with all Ippolito's other Tibetan work, on the bookshelves of a country villa in Italy.

Seventy years later, in 1785, Major James Rennell, Surveyor-General of Bengal, reached the same conclusion as Ippolito. Known as the 'father of Indian geography', Rennell wrote, 'This river must needs have a very long course before it enters the Bengal provinces, since four hundred miles from the sea it is twice as big as the Thames . . . [There is] the strongest presumptive proof possible of the Sanpoo and the Burrumpooter, being one and the same river.'

However, to dispel the more popular belief about their being two entirely separate rivers, positive proof was needed. At the beginning of the nineteenth century, having annexed Assam in India's north-east frontier after the Anglo-Burmese war, the British launched a two-pronged attack. While continuing to trace the course of the river downstream from Tibet, they now started sending expeditions upstream, to follow the tributaries of the Brahmaputra from the south through the unexplored and inhospitable jungles of what is now known as Arunachal Pradesh.

There the British endured terrible hardships and danger, not only from the fever-ridden forests, but also from the indigenous tribal people, particularly the Abors – a fierce tribe described as 'a very rude barbarous people of open manners and warlike habits' and 'very averse to receiving strangers'. The Abors, or Adis as they are known today, continued to be a thorn in the side of the British for another century.

By 1878, nonetheless, the gap was closing. There now remained only about three hundred miles of territory left to explore, where the river itself seemed to disappear into the bowels of the earth, through the great range of the eastern Himalayas.

It would be another thirty-five years before British explorers effectively established the Tsangpo and Brahamputra connection, though even then large sections of the Tsangpo Gorge remained unpenetrated. The speed with which the river fell in those unknown stretches was so rapid that it gave rise to one of the great romances of geography: the belief that hidden in the depths of the gorges must be a Tibetan equivalent of the Victoria or Niagara Falls. It took a further eleven years before the myth of the 'fabled falls' of the Brahmaputra was exploded.

There then followed a hiatus of some sixty years or so before any further exploration of the Brahmaputra was undertaken. This owed as much to politics as anything else. China invaded Tibet and refused to recognise the McMahon Line, the disputed border that divides Tibet and India along the eastern Himalayas, drawn up at the Simla Conference of 1914 between the British and the Tibetans. Then in India, after Partition in 1947, Prime Minister Jawaharial Nehru instituted a policy of restricting all outsiders from the region known as NEFA (North-East Frontier Agency), now Arunachal Pradesh, in order to protect the unique culture and autonomy of the indigenous tribal people. Further south, meanwhile, Bangladesh and India, never the most harmonious of neighbours, continued to squabble and differ over control of the subcontinent's greatest river.

By the late 1980s the political situation had if anything worsened. In 1962, China had blitzkrieged into India. Now rumours of war were again rife. Once again, Chinese and Indian troops had massed along the McMahon Line as India had recently declared Arunachal Pradesh a federal state. Farther south in Assam, another conflict was gaining notoriety – traditional guerrilla factions were fighting for autonomy. Foreigners were hardly welcome in any of these areas.

But by the 1990s the political climate had changed dramatically. Tibet had become more accessible and a limited number of Indian pilgrims and even some foreigners were once again allowed in to visit Mount Kailash. Further east explorers, mountaineers, climbers, rafters, white-water kayakers, trekkers, canyoneers, Tibetan scholars and scientists were flooding into the Tsangpo Gorges. However, the border area below the gorges where the Tsangpo/Brahmaputra leaves Tibet was still completely out of bounds.

India too was beginning to relax her grip, a little. From 1994, permits for groups of four or more foreigners could be obtained, with difficulty and great expense, to visit a few carefully monitored areas of Arunachal Pradesh. But not for where I wanted to go. And

I certainly did not want to travel in a group. Apart from joint foreign rafting expeditions with the Indian army and border police,
the border area where the Brahmaputra entered India was, like
Tibet, forbidden territory, as was farther south.

Assam, more auspiciously, although still volatile and carefully
monitoring foreigners, was now open. And poor old Bangladesh
suffered from completely the opposite problem – a lack of foreign
visitors. I did not foresee any difficulties there.

Over the years since the late 1980s, I had monitored the situation quietly, gathering research and information, making contacts
and biding my time. Meanwhile I had been involved with much
more important things – getting married and having a daughter.
But the river was waiting, and I was getting impatient. And the
moment I decided that it was time to get going, things began to fall
into place. One thing in particular was the final catalyst I needed to
embark on what for years had seemed a totally overambitious
dream. It was a meeting with the man who had given me the inspiration, who had in effect thrown down the challenge all those
years ago – Charles Allen.

It was spring 1996, and I was living in the English countryside
writing another book about elephants. My former travelling companion and great friend from India, the photographer Aditya
Patankar who had accompanied me on all my elephant journeys,
was staying with me recovering from a hip operation. Charles
was coming to see Aditya to discuss the photographs for a new
book on India, though Aditya was a little worried that he might
not turn up. 'Charles,' he explained, 'can be a little vague. He once
flew out to India to attend an important wedding. The son of a
maharajah friend of ours was getting married. Charles arrived a
day late.'

I admit I was apprehensive too, but for different reasons. I was
about to meet a legend: a man who had grown up in the jungles of
Assam; who had already written a dozen or so books; who'd been

one of the first foreigners to reach the Cow's Mouth, the traditional source of the Ganges; and who had trekked and climbed extensively throughout the world, including an arduous solo walk through the Himalayas. He was one of my heroes: a gifted writer, an explorer, and a scholar to boot.

At least I knew now that he was vaguely human, fallible, for over the years I'd built up a rather frightening mental portrait of my hero. I'd imagined a man who would not suffer fools gladly – one of those dry, silent, mountaineering types, bearded, weather-beaten and flinty-eyed, with perhaps a finger or two or a toe missing from frostbite, and a half-translated Sanskrit manuscript stuffed casually in his pocket. I was convinced that he wouldn't take me seriously.

As it turned out, neither Aditya nor I need have worried. Charles arrived bang on time, and he didn't have a beard either. In fact, he was meticulously clean-shaven, trim and fit, with an alert, upright, almost military bearing – a real pukka sahib. A pair of running shoes peeked out incongruously from under his neatly pressed corduroy trousers and behind metal-framed spectacles his eyes glistened with curiosity, humour and excitement. I could tell instinctively that this was a man who was up for adventure, and the minute he opened his mouth I was spellbound.

It was like being pulled along in the slipstream of a shooting star. Over lunch Charles talked, and talked. All I did was listen as one extraordinary story dovetailed into another and then flashed off at a tangent. It was both fascinating and frustrating trying to follow him: in about twenty minutes we had been up the Himalayas, down the Himalayas, into tantric rituals and out through the unimaginable splendour and extravagance of the great Indian durbars in the days of the British Raj. But there was only one place I wanted to go – down the Brahmaputra. And I had the world's greatest historical expert sitting right here. I couldn't contain myself any longer.

'Charles,' I interrupted. 'In your book, *A Mountain in Tibet*, there is that line you wrote about the last great Asian adventure.'

He looked at me, confused.

'Hang on,' I said, 'I'll show you.' I rushed out and returned with a huge plastic folder that I slapped down in front of him. 'Take a look at this,' I said proudly. 'I've researched every inch of the river. Do you think it's possible to do?'

It was as if a tap had been turned off hastily, the silence only broken by the sound of the occasional drip as Charles very slowly, very methodically started to turn the pages of my Brahmaputra file. He had turned, I noticed, a strange ashen colour.

The silence continued. I looked at Aditya. He looked back at me, and shrugged, a puzzled expression on his face.

'Er, Charles,' I ventured at last. 'Is there a problem?' Perhaps he had found a mistake.

Charles closed the file quietly. He stared at its cover for a moment, and sighed.

'Yes, there is a problem,' he answered finally, his voice a mere whisper. He seemed suddenly to have shrunk in size. 'But it's not about the river. I've always believed it's possible. Your file confirms it more than ever. The problem . . .' He paused, as if he were search-ing for the words. 'The problem is that I was planning to do it. I've dreamed about making this journey ever since I wrote my book.'

Oh fuck, I thought. So that explained his strange reaction. I couldn't believe it. I was gutted.

There was another long, awkward silence.

'Perhaps we should all have a drink,' Aditya suggested diplo-matically, hobbling out of the room.

'Well, Charles,' I said at last through gritted teeth, wishing he had never entered my door. 'You must do it. It's your story, and you're the expert.' It was a struggle to sound gracious. In the past, in the tradition of the great Victorian explorers, we would proba-bly either have stood up, shaken hands solemnly, wished each other fame and fortune and agreed may the best man win, or challenged each other to a duel. At that moment I was mentally selecting my choice of weapon.

Charles shot to his feet and eyed me intently, as if he were making a momentous decision. Thinking he might attack me, I prepared to defend myself. But unlike me, he was a true gentleman, a pukka sahib. A wry smile flickered across his face. 'What a buggers' muddle,' he said suddenly, and then he laughed. 'Although it really pisses me off and I'm as jealous as hell, you must do it, Mark. I think you're just mad enough to pull it off. And, to be honest, I'm working on something else at the moment. Something *really* extraordinary.'

'What?' I asked, intrigued.

He laughed again. 'Forget it. Knowing you, you'd steal that as well.' Charles was back to full speed, bristling with energy: the tap turned on as suddenly as it had been turned off. 'Now, let's look at maps.'

For the rest of that afternoon, Charles told me everything he knew. He brought the river to life: its colour and size, its smells and moods, the stories I would never find in a library, a wonderful, evocative alchemy of strange tales and bizarre anecdotes that only someone who'd lived there could create.

'You must try to find the lost copper temple and what the British troops called "the penis park",' he announced, stabbing his finger on an old map of Upper Assam. 'They were somewhere near here. I remember my father talking about them when I was a child. And if you go to Shillong, see if you can track down Million, Billion, Trillion and Snow White. They'll be very old, though – probably dead. It was a long time ago.'

He noticed my astonishment.

'The war was on and Shillong was full of troops,' he explained, 'and they had a ball, because the women there, the Khasis, were, how shall I put it, pretty liberal with their favours. Particularly these four beautiful girls. They were infamous. Of course I was only a young boy. I named my chickens after them.'

As the afternoon wore on, Charles and I also discovered that we shared a common hero – the indomitable Kinthup, one of the extraordinary nineteenth-century Indian pundits, the geographer-spies employed by Her Majesty's Government. Kinthup's mission was to trace the course of the Tsangpo/Brahmaputra by throwing five hundred marked logs, each a foot long, downstream. It took him four years of almost inconceivable hardship, determination and bravery, and he was all but forgotten at the end of it. His resolve, his tenacity, his devotion to duty – and his attachment to the river – inspired us both. He never let it get the better of him: he never gave up. If I had only a fraction of Kinthup's courage on my own journey, I realised, I might just succeed.

By the end of the day, Charles and I had become firm friends, and although he wouldn't be coming with me, he was, I sensed, a man I could travel with. There are very few people one can say that of. And, without being presumptuous, I had this curious feeling that he thought the same about me. As I waved him goodbye, he wound down the window of his car. 'I just might join you in Assam,' he said wistfully. 'I've always wanted to find that penis park.'

TWO

The meeting with Charles was just what I needed to get going in earnest. The dreaming was over: it was time to start organising, and that meant applying for permits. It is what I call the paper journey: every traveller's nightmare but a necessary and unavoidable preamble. I was an old hand at bureaucracy, having dealt with the labyrinthine intricacies of Indian officialdom in the past, but this turned out to be something quite surreal. The problem was that my river journey was going to take me from Chinese-controlled Tibet into India, never the most harmonious of neighbours, and across a border that had been closed on both sides for centuries, the disputed McMahon Line.

I'd worked out that the journey itself, about 1800 miles, would occupy around six months: three for the upper stage in Tibet and three for the lower stages. Incredibly, the infamous, interminable paper journey took four times as long: two whole, grinding years. And the worst of it was that, in the end, it failed. I was not, it finally became clear, going to be allowed to cross that border. Because of the tension between two countries, I would have to make another journey, an immense detour, to avoid a stretch of land a few miles wide that lay between them. There was no entry to this no man's land. Instead, staggeringly, I was going to have to go down the river in Tibet to the border; then back up to Lhasa; then by plane to Kathmandu and thence to Delhi; and from there, in stages, back to the Indian side of the border a short distance from where I'd left. I could have waved at myself on the other side. But politics are politics. I was going to have to do it their way.

So, I would do the journey in two halves. It still was not going to be easy to get all the permissions, but by circumventing the border issue at least I had removed the major obstacle to progress. By now it was early 1998 and, with the end of the most painful bureaucracy distantly in sight, I could begin to concentrate on the practicalities of departure.

The logistics I left in the experienced hands of friends at Tiger Mountain in Nepal and India. Their company had pioneered Himalayan and jungle treks in Asia and if anybody could keep me alive they could. For the upper course of the river in Tibet they told me I would travel with a substantial support team: a Tibetan-speaking Nepalese Sherpa, a cook, an assistant cook and an assistant to the assistant cook, plus a truck to carry supplies and two drivers. I thought this a little excessive. It sounded as if it were a culinary expedition I was embarking on.

I got a curt reply from headquarters in Kathmandu, telling me that Tibet was cold – numbingly cold. The wind would flay me to the bone. And it was high, bloody high. Once in, I was on my own. Blah, blah, blah, I thought. And then they told me there was no food. 'Food,' they wrote, 'is fuel. Without fuel you die. Think about it.'

I didn't need to. It was the killer punch. I felt better when I read a nineteenth-century account of Tibetan travel by one of those hardened Victorian explorers. This gentleman travelled with thirty porters for his luggage and another thirty just for his food – all supplied by the Bovril company.

For the lower course of the river, I was informed I would be accompanied by what was described to me as 'a solid, dependable trekking type' and one cook. In the tribal areas of Arunachal Pradesh where the river was completely unnavigable we would pick up a local guide and porters. Food there, I was assured, was not a problem. The Adis were superb hunters – they shot and trapped anything that moved. Rats and beetles were apparently a great delicacy. And in Bangladesh a major tea company had offered the services of a planter as a guide.

The next question was one of timing, and that, permissions aside, was going to be determined by weather. The window for travel in Tibet is very small, but for what I was trying to do it was minuscule, almost impossible. The best time to reach the Chang Tang plateau in western Tibet is between May and July, after the snow melt, when access is possible over the high passes. And realistically the only time to negotiate the gorges in eastern Tibet is from September to November, after the monsoons, when the river is low. To attempt those deep gorges in the heavy monsoons is to invite disaster. The torrential rain makes the tiny, dizzy tracks that cling to the sides of the precipices almost impassable, if there are any tracks at all: landslides are a daily hazard.

So, ideally, the upper course of the river in Tibet should be travelled in two stages: during the summer in western and central Tibet, and the autumn in eastern Tibet. But for me, this was out of the question. Logistics, permissions and, above all, expense prohibited such a lengthy option.

I had given myself three months. I was going to have to take a risk. I could either hope for an early snow melt, get into western Tibet at the beginning of April and make my way down the river and through the gorges by the end of June before the monsoons; or leave in September or October, hope winter came late and get down the river and the gorges by the end of November before Tibet was sealed in its icy grip.

Nowadays, weather conditions change alarmingly suddenly. But on the roof of the world, they are notoriously unpredictable. If I got it wrong, I could either end up in a watery grave or an icy tomb. It was a gamble, but I had to make a decision because I only had a month left for the spring window and it was closing fast. I opted for the icy tomb. I would go, whatever happened, in September, and pray to the gods for clement weather. I would return and embark on the second part of the journey through India and Bangladesh in January. There, short of an earthquake or a cyclone, the weather conditions should be more agreeable.

Eighteen hundred miles through three countries. From 5715 metres to sea level through arctic conditions of snow and ice, to the fever-ridden humidity of jungle and river delta. I had all the gear for the bottom part of the river from my previous travels, but the mountains were a new challenge to me. It was time to go shopping, I thought happily – the only kind of shopping I really like.

When it comes to travel gear, I'm an addict. I'm like an 'It Girl' on speed during fashion week. I try to fight it every time, but it always gets the better of me. Imelda Marcos' fabled shoe collection pales in comparison to Mark Shand's 'how-to-stay-alive-in-extreme-conditions', extremely useless accessories collection. And like Imelda Marcos' shoes most of these items remain unused and unopened gathering dust in the back of a cupboard. Then, at Christmas or birthdays, family and friends become the unfortunate recipients of multi-bladed pen knifes, digital map readers, heated earmuffs and combination alarm-stopwatches that measure your pulse rate and tell you the time in a hundred zones.

But this time, I was after really extreme kit. Extreme kit for extreme weather. Ranulph Fiennes, Robert Swan, Chris Bonington, Robin Cox, Rheinholt Messner type of kit. The kind of kit that separates the professional from the amateur, the men from the boys.

My heart racing, I entered an adventure emporium that I'd visited on many occasions.

'G'day, Mark. Welcome back. Good to see you,' a young, impossibly fit Australian greeted me enthusiastically. 'Off on another one? Where to this time? Back on the old ellies?'

'Not this time,' I replied wistfully, remembering the simplicity of a lunghi and a pair of flip-flops on those long, warm elephantine days. 'Going a bit higher, to start with anyway. Himalayan region. Beyond actually. Tibet. Following a river . . . '

'Tibet, eh?' he interrupted excitedly. 'Never been there myself, but friends of mine tell me it's cold, bloody cold. Apparently it freezes the nuts off a polar bear. It's the wind, they say. Drives you mad. Never stops. Gets into your bones. We're going to have to seal you up.' He rubbed his hands together briskly. I wasn't sure if his gesture was prompted by the thought of that wind or the anticipation of what it was going to take, as he put it, to seal me up. I soon found out.

'It's all about layers nowadays,' he continued, plucking garments off racks like apples from trees. 'We'll work inside out. First, thermals – top and bottom. But not silk. Silk's out. Sweat like a sheila in silk, causes an icy layer against your skin. Makes you crook. Polyester perforated with small breathing holes is the new stuff. You'll need two sets. On top of that trekking trousers. Must be wind-resistant with plenty of pockets. Neutral colours are best. Take three pairs. Then over-trousers. I suggest Mountain Equipment Ultra Fleece. Two pairs. On top of that fleece or flannel shirts. Fleece is more expensive but better. Take two. On top of that, a fleece jacket. Fleece again, eh?' he grinned. 'I'm fleecing you, mate,' he said, and laughed uproariously at his own joke. 'Now, on top of that a good duvet jacket. Synthetic, not down. Down is useless when wet. And finally,' he paused dramatically for effect, 'we're going to seal you up. Gore-Tex – top-of-the-range shell suit, top and bottom with fixed hood and decent underarm movement.'

I eyed the growing pile with alarm. I doubted whether I would be able to move anything, let alone my arms.

'This is your barrier, your shield, your cocoon against that bloody wind. Very, very expensive though,' he said wistfully, caressing the sticky surface of what resembled a giant crinkled prophylactic. 'Colour?'

'Black,' I said emphatically.

He shook his head disapprovingly. 'Black. Not a good choice. What happens if you get lost or take a tosser? Black against snow? You'll just look like another bloody rock. They'll never bloody find you. Get something really bright, like red or yellow.'

'Black,' I repeated again firmly. I had to begin to assert my own authority. 'Black absorbs heat.'

'Well, if you say so,' he replied huffily, clearly miffed that his expertise had been challenged. 'But don't come back here and say I didn't warn you.'

Unlikely, I thought. If he was right, I'd just be another frozen rock on a Tibetan glacier.

'Now?' he continued, eager to regain the upper hand, 'you'll need a sunhat with legionnaire-style neck protection. Nothing worse than a burnt neck. Can't bloody sleep. White is best,' he added pointedly. 'It reflects the heat.'

I didn't bother to argue.

'And several pairs of fast-drying gloves, and mitts with windproof shells. And, oh yeah, a warm hat, of course. Lowe Mountain Cap with earmuffs. Well, that just about does it,' he grinned triumphantly. 'Now try it all on, mate.'

In the cramped confines of the changing room I pulled and heaved and tugged and sweated, really sweated. It was pouring off me when I finally emerged. Furtively, I peered around the door, praying the room was empty. The coast was clear and I struggled out. Then I caught a glimpse of myself in a large floor-to-ceiling mirror. I reeled back, nearly tumbling over. What loomed back in the reflection clearly wasn't me, and it clearly wasn't human. Sheathed in a shiny black condom was a giant tropical beetle.

'Got you all sealed up mate, haven't I? Couldn't squeeze a fart out of there, could you? How does it feel? Hot, eh? See you're sweating. Good.'

'Are you sure I need all of this?' I gasped. 'I can hardly breathe, let alone walk.'

'Remember, what you don't have, you don't have. Now, accessories, let's see . . . '

'I think I'll just change first,' I told him. Accessories. The mere mention of the word was enough to set my adrenaline racing. I had to control myself. I shed my skins, and as we moved slowly around the store, the battle commenced.

'Kathadyn water filter. New design. Light. Easy to use. Pump action. Comes with six spare filters.'

'No, got one.' Fifteen-love.

'Water bottles.'

'No, got them.' Thirty-love.

'Stove, MSR Whisperlite. Excellent. Never goes out. Cook a yak on it.'

'No.' Forty-love. I was winning, I was actually saying no. My confidence soared. Now he was beginning to panic. He changed his tack.

'Sunglasses,' he suggested seductively, taking a pair out from a small display cabinet. 'UV/IR resistant. Unbreakable. Lenses come in four different colours. Bloody bright where you're going. Sun slams off the ice. Burns your eyeballs out. Nothing worse than snow blindness, believe me. Try 'em on.'

I slipped on a pair of bright metallic-blue reflector shades. I looked cool, very cool.

'OK, I'll . . . '

'Two pairs,' he said quickly. 'Always take a spare pair.' Forty-fifteen.

'Now, you mentioned rivers,' he went on, not wanting to lose momentum. 'Well, these,' he held up a selection of thick, shiny black bags in different sizes, 'are 100 per cent waterproof. Made by Ortlieb. You could stuff your mother in one and throw her overboard. She'd float. Guaranteed.'

They might be useful, I thought. After all, this journey was all about water. But . . .

He sensed my hesitation. 'Imagine if your boat capsizes. All your notes, diaries, films, cameras . . . ?'

'OK, OK.' Forty-thirty.

'Better take six, different sizes.'

'OK.' Deuce. I began to panic. My mouth went dry.

'Trekking poles. Essential for balance. Force you up those long, hard, cold passes.'

'Nnnnnnnn.'

'You all right mate? You look a bit crook?'

'Om fone,' I mumbled.

'You ought to think about those poles.' He could sense victory. 'They're not just for geriatrics. All the explorers use them. Fiennes, and Swan in the Antarctic. All the climbers . . . '

I nodded quickly.

'Bob,' he yelled, 'chuck us down a couple of Leki Trekkies.' Advantage, young, impossibly fit Australian salesperson.

We were now reaching the check-out desk. I could see the welcome light of the street. I was so nearly there. I felt I had resisted. I hadn't really bought anything I didn't need. But there was one last obstacle to overcome: the large glass display cabinet where the gadgets, the toys, the really useless, expensive items were displayed. I heard the lock of the cabinet click open.

'What's that?' I whispered. My eyes zeroed in on a small rectangular object that resembled a mobile telephone. 'It's beautiful.'

'Ahh,' he said. 'That is the latest in survival technology. It's a real winner. It's a GPS. A global positioning system. You can't get lost. It's accurate to within thirty feet, anywhere in the world. You just turn it on and point it at the sky. It'll lock on to a satellite and bingo, your position is pinpointed. Here, try it.'

I felt like kissing it. It was lovely – smooth, small and snug in the palm of my sweaty hand. I turned it on. It chirped pleasantly and lots of numbers danced magically across the pretty, bright green LCD screen. I had no idea how it worked or what it did. It didn't matter. I was hooked. It chirped again. 'Buy me, buy me. I'll keep you alive, alive, alive . . . ' Game, set and match. I definitely needed counselling. Me and Imelda . . .

I had one more very important decision to make. I wanted to travel with an animal. After my journeys with elephants, I couldn't imagine being without one. They add another dimension to your travels, they take you away from yourself, and they ensure that you never get bored. Animals are always up to something. They give you something else to worry about, to care about. And in my experience, they care about you.

An elephant was obviously out of the question. There was only one animal that could hack a journey like this, given the geography, the climate and the terrain: a dog. Their fidelity is unquestionable, unlike man's; they comfort you and keep you warm at night; and in case of danger they are the ultimate alarm system. Plus, if the worst came to the worst and I was dying of hunger, I could always eat it. I've eaten dogs before and they're not bad, if a little tough. I'm sure it would understand, after all, they are called man's best friend.

There was, too, a certain doggy tradition to honour. Faithful canine companions had accompanied many of the travellers in whose footsteps I would be treading. There are splendid tales of exploits with Bingo, Bongo, Roarer, Sadie, Rover. For instance, the British-Hungarian explorer, Sir Aurel Stein, who always took his black-and-white terrier, Dash, on his journeys of discovery in central Asia at the turn of the twentieth century. Not one Dash but seven of them: Dash one, two, three, four, five, six and seven, one succeeding the other as each succumbed to the hardships of these arduous journeys. But few of the stories has a better outcome than that of the expedition of Mr St G. Littledale and his dog, Tanny. This was the stuff of doggy legend. It set my heart racing.

In 1895, Mr St G. Littledale, an English gentleman, bravely set out for the forbidden land of Tibet with his family and a little dog, Tanny. Constantly fearing detection from Tibetans, the family withstood blizzards, deserting servants and dying pack animals. Finally they were stopped by five hundred armed Tibetans only forty-nine miles from Lhasa. Neither a proffered bribe, nor Mrs Littledale's declaration that she was Queen Victoria's sister could save them from expulsion. But the Royal Geographical Society awarded Mr Littledale its Gold Medal, and Tanny was made an Honorary Fellow with a silver collar.

My fantasy was now in full flow and I could already imagine my own triumphant destiny. Fast forward a century and a half to a glorious evening at the RGS. I step forward and bow my head to tumultuous applause. From a plump velvet cushion the President takes the gold medal and places this most prestigious exploration award carefully around my neck. And then he stoops and fastens a magnificent silver collar around my faithful companion's furry neck . . .

But that was fantasy. Reality was a very different story. Although I had been brought up with dogs, I had never actually owned one. What's more, they didn't seem to like me very much. I've been savaged by them on four separate occasions and still bear the scars. There was one, though, of whom I was enormously fond, and he of me: a jet-black bull terrier called Satan, thirty kilos of pure muscle, who bore an uncanny resemblance to Mike Tyson. I had looked after Satan for a while for a friend. He and I had got on famously. His brother had killed a postman in Spain. Unfortunately the same homicidal genes ran in Satan. He was a serial dog killer. During our

all-too-brief relationship he cannibalised three Yorkshire terriers
and a Sloane Ranger's spaniel.

Obviously I had to find a different kind of dog now. Somewhere,
I was convinced, there was another one with whom I could establish a wonderful rapport. After all, I knew I had a way with
animals. I'd got an elephant to love me. A dog couldn't be *that* difficult.

I started looking first in Nepal through my friends at Tiger
Mountain. They suggested a Tibetan mastiff. But after a bit of
research I was not sure I wanted to share my three-month journey
with one. It turned out that they were a bit like Satan: large and
extremely fierce. They were splendid watchdogs, but sulky and
perfectly capable of killing and eating a thief, and the largest on
record measured well over a metre. I couldn't exactly conjure up
cosy evenings in my tent with such a monster. It was more likely
that it would end up eating me.

I turned to India, where I had found Tara my elephant, and
rang Aditya Patankar. Aditya was a Maratha nobleman, a direct
descendant of the fierce clan that had ravaged India in the seventeenth and eighteenth centuries. A man of legendary ingenuity and
resource, he would not, I knew, consider my request in any way out
of the ordinary.

'What do you want now?' he asked rather irritably when he
heard my voice.

'A dog,' I replied.

'You can't have mine,' he barked. 'Anyway, what do you want a
dog for? You've already got an elephant.'

I told him about my dog idea.

'That's easy,' he said, with just a hint of sarcasm. 'Any particular kind? Sex? Breed? Take your pick. They're everywhere –
millions of them. In fact, I'm looking at some right now out of my
window. You can have one of them. Bloody scavengers!'

'What!' I exclaimed in horror, 'You mean one of those street

dogs – a pi-dog?' I hated those curs. They had nearly driven me
mad on my elephant journeys, yapping at the heels of the elephants. My greatest pleasure had been picking them off with a
catapult.

'Get real, Mark,' he replied curtly. 'Nobody, and I mean nobody,
is going to lend *you* a dog. God knows what would happen to it. A
pi-dog would be perfect for your journey. They're as hard as nails.
They eat anything – anything. They're survivors.'

'Aren't they a bit savage?' I asked tentatively.

'No,' he said. 'Treat them well, and they'll follow you to the
ends of the earth.'

'How do you know?' I asked.

'It's in my blood,' Aditya replied. 'Marathas know about dogs –
trust me.'

'All right,' I said, hesitantly. But I was not convinced. 'How are
you going to find me one?'

'I'll catch it, of course.' He made it sound a very stupid question.

'Catch it? How?' I was intrigued.

'Leave that to me. Now, how soon do you want it?' That was
typical of the Maratha. He didn't hang around.

'Well, there's no particular hurry,' I stammered. Things were
moving alarmingly fast. 'My permissions haven't come through
yet.'

'OK.' He cut to the chase. 'What do you want – a dog or a bitch?'

I really hadn't given this much thought. In fact, no thought at all.

'Take a male,' he said authoritatively. 'Better guard dog. A bitch
is bound to come on heat. You'll be chased all the way down the
Brahmaputra.' He laughed. 'Right, I'll deal with it.' The phone
went dead.

Shit, I thought. A pi-dog. What had I let myself in for? Knowing
my luck, it would bite me, and I would die of rabies. I needed to do
some more research. First I consulted my dictionary. 'Pi-dog n.
(also pye-dog, pie-dog) an ownerless or pariah dog, esp. in Asia.

[Anglo-Indian *pye*, *paë*, Hindi *pahi* meaning "outsider".]' That was helpful. Then I looked up 'pariah'. 'Pariah n. a member of a caste in southern India, lower than the four Brahminical castes; one of low, or no caste; a social outcast; an ownerless cur of eastern Indian towns, in full, pariah dog, or pi-dog.'

It didn't sound too good. I turned to Lockwood Kipling, Rudyard's father, always, I'd found, a reliable source on all things Indian, and a champion of the downtrodden.

We say that one may as well hang a dog as give him a bad name, thereby admitting the possibility of a good one. But no such allowance seems to have been made for the Indian pariah dog . . . Tainted with the worst of the philosophy to which he gave his name some centuries ago in Greece, he reveals more of the currish side of canine character than English dogs and dog lovers are aware of. He uncovers more of his teeth when he snarls – and he often snarls – than the civilised dog; he slinks off with inverted tail at the mere hint of a blow or a caress, and his shrill bark echoes the long note of the great dog-father, the wolf, and the poor cousin, the jackal. In a fight he does not abandon himself to the delight of battle, the stern joy of the English dog, but calculates odds and backs down with an ignoble care for his skin. In short, he is a *lendi*, a cur, a coward.

For once, Lockwood Kipling had let me down. What on earth was Aditya thinking? I didn't give up – someone, somewhere must have something good to say about pi-dogs. After a lot of research I unearthed the greatest authority on them, Mr W. V. Soman. In his book *The Indian Dog* he observes that:

Practically every writer speaks of the pariah dog as ill-bred, considers it a scavenger and gives it a hideous aspect. But if reared and brought up, they turn up the best dogs. They possess the best qualities which are expected in a good breed, so they deserve meriting admiration rather than simply creating a disgust and contempt for them. Considering all the qualities of the pariah dog, such as habit, character, temperament (which may appear unpleasant when in its wild stage), we must admit that they are in no way inferior to the most favoured breeds. Their sagacious and cautious behaviour adds to their qualities. Their senses are very acute. They eat anything, from a decomposed body to vegetation.

This was great – a dog that ate everything from a decomposed body to vegetation. It was perfect in fact.

And it was from this same splendidly comprehensive work on Indian canines that I came to understand Aditya's connection with dogs. It was indeed hereditary. It was, as he said, in his blood. Aditya was a Maratha. Marathas, I learned, were dog worshippers. Not only had I found the perfect dog, but I had also found the perfect dog catcher.

Unfortunately, from the fax I soon received from him, it seemed that Aditya's obeisance to the dog gods was not up to scratch. Things were not going to plan.

'A few days ago, I found the perfect dog for you. But not a dog – she's a bitch. I feel she's just right: she's pretty, small, well built and intelligent. She has a tan coat and isn't in bad condition. She hangs around my local booze shop. The thing is, how to catch her? She's skittish and, not surprisingly, very suspicious.

'I nearly got her the first time. I parked my car near the shop. Now, you must realise Mark, this is all quite difficult. I'm not too sure of the legalities. I don't want to be arrested, so it has to be a covert night operation. Anyway, I opened the back door of the car and put some bread on the back seat, and then laid out a line of bread leading towards the back of the booze shop. I then hid behind the car. She came slowly forward, picking up the bread. She hesitated for a moment when she reached the car, and then jumped inside. I quickly slammed the door shut. I'd got her. Well, I thought I had. Unfortunately, one of the windows was open and she jumped out.'

It was hard to keep a straight face. I read on.

'I left her alone for a couple of nights, to let her settle down. Then I returned. This time I employed an ancient Maratha guerrilla-warfare capture technique, which we used when we terrorised northern India: the net. I laid exactly the same trap, not forgetting to close the windows. But instead of hiding behind the car, I lay on the roof, not with a net – with a blanket.'

I was beginning to laugh out loud. A more absurd situation for the Maratha was hard to imagine.

'Everything went exactly to plan. As she approached the back door, I dropped the blanket on her. Well, I can tell you, all hell let loose. She started to howl. Lights started to go on in the sur-rounding buildings. I had to move fast. I tried to bundle her up, but she went for me. I nearly got bitten. You've got to understand, these dogs probably all have rabies. It's bloody dangerous. Anyway, she escaped again. But don't worry, I'll think of something else.'

I couldn't resist it. I rang him. He sounded irritated and tired, and he must have sensed the mirth in my voice.

'This is not a joke, my friend,' he insisted crossly. 'I can hardly sit down. I've just had a rabies shot. The things I do for you. Finding Tara was a piece of cake compared to this.'

'Why don't you try a bit of worship,' I suggested lightly.

'What the hell are you talking about?'

'Dog worship,' I answered. 'I found out that you lot worship dogs. Get down to your temple and pull in some of that power. Hypnotise the dog. It's in your blood, after all. You told me that.' There was a long silence.

'Look,' he replied wearily, 'I'm trying to help you. I don't need another of your far-fetched stories. You're at it again. You should write fiction. Marathas were warriors. They were certainly *not* dog worshippers.'

'Oh yes they were,' I insisted. 'Well, according to the book I just read.'

'Which was probably written by another of your bloody English colonials,' he parried. 'God, they talk bollocks.'

'Not at all,' I replied smoothly. 'It was written by an Indian. Your country's greatest authority on the Indian dog – Mr W. V. Soman. 'Listen to this.' I picked up my notes. 'Apparently, at one of your shrines the ministrants used to dress up in blue woollen coats, tie belts of skins round their waists, and meet the pilgrims, barking and howling like dogs. They endeavoured, in fact, to assimilate their appearance to that of the god – your god – whom they served. Each ministrant had a bowl into which the pilgrims put food. The ministrants laid these down, fought with each other like dogs, and then, lying on the ground, put their mouths, as animals do, into the bowls and ate the contents. You see . . . ' The telephone went dead.

I was about to ring him back, but decided against it. Aditya was one of my greatest friends. We'd shared so many adventures together. I knew he'd see the funny side. No one I knew had a better sense of humour. I also knew he would find me that dog. I had now laid down a bit of a challenge. No one liked a challenge better than Aditya. He was the most determined man I'd ever met.

THREE

I wasn't to hear more from Aditya and his quest to find me a dog for some time. Instead, and quite unexpectedly, I was about to be taken to the very beginning of my journey by the man from whom I'd hijacked it. Out of the blue, and cutting across all the bureaucratic obstacles that had delayed me, Charles Allen invited me to join him on an expedition that would take in Lake Manasarovar, Mount Kailash and perhaps even the very source of the Brahmaputra.

Charles and I had kept in touch since our fateful meeting, though fitfully. It was difficult to keep track of him. He was like a wraith, mysteriously disappearing and then, just as mysteriously, reappearing. He was vague about his whereabouts, probably deliberately, considering I had stolen his last dream. He'd been playing his cards close to his chest. But now he was ready to reveal his hand. And what a hand. It was the full house. After years of research and several perilous forays, Charles was convinced he knew the whereabouts of a legend – the most romantic legend of all. It was the fabled lost city of Shangri-La, and Charles believed it lay in a deep gorge in a remote corner of western Tibet.

Charles had already made three journeys into Tibet, each one drawing him closer to that earthly paradise, that lost idyll – a place where everything is perfect, tranquil and peaceful, a place where you never grow old. On his last journey he had actually reached what he believed to be the gateway to Shangri-La. There, in the dark confines of a meditation cave, in a monastery hanging dizzily from the side of a cliff, he had met the guardian of what was known locally as the Garuda Valley, a powerful Tibetan Rinpoche or reincarnate lama. He had learnt that his Shangri-La was just two days away, over two passes and a river. But Charles had run out of karma. Sickness, appalling weather conditions and Chinese politics had forced him to withdraw.

At the beginning of May Charles rang to tell me that he was now about to embark on a final assault. An independent production company was near to finalising a deal with the BBC to make a documentary. I was surprised that they hadn't commissioned it immediately. After all, Charles was close to finding something as important as the Holy Grail. And amazingly he wanted me to go with him.

'You see, Mark,' he explained, 'the producers think the film needs two sides of the coin, two characters, to make it more effective. They want me to be the scholarly professional explorer – the expert – and they want someone else to be the grumbling sceptic, the doubting Thomas, the novice. In a nutshell, the film needs lightening up. It's a bit like *The Odd Couple*. I thought of you.'

I admit, I wasn't particularly flattered by my role in this upcoming epic – I even wondered if there wasn't a certain element of revenge on Charles' part – but I had to put vanity aside. This was the chance of a lifetime. I couldn't turn it down. It would take me exactly where my journey began. It would get me acclimatised and in shape for September. I'd be travelling with the expert. I'd have a chance to wear in my kit and best of all test my new 'impossible-to-get-lost-with' gadget. I told Charles excitedly about my latest acquisition. He wasn't at all impressed. In fact, he was rather scornful.

'Look, Mark. I've got a first-class support team, and a young man called Binod Rai as my expedition leader who's the best there is – an expert in mountain survival. Binod's already saved my life once. Not to be impolite, I think I'd rather put my life in his hands than yours. And remember, I have been there three times. So I don't think we'll need your toy.'

But I wasn't too sure about that. Charles, as I knew from Aditya, could be a little absent-minded. Aditya had once accompanied him on a rail journey of epic proportions – three times round the Circle line. Charles had simply forgotten to get off. Shangri-La would be a lot harder to find than Victoria station.

'Out of interest, Charles,' I said, 'you haven't actually found Shangri-La yet, have you? I mean, are you sure it really exists?'

'Don't worry about that,' he said airily. 'Leave all that to me. Now, much more important, have you got the proper kit? It's pretty cold up there.'

'I've got everything,' I announced smugly.

'Got good boots?' he asked. 'Well worn-in boots? Nothing worse than new boots. They'll cripple you.'

I gulped and looked down at my feet. They were encased in two brand new, bright yellow boulders, each weighing about five kilos. They looked exactly like Noddy's boots. I was trying to wear them in, in preparation for my own journey. They had already effectively cut off the blood supply to my feet. They were agony.

'I actually don't like boots myself,' he continued. 'I wear trainers as long as I can, until it gets too cold. Boots slow you down, especially if you're in a hurry. I learned that after jogging from Kathmandu to Everest Base Camp and back.'

'You ran,' I gasped, 'through the Himalayas?'

'Well,' he replied modestly, 'I was a bit younger and fitter in those days. It was a long time ago.'

This was turning into a nightmare. Forget *The Odd Couple*, it was more like *Raiders of the Lost Ark*. I was going to be travelling with Harrison Ford.

I tried another tack. 'So, we fly into Tibet from Kathmandu and then start driv—?'

'Flying? Driving?' he interrupted. 'What's wrong with walking? The Chinese have just opened up one of the old pilgrim trails out of Nepal. We'll be following an ancient route up the Karnali Valley and then through the Himalayas. It's a bit of a climb. Over a fifteen-thousand-foot pass. But most importantly it allows us to acclimatise to altitude. Altitude can be a killer. I've watched two Indian pilgrims drown from pulmonary embolism because they hadn't acclimatised. Their lungs filled up with fluid. Poor guys. Then we cross into Tibet.'

'And then . . . ?' I asked tentatively. Maybe things would get a bit easier there.

'Then? Oh, then,' he continued impatiently, 'we're on our own. Tibet really is like the Fourth World. It's hermetically sealed in a kind of time warp. There are no doctors or drip-feeds, no helicopters to get us out, up there. From the border we'll go by truck on to the roof of the world. We'll make our first camp at Lake Manasarovar in preparation for our *parikarama* – that's our holy circuit around Mount Kailash. I must admit, it's a bit of a slog. About thirty-two miles around the mountain. The highest point is 18,950 feet. The air gets a bit thin up there. You really feel your age.'

My mind was reeling. 'Charles, are you sure we need to endure all this religious mumbo-jumbo? I mean, I thought we were just going to find Shangri-La.'

'It's not wise,' he warned me ominously, 'to poke fun at the gods up there. Remember, this is the fountainhead of your river. You must show respect if you want to make your journey. All that mumbo-jumbo, as you so rudely describe it, is an essential strategy for survival. The Kailash region is not only one of the holiest places in the world, it's also one of the most hostile. That means it's full of demons and spirits. So if you want to survive you show them respect. The other thing to remember, for my sake, is that only the pure in heart can hope to enter Shangri-La. So I propose a full immersion in Lake Manasarovar and a circuit around Mount Kailash. In theory, that wipes out the sins of a million lifetimes. And considering your past life,' he added piously, 'it's essential.'

'If you say so,' I replied meekly. After all, he was supposed to be a leading authority on the subject.

'Oh, just one other thing, Mark. Get yourself a bedpan. Well, not a bedpan, but one of those plastic bottles you pee into when you're bedridden in hospital. They're vital.'

'Vital for what?' I asked incredulously.

'Vital for peeing into at night, in the confines of your tent. Believe me, you do not want ever, *ever*, under *any* circumstances, to leave your tent at night. It's so cold up there that things just snap off. I think I'll send you my survival manual.'

We were to leave at the beginning of June, and over the next few weeks everything fell into place. The BBC commissioned *The Odd Couple*. Charles and I were to be accompanied by a skeleton film crew – two friends of mine with whom I had filmed before, hardened veterans of a hundred documentaries: the legendary director and cameraman John Bulmer, and Alastair Kenneil, the wizard of sound. Charles' young son George was coming as John's assistant, and all the logistics and back-up had been arranged with military precision by Charles' brother, a retired Gurkha colonel who ran a travel outfit in Kathmandu. Meanwhile, I studied Charles' survival manual with growing alarm (it was called 'Charles Allen's Guide to Coming Back from Tibet Alive'), filled up a sea-chest full of drugs, and put myself in the hands of a sadist – a personal trainer.

I was dreaming. In my dream, I was floating happily in a warm pool in the tropics, gazing up at a vast orange sky that was gradually darkening to burnt ochre from the last rays of the setting sun. Against my brow I held a long, cool drink. Then everything went black – that absolutely you-cannot-see-anything kind of black. I awoke with a start, gasping for breath, banged my head on a cold, hard object and found my lower body rapidly being encased in what felt like a layer of ice. It had been a wonderful dream. Reality was a nightmare.

The rays of the setting sun that had caused the vast orange sky to darken to the colour of burnt ochre were in fact the dying beam of my torch. I had left it on accidentally during the night, illuminating the orange nylon ceiling of my small geodesic tent. The long, cool drink had transmogrified into my tin medicine chest, against which I had banged my head. And, worst of all, the warm pool I had been happily floating in was my sleeping bag. Sometime during that long, never-ending night, the lid of my 'top-of-the-range' plastic urinary receptacle (purchased on the advice of my good friend Charles Allen, with great embarrassment and even greater subterfuge – I had told the salesperson that it was for an incontinent relation) had sprung open and liberally deposited one and a half litres of my own urine into the warm confines of my brand new Anjungilak down sleeping bag.

And the reason I was gasping for breath? I was desperately short of oxygen. I was camping 4560 metres above sea level on the roof of the world, in a remote corner of western Tibet.

Surrounding me in similar constructions of different shapes and sizes were twenty-three men and one woman – also of different shapes and sizes, and different nationalities. All, I may add, judging from the variety of snores intermittently breaking the silence of what must be one of the quietest places on earth, were annoyingly fast asleep. This was the Shangri-La expeditionary force. And among them somewhere, also no doubt sleeping peacefully, was our leader, the man who was responsible for me being here –

Charles himself. If it hadn't been minus fifteen degrees outside, which in my condition would have instantly turned me into a block of urine, and one of the most sacred places in Asia, I would have happily slipped out and slit his throat.

All of us were exhausted. Precious time – nearly a week, when every day counted – had been wasted in Kathmandu obtaining our film permissions. And time is everything in the People's Republic of the Autonomous Region of Tibet, due not only to the unpredictable weather conditions but also to the heavy fines – or worse – that the Chinese can enforce on those who overstay their welcome there. Our visas were valid for just one month. We were pushing it. The time lost in Kathmandu meant we had to get in and out of Tibet in less than three weeks.

In a series of numbing end-on-end journeys we had leapfrogged by aeroplane from Kathmandu into the cauldron of the Terai – 60 degrees Celsius – to Nepalganj in western Nepal. From Nepalganj we had been shaken, stirred and deafened in a battered Russian helicopter that took us north, weaving and lurching through the valleys and sheer chasms of the vast Himalayan barrier, to Simikot.

From Simikot we had endured a five-day forced march from two to four and a half thousand metres, up the Karnali Valley, to the Nara Lagna – the 'pass of the blue sheep' – ironically considered one of the easiest crossing points into Tibet in the western Himalayas. None of us had found it easy. The higher we climbed, the colder it got. Packed ice covered the ground. My raw and blistered feet had burned like fire inside my trainers as I staggered up and down vertical inclines (Charles was right about boots, they were far too heavy – my Noddy boots had long been despatched to ride in state on the back of one of the pack animals). The beginnings of a headache were starting to hammer at the back of my head. Even more worryingly, my fingers had begun to swell. They looked like a slab of uncooked sausages.

We crossed the 'pass of the blue sheep', a large cairn of frozen stones decorated with the bleached bones of yak skulls and wind-torn prayer flags marking the summit. A vicious wind got up, bringing with it a flurry of icy snow and homing in through every crevice of my clothes like an Exocet missile. It was like a warning from the gods, a reminder that this was the point of no return.

Ahead and below us lay Tibet. We descended towards the border across a treacherous, dirty grey-green glacier. The frontier was a simple wooden bridge over the Karnali, or as it is known in Tibet the Mapchhu Khambab: the 'peacock-mouthed' river. We climbed a steep hill to the guard post. I was most disappointed. I had expected something more dramatic, even a sign, saying 'Welcome to Tibet'. Perhaps that was pushing it. At least a sign announcing we had entered Tibet. All we found were a couple of wind-blasted concrete buildings, above which fluttered a torn red flag with five red stars, and a group of miserable-looking Chinese soldiers, dressed only in thin cotton, ill-fitting green uniforms decorated with a few shoddy red epaulettes, peaked hats and white plim-solls. They weren't even carrying guns. They made a perfunctory check of our enormous amount of luggage, listened for a few moments to my Walkman, bummed some cigarettes off me, and then returned to the relative warmth of their barracks.

We waited and waited for the vehicles that were to carry us across the vast expanses of the Tibetan Steppe. I had lost it by now. I felt ill, cold and bored. I did not believe that any vehicles of any kind were coming to pick us up, let alone the two Landcruisers that Charles had been promised. It just sounded too good to be true, considering that it was only forty-four years since the first motorised vehicles of any kind – two ancient cars owned by the fourteenth Dalai Lama – had arrived in the entire country.

While everyone else tried to sleep, wedged amongst the baggage for protection against the icy wind, I drove them all mad by looking for something or somebody to play with. My first victim was a raven perched on top of the Chinese flagpole, which I tried unsuccessfully to dislodge in a flurry of stones – perhaps, in retrospect, not the most diplomatic of actions considering where we were.

Bored of that, I pulled out our illegal satellite telephone, only ever – we had been instructed by the production company back in England – to be used during emergencies (calls cost about twenty pounds a second). As far as I was concerned this was an emergency and I woke up a very disgruntled John Bulmer to show me how to use it. I telephoned home, or tried to. At last I finally got through. To my alarm, an unknown male voice answered. With some relief, I found that I'd been connected to a Kwik-Fit tyre service in Acton. Still, I felt like throwing the bloody thing into the Karnali River.

The timely arrival of our transport prevented an expedition homicide. It was one ancient Chinese lorry, manufactured by a company called Dong Fen. I eyed it with dread. For twenty years my life and bank balance had been ruled and ravaged by an extremely temperamental second-hand generator from the same company, which was supposed to supply power to a house I once owned in Bali. It made so much noise that it had to be buried six metres underground. It constantly broke down, even resisting the powers of the high priest of Bali, hired, at great expense, to breathe some spiritual life into this dragon. To my relief, it finally exploded like a nuclear device, sending a mushroom of oily smoke and shrapnel into the stratosphere.

With Dong Fen came the next contingent of the Shangri-La expeditionary force – the Chinese. Two of them were sort of official minders, who had been sent from Lhasa to keep an eye on us. I called them Mr Cross and Mr Cunning. I observed them closely. Paranoid, hysterical and obstructive, these were the kinds of people I'd have to learn to deal with in September. There were also four drivers, one woman, and a goose. The woman was the wife of one of the drivers. The goose, I was led to believe, was their child. Although as far as I know it survived the trip, tied up by a piece of string, living in a basket in a roof-rack above the driver's cab, I somehow felt that its future was of a more culinary kind than that of a doted-upon surrogate child.

Somehow nearly twenty people and twice as much equipment squeezed into Dong Fen. Steaming, hissing, crunching and grumbling, it carried us the few miles to Purang, the Regional Headquarters of the Ngari district. This was the real customs post. Here our papers and passports were checked thoroughly, and our baggage even more so. They were looking for images of the Dalai Lama. It is a criminal offence to carry any image of the Dalai Lama in the People's Republic of the Autonomous Region of Tibet.

Leaving Binod to deal with Chinese bureaucracy, we decided to check out Purang. It had nothing to offer. It was a typical frontier town – one long street through which an icy wind blew intermittently. Empty plastic bags crackled eerily through the air. Shutters banged. A few Chinese soldiers lounged around in groups, looking bored, cold, and chain smoking. A cluster of high-heeled, heavily rouged hookers looked even more bored and even more cold, our presence causing no more reaction than a series of soft pops as they blew balloons of pink bubble gum through bright scarlet lips. Business, it seemed, was slow today in Purang, but perhaps that was unusual: the street was littered with empty condom packets. Where, I wondered, was the real Tibet, that 'forbidden land', the land that for millions is the most sacred place on earth, the land of the gods. We were soon to find out.

The rest of our transport had eventually turned up: another wheezing, hissing, puffing Dong Fen and, as Charles had promised, two lovely warm Landcruisers. We loaded up quickly. A few minutes later, as the skies rapidly darkened, the Shangri-La expeditionary force set off in convoy northwards, climbing out of the Karnali Valley, on to the roof of the world.

If I had wanted to slit Charles' throat that first hideous night under canvas, by the early morning, I wanted to kiss him. As I unzipped

my tent and hung my stained and smelly sleeping bag out to dry
(my plan was to tell everybody that I'd spilt a cup of tea over it
during the night), a panorama unfolded in front of me of such
beauty that it would have taken my breath away, if I had had any
breath to be taken away. Everything that Charles had described in
his book and in person was pinpoint accurate. I was finally standing where those great explorers had stood before. And nothing
had changed.

Behind me lay the great white necklace of the Gurla Mandata
massif. To my right, just a few steps in fact, lay Manasarovar, or
Mapham Tso, the 'turquoise lake' – a sphere of sapphire so bright,
so blue, so enticing that I felt I could pick it up and hold it in my
hand. No wonder it was venerated and revered by both Hindus
and Buddhists. The Buddhists believe that Queen Maya was carried here to be washed in its sparkling waters before giving birth to
the Buddha himself. The Hindus believe that it was formed in the
mind of God, the great God Brahma, who breathed its creation so
that pilgrims going to Kailash could purify themselves before visiting the holy mountain. I had begun to believe that it was formed in
my imagination. The lake had been just a blue smudge on an old
map that had haunted me for twenty years. But no longer. I had
finally reached the mythological source of the Brahmaputra, and in
doing so had taken that first vital step on my journey down the
river.

To the north, over the far horizon directly in front of me, soaring above a range of desolate, brown and wind-blasted hills, was
the crown jewel: Kailash itself, a perfect cone of ice, the holiest of
all mountains, the axis of the universe, the navel of the world.

Most of us have experienced a moment in our lives when we are
humbled by the sheer power and beauty of nature. But Kailash
blew my mind. I was rooted to the spot – hypnotised. I'm not
really a religious person, but I could well understand why devotees
for thousands of years had prostrated themselves in awe on their

first glimpse of the mountain. It was impossible not to believe that if there was a god, this was where he lived. And it seemed to have the same effect on everybody else. I'd been standing there so long that I hadn't realised that the entire camp had woken up. Many of them had gazed upon Kailash before. But they all stood silent in the mountain's spell. However hard the journey had been, I could never thank Charles enough. He had given me a moment that would last a lifetime.

But not for long. 'Eat a large, hot breakfast, Mark,' Charles said with a certain relish, 'because it's time to wash away all those sins. It's time for your little dip.'

To be fair, Charles did not impose the heart-stopping penitence of doing a full Monty in the icy waters of holy Manasarovar. Instead he gave me a choice. There were, he explained, two ways of doing it: the Tibetan way, and the Hindu way. The Tibetan way was simpler and infinitely less painful – just a quick handful of water splashed on to the face, while muttering your mantra. For the Tibetans this symbolic gesture in the holy, healing waters is enough. The Hindu way was more literal – total immersion three times.

I chose the latter, not because I am macho, or more likely masochistic, but for what I thought were several very good reasons. First, it was Charles' view that my purification was essential if we were to have any chance of finding Shangri-La, and I didn't want to let Charles down. But, perhaps more importantly, it was essential for my journey. I needed to pay my respects to ensure good luck, and anyway, if I didn't do it now I'd have to when I came back in September. By then it would be a lot colder, if that were possible. Charles had made his full immersion the previous year, though worryingly he told me he'd nearly died in the process. He thought his heart had stopped, and his head had been totally numb for three days afterwards. But I felt I should follow him – it was a question of follow my leader. And, finally, I'm nearer to the Hindu religion than to Buddhism.

Often during my past journeys in India with my friend Aditya Patankar, we had plunged into icy torrents first thing in the morning to cleanse our souls, evoking the name of the great Lord Shiva, 'O Bholay. O Bholay Shankar. O Bholay.' I had become quite a fan, in fact a devotee of the great Moon God of the Mountains. And what was more important was that I would be paying my respects right under his holy nose. For the Lord of the Mountain's home was on the summit of Mount Kailash. Here he sat, reclining on his tiger-skin rug, as white as the snow in which he resides, as white as the bright moon of wisdom in his hair, looking directly at me – south – towards India. How could I not honour him?

Fuelled up by an immense breakfast, I stripped down to a lunghi, ran towards the edge of the Holy Lake, evoked the name of the great God, and prepared to launch myself into the icy waters. Except there weren't any icy waters, just a crust of ice covering a spongy bog. I ran farther out, and farther. By now the tents were mere specks on the horizon and my feet had turned into blocks of lichen-covered ice. A few yards ahead a group of terns exploded into the air, panicked by this strange pink apparition crashing towards them. Water, I thought. It must be water, deep water. The wind had now picked up, a cold, cruel wind. My mind and body had almost shut down. I was shaking so hard that I felt my teeth would fall out. The water was up to my calves. A little voice inside my head whispered Yes! But a much louder one screamed No! I just couldn't do it. Bending down quickly, I scooped some water on to my face, chanted a mantra, and sprinted back to my tent.

Charles and Binod came to comfort me with warm cups of tea. But I was inconsolable. I felt that I had let everybody down and that at any moment the Lord of the Mountains would open his third eye, the eye that sees the hidden truth, and incinerate me into a pile of ashes. It was bad karma, of this I was convinced.

Still, I had another chance to redeem myself, in both mortal and godly eyes. We struck camp and headed northwards in our vehicles, climbing across the Bharka Plain towards the Crystal Mountain, to start our thirty-two mile *parikrama*. One circuit, it is said, wipes out the sins of a lifetime. And that was good enough for me.

As we got closer, the great mountain loomed bigger. And the bigger it loomed, the smaller I felt. Not small in a literal sense, but humble. It hypnotised me. Its power sent out icy tentacles that drew me in, like a giant white magnet. It is a magical mountain. And, unlike any other mountain of comparable height, it stands alone. It soars straight out of the plain like a giant pyramid, separated from the rest of its range, the Kangri Tise, by two vertical chasms on either side. It seemed to me to be accessible, yet inaccessible. As it was summer, only Kailash's summit and narrow shoulders were covered in ice. Its torso lay bare – a massive pile of sculpted black and brown rock.

It has four clearly defined walls that match the points of the compass. On its southern face, which we were approaching now, it has a deep gully that runs down vertically from the summit, crisscrossed by a series of horizontal strata. It really does seem to form a cross, or more a swastika, from which Kailash earned the title of the Swastika Mountain.

'Those horizontal strata,' Charles explained patiently, 'are, according to legend, supposed to be scratch marks made by the fingernails of the great Bon priest, Naro Bon Chung, when defeated in an epic battle for supremacy by the Buddhist yogi and Tibetan poet, Milarepa.'

I'm afraid he had lost me by now. Not because I wasn't interested, but because my head felt like it was going to explode. We were now nearly 300 metres higher, at 4700 metres to be precise.

We made camp at the bottom of the Lha Chhu Valley, where the Lha Chhu, the Divine River, debouches on to the plains, our bright, orange domes adding to the colour of the little tented city of fellow pilgrims. This was the gateway to the Crystal Mountain, the jumping off point for the *parikarama*.

We were to start our *parikarama* early – very early – the next morning. Most Tibetans can complete the circuit in just one day, but foreigners usually take three days, and sometimes more.

I barely slept at all that night. My headache had gained in intensity, and my heart raced alarmingly, thumping against my ribs as if it were trying to force its way out. Perhaps I should have gone and told Binod how I was feeling, but it just seemed too pathetic. By morning, when I poked my nose outside the tent, it was viciously cold. The air was filled with dust and flying grit hurled by a bitch of a wind that seemed to have gathered its power at the north end of the Lha Chhu Valley and was now storming towards us in all its fury through the high, narrow chasm. Ippolito Desideri, the young Italian Jesuit priest who reached Kailash in 1715, described it as 'horrible, barren, steep and bitterly cold'. At that particular moment, I agreed with him.

It was now time to dress up, really dress up. It was time to bring out the black, crinkly prophylactic: the tropical-beetle costume. Half an hour later, after much pulling and tugging, which sent my heartbeat off the scale, I squeezed out of my tent. I could hardly stand up I had become so bulky, let alone walk. Not even with the support of my two brand new Leki Trekkies. With firm resolve, I slipped on my UV/IR-resistant blue shades, tied a silk scarf around my face, pulled on my ski mask, gloves and outer shell mitts, struggled into my backpack and set off slowly up the long valley.

The others had gone ahead to film, and I could just make them out in the distance, tiny dots dancing in and out of the plumes of dust pushed up by the feet of the convoy of yaks that was transporting our camping and film equipment. It was like walking into a wind tunnel – one foot forward, two feet back; one foot forward, three feet back. To my right, above me, far above me, the Holy Mountain showed a glimpse of its west-facing façade, guarded by its sheer, wind-scarred granite flanks.

This, now, was the easiest stage of the our *parikarama*. It was really just a gentle incline. But for me it was like climbing Everest. I didn't realise it but I was beginning to get seriously ill. In fact, I was hallucinating. I was convinced there was a small man sitting on my right shoulder, bashing the back of my head with a hammer. I kept on trying to knock him off with one of my Leki Trekkies, and in the process nearly impaled Binod, who I hadn't realised was walking right behind me. Good old Binod, he clearly knew that I was struggling, and had been shadowing me up the valley. He produced a water flask and forced me to drink. He told me that I was retaining fluid. That was dangerous, but for me it was the lesser of two evils. The very thought of extricating myself from the confines of my tropical-beetle outfit, and then fumbling around through a further eight layers of clothing to find the necessary part of my anatomy to allow me to relieve myself was too ghastly to imagine. I was also beginning to doubt the efficiency of my Gore-Tex outer shell. I remembered the words of the young, impossibly fit Australian salesperson in that friendly London emporium. Though it was only a few weeks ago, it seemed like two years.

'Got you all sealed up, mate, haven't I? Couldn't squeeze a fart out of there, could you?'

I wasn't concerned about squeezing a fart *out*. I was much more worried about the fart or, more appropriately and politely, wind that seemed to be squeezing *in*. I came to the conclusion that unless one was hermetically sealed, there was nothing one could do. This wind *could* cut the nuts off a Polar bear.

We struggled along, with Binod gallantly supporting me. Half an hour later we found Charles sitting on a rock, coughing.

Worryingly, he didn't sound or look too good either. He thought he had picked up a chest infection which the increasing altitude wasn't helping. But Charles was made of much tougher stuff than me and tried to cheer me up by telling me that a few months before, in exactly the same spot as we were sitting now, two German trekkers had expired in a blizzard. It wasn't exactly what I wanted to hear at that particular moment. Now Binod had two cripples to care for.

A little farther on we came across an extraordinary sight – well, for me at least. A Tibetan was lying flat on the ground on his stomach, wearing a kind of hide apron and a pair of plimsolls on his hands. He got up suddenly, marked the spot where his forehead had touched the ground, and fell forward again, and so on. It was a bit like watching a caterpillar.

Charles explained that this was the most devout form of obeisance, known as *gyang chatsel*, meaning to salute stretched out. The pilgrim's prostration, over snow, ice and grit, would take him thirteen days around the Holy Mountain. We learnt that he had already completed two *koras* and hoped to complete another eleven. Thirteen *koras* of the Holy Mountain would not only wipe out the sins of past, present and future lifetimes, they would also allow him to undertake the holiest of all *koras* – around the inner sanctum of the Holy Mountain, which only masters or adepts perform. I was awed – no, humbled. Actually, to be more precise, I was shocked by such devotion, by such belief. It also made me feel pathetic, particularly when he overtook me a mile or so farther on.

I can't really remember the last few hours, I was so ill. Eventually, at around 5000 metres, we reached the top of the Lha Chhu Valley, where it divided. Straight on led to the source of another of those four great Asian rivers, not mine but the Senge Khambab, the 'lion-mouthed' river, the Indus. We veered right around the corner of the Kailash massif and across the Lha Chhu River, which was by now just an iced-up stream. There was the camp. A yak dung fire burnt brightly. I followed the smoke upwards and upwards until it dissolved into the gauzy clouds that raced across a twelve-hundred-metre vertical slab of snow-streaked rock: the Crystal Mountain's dark, forbidding north face. It was the most frightening thing I had ever laid eyes on in my life.

Headache and fatigue, undue breathlessness on exertion, the sensation of the heart beating forcibly, loss of appetite, nausea, vomiting, dizziness, difficulty sleeping, and irregular breathing during sleep – these are the symptoms of AMS or Acute Mountain Sickness. That terrible night I had them all, especially the nausea. I hadn't bothered to eat, drink or even undress on reaching camp. I had just collapsed into my tent, wrapped myself in my sleeping bag and prayed to the great God of the Mountains twelve hundred metres above to ease the pain and allow me to complete my *parikarama* of his holy abode, thereby absolving me from the sins of my lifetime. Surely I didn't have that many sins? Apparently, I did. The suffering just increased throughout the night. Not wanting to soil Binod's tent, I spent most of it outside on all fours, throwing my guts up. It was in this pathetic, frozen state that the others found me early the next morning.

What I could not understand was why nobody else was suffering, although admittedly Charles didn't look too good. Not only was his face swollen, but his cough had now turned into an alarming chesty rattle. Nobly, he tried again to cheer me up by telling me that when he'd looked into his shaving mirror that morning, he had seen his granny looking back at him.

'It can happen to anybody, Mark,' Binod reassured me. 'I have experienced it myself. I've seen it strike down lots of people – fit people, young people, old people. Or even people who smoke,' he added disapprovingly, noticing me fire up my fifth Benson & Hedges of the day. It was only 5.30 a.m. 'AMS is still really a mystery. It's not choosy who it affects. Now,' he continued, 'I'm going to try one last procedure – I'm going to try and compress you. If that doesn't work, you'll have to descend. Your life is my responsibility, and going back down is really the only reliable cure.'

Half an hour later, I found myself entombed like an Egyptian mummy in a large, red cylindrical frankfurter – a portable compression chamber. Basically, without getting technical, what it does is fool your body into thinking that it's a thousand metres lower. I had company in the frankfurter to begin with – a fly. Worryingly, it expired after a few minutes. I spent an hour or so in this chamber. It was really rather relaxing. My vision was limited to a small rectangle of clear plastic an inch above my nose through which I stared at my own bloated reflection in the lens of John Bulmer's camera. The ultimate professional, he was never one to miss a good filming opportunity. Occasionally Charles' equally bloated face swam into view as he leant down and tried to communicate to me the latest score in the Test match that he'd picked up on his radio, by yelling through the thick plastic.

I felt better when I eventually climbed out, but unfortunately only for a short time. I was soon back on all fours, in gut-wrenching misery. There was nothing else that anybody could do: I had to descend. I couldn't look any of them in the eye. I felt I had let them all down. Miserably, accompanied by one of the Sherpas, I returned slowly down the Lha Chhu Valley to the base camp while the others struggled bravely on.

As matters turned out, no one made it round the mountain. They all returned later that evening. Apparently the yak herders had refused to continue, saying that the snow was far too deep for their animals around the 5760-metre Drolma Pass. Whether this was a genuine concern or a ploy for more money, one will never know. In fairness, though, yaks were at a premium that year. Thousands had died from starvation after the heavy early snows that wiped out many of Tibet's nomadic communities in the late autumn of the previous year. But in my heart I really believed that the team might have made it by carrying only the basic equipment themselves. They had returned, I felt, just to be kind to me.

That wasn't the worst of it, though. I had failed completely on all counts – spiritual, mental and physical – first at Manasarovar and now at Kailash. I'd missed the best opportunity, the perfect opportunity, when the weather was at its most clement. I was going to have to do it all again in winter. I realised that I'd taken this far too lightly. As Charles had said, it wasn't wise to poke fun at the gods. This had been bad enough; in winter it would be one of the most inhospitable places in the world.

We spent a night resting and regrouping. We'd have liked longer, we were all exhausted, but there was no time and early the next morning we set out north-west in search of Shangri-La. I took one last look at the Crystal Mountain. It had almost disappeared behind a veil of mist. Just its icy tip was visible, from which spewed a feather of vapour, as from an active volcano. It seemed to be laughing at me.

What happened over the next few days is not my story to tell, it is Charles'. It took us a week's long and arduous journey by vehicle, foot, pony and yak. In a remote valley in the north-west of Tibet, Charles made an important archaeological discovery: the remains of an ancient and lost Tibetan civilisation. Whether we were actually in Shangri-La is debatable. It's now up to Charles, the archaeologists or the historians, to pick up the pieces and complete the jigsaw. However, if it *was* Shangri-La that we found, there is one myth about it that I can debunk with the utmost authority – the legend of eternal youth. When I left, I felt about 150 years old.

It was at the end of our expedition, on our way out of Tibet, that Charles – perhaps inadvertently – made up for making my life hell for the last month. We had stopped just short of the summit of one of the highest passes that the vehicles could cross – the 5150-metre Maryam La Pass. In fact the pass is the only way out of western Tibet, but only at certain times of the year. If you get your timing wrong, you will be sealed in until the snow melt the following spring. A little rivulet, hardly a foot across, gurgled happily beside us as we ate our lunch.

'What's this river called?' I asked Charles.

'Oh,' he replied casually, 'this is the Tsangpo, the Brahmaputra. Well, the beginnings of it.'

'It's the what??!' I exploded, in a fine spray of corned beef sandwich. 'You mean this is the beginning of the river? The source of the Brahmaputra?'

Politely, Charles handed me a handkerchief. 'Well, now that you mention it,' he said, 'that's an interesting point. It's actually a feeder, although certainly one of its highest feeders. Its recognised source, as you well know, Mark, from all your research,' he added pointedly, 'has been established sixty miles or so south-east of here in the Chemayungdung glaciers. I suppose it all depends on what constitutes a source.'

This was a good question and it set my mind racing. I knew indeed from my research that the Chemayungdung glacier had been measured at 5120 metres. But I was now near the summit of the Maryam La, which stood at 5150 metres, and that was indubitably higher. So who was right?

'Do you think I can claim this to be the source?' I asked Charles, excitedly.

'Well now, that's again debatable, Mark,' he replied, rather more soberly. 'It would be up to the RGS. And all sorts of other experts. We're not exactly geographers or surveyors.'

But I wasn't concerned. I had now reached one of the highest feeders or sources of the great river, and that was good enough for me. I was jubilant. It meant I had effectively already started my journey. I got up, did a little jig, straddled the tiny stream and, adopting the pose of an intrepid explorer, asked Charles to take a picture of me.

'All you need now is a straw hat,' he remarked, 'and you could be Henry Savage Landor.'

That might have been true, but I felt it was a little below the belt. Henry Savage Landor had also claimed to be the first person to have discovered one of the sources of the Brahmaputra. And he usually wore a straw hat. It featured prominently in an unfortunate incident described in his extraordinarily violent and far-fetched 1898 bestseller *In the Forbidden Land*, an account of his travels and adventures in Tibet. One of his 'coolies', as he called them, who was carrying goose eggs in Landor's hat, had slipped and fallen, smashing both hat and eggs.

I hate to think what happened to the poor man, considering the utter contempt and hatred Landor felt for Tibetans. He thought they were all dirty, degenerate and cowardly, basically villainous savages. In another incident an unhappy Tibetan he encountered fell foul of his violent temper: 'Throwing myself upon him, I grabbed him by his pigtail and landed his face a number of blows, straight from the shoulder. When I let him go, he threw himself down, crying and imploring my pardon. To disillusion the Tibetan on one or two points, I made him lick my shoes clean with his tongue, in the presence of the assembled Shokas (Bhotias). He tried to scamper away but I caught him once more by his pigtail and kicked him down the front steps.'

At one stage during his journey, the Tibetans took Landor prisoner. He was beaten up, starved, tortured, shot at, and then nearly executed. He was the worst kind of English colonial: vain, arrogant and utterly merciless. But he was a true eccentric, and if you believe his stories, remarkably brave. Although he undeniably reached this spot, almost every reputable geographer dismissed Landor's claims and tales as works of pure fiction.

I was now standing at the very source that Landor had modestly named after himself. In his book he had written,

A little rivulet, hardly six inches wide, descended among the stones in the centre of the valley we were following, and was soon swollen by other rivulets from melting snows on the mountains to either side. This was one source of the great Brahmaputra, one of the largest rivers of the world. I must confess that I felt somewhat proud to be the first European who had ever reached these sources, and there was a certain childish delight in standing over this sacred stream which, of such immense width lower down, could here be spanned by a man standing with legs slightly apart. We drank of its waters at the spot where it had its birth.

Now, almost exactly a century later, another Englishman, admittedly not so young, and certainly not possessing the same qualities, felt that same childish delight, standing over this tiny sacred stream which, of such immense width farther down, could be spanned by a man standing with his legs slightly apart. He also drank from its waters at the spot where it had its birth but performed one other symbolic little gesture. He plunged his hands into the icy, clear water, extracted a small, smooth round pebble, wrapped it in a handkerchief, and put it carefully into the inside pocket of his jacket.

Once over the Maryam La Pass, I became obsessed with the river that ran almost next to the little dusty track along which we were travelling. Gathering width, volume and speed from the snow melt of the high passes, the river raced westwards, a smooth, twisting ribbon, its cold, satiny surface the colour of burnished steel – the highest river in the world, protected by the vast massif of the Himalayan range towering majestically to our right.

We had precisely two days left on our visas and hundreds of miles to go in our Landcruisers. It was during these endless bone-shaking days of travel, as the Tsangpo flickered in front of my eyeballs like an old silent movie, that I began to plan how I was going to get down the river. Suddenly it came to me. I realised now that apart from the high, glacial top section and the bottom section where the river plunged its staggering ten thousand feet in a hundred miles through the awesome Tsangpo Gorges, the middle section, the longest stretch of river – five hundred miles or so – should be navigable by boat. Here, as far as I knew, the Tsangpo entered a long, flat, winding valley, where it became a typical braided river, meandering its way benignly through the sandbanks.

My problem was the type of craft available. This wasn't exactly the London Boat Show. The choice was either oblong, wooden 'box boats', a bit like floating coffins, or small round coracles made of yak hide and willow. I'm all for using traditional transport on my travels, but this was pushing it. One tiny mishap would end my journey and, more importantly, my life. A few seconds in those icy waters was all it would take.

What I needed was one of those top-of-the-range, portable, inflatable rafts – the kind that seem to defy gravity even in the most turbulent river rapids of the world – with a couple of added extras: a dog kennel and a powerful outboard motor. The outboard would give me the advantage of speed. Time, as I'd found out, was not on one's side in Tibet. I was pretty sure I could find this type of craft in Nepal – a haven for white-water rafters.

At the little township of Saga, I bid the Tsangpo farewell for a few months. We crossed the river on an ancient, flat-bedded barge operated by a winch system, and headed due south, down the roof of the world, towards Nepal.

It was here that I realised again what a narrow weather window was available to me. The sheer, precipitous track through the main core of the Himalayan range that we were inching down had only a month ago been impassable, encased in a sheet of snow and ice. Now it had become a river – an extraordinarily dangerous, muddy slide of a river. The monsoons had hit, and hit hard. We were soon blocked by an immense landslide that had, earlier that morning, swept a bus full of people and children over the edge – a thousand-foot sheer drop to the valley floor. Tragically, there were no survivors. We spent a nerve-racking day, expecting any moment to be hit by another landslide, transferring equipment from our vehicles across the blocked track and into other transport that had managed to inch up from the Chinese border town of Zhangmu.

After the crossing the Friendship Bridge that acts as the border between Tibet and Nepal, we stopped at Khodari, a small Nepalese frontier town, to clear customs. I bought a cup of chai and wandered back on to the bridge. I looked upwards, through the driving rain, upwards through the high, misty passes and beyond, on to the roof of the world. I started to shake – not from cold, but from fear. In two months, I would be returning.

Charles and the others flew straight back to London from Kathmandu. I stayed on a few days, discussing logistics with the guides at Tiger Mountain: the availability of white-water rafts, and arrangements to fly my dog from India into Nepal and on to Tibet. Then I joined my family in the tropics for a spot of R & R. After what I'd been through, I needed not only their warmth and comfort but some real heat in my bones before I could face returning to the cold.

FOUR

I returned to London at the beginning of September to good news and bad news. The good news was that all my permits had been approved. It should have been a time to celebrate – the seemingly interminable paper journey was finally over. But the bad news was far too disturbing. It came from my friends in Nepal. Winter, they reported, had arrived early – unseasonably heavy snow had already begun to fall in the Kailash region in western Tibet. That narrow window was closing fast. It might even have shut already. I could give it a go, I was told, but they advised strongly against it. The problem, they told me, lay with my supplies, no doubt, I suddenly realised with dread, to be carried by another member of the Dong Fen family. There was no guarantee that the vehicle could get up or down the icy high passes. I could effectively be sealed in for the whole winter. Food is fuel, I remembered them saying: without food you die.

I shivered violently. The last time had been bad enough, the experience was still horribly fresh in my mind. Mountains and me, it seemed, did not as yet enjoy the most convivial of relationships;

more importantly, I had a family to think of. But just to make sure that I wasn't overreacting or being a wimp, I rang the expert – Charles. Charles wasn't well, not well at all. The chest infection he had picked up in Tibet had turned into pleurisy and infected his lungs.

'Don't even *think* about it,' came his wheezing reply.

That did it. Yet it was so hard for me to accept that having got this far, an obstacle of this size should suddenly be thrown in my way. It was almost surreal. What the hell was going on? Was I carrying bad karma from my failed obeisance to the gods? Or was it something more personal between me and the river? Its power was uncanny, and not just in the physical sense. Maybe I was becoming paranoid, but I began to think that the river was manipulating me: actually sending me a clear message to keep away. However, I wasn't going to be beaten. I would catch it unawares. I would sneak in its back door: I would do the journey not simply in two halves, but back to front. Instead of starting in Tibet, I would attempt the lower part of the river first, the nine hundred miles from where it thunders into north-east India over the McMahon Line to its end in the Bay of Bengal. Then, better versed in the river's whims, I would return to Tibet in the early spring to renew my assault on its upper course.

If one is patient, I'd always found in my travels in the East, the wheel, however slowly, turns in one's favour. As if by magic, everything now fell neatly into place. I called Tiger Mountain in Delhi. From past experience, I was pretty sure they wouldn't let me down. If I was ready, came the reply, they were. And then, just a few days before I was due to fly out to India, I received excellent news – the best news of all, in fact.

It came from that great country's ace dog catcher, Aditya Patankar. Apparently he had been spending time in the temple in obeisance to the Maratha dog God, Bhairoba. Aditya had regained his powers. He had found me a dog. His fax read,

Pie (I've named it Pie. Suitable, I think, and short enough so you won't forget its name) is in my house! However, it is not the one I tried to capture. This is a big, black male. This morning, he walked into my house, trailing the scent of my bitch, Coffee. I guess it was meant to be – there are, as you know, no mistakes in life! He's a street fighter and reminds me of a battle-scarred Maratha warrior. He is reacting to me very well and will look after you. Training will commence this evening, Aditya. P.S. Buy some good, strong chain leads, they're difficult to get here.

I couldn't believe it. I finally had a dog, I thought excitedly. And what a dog – a battle-scarred, Maratha warrior type of dog. He sounded the kind of dog that could look after himself.

I set off to Harrods' pet department to buy Pie his chains. Harrods' pet department has changed drastically since my childhood days when I used to slip into this deafening and exotic emporium that smelt of hay, bird seed and fur to escape my mother's shopping expeditions. I spent some of my happiest times here, wandering through the bewildering and magical labyrinth of cages that squawked, squealed, chirped, grunted and dazzled with a myriad exotic species that conjured up to me the mysteries of far-flung lands. It was here that I bought Charlie, much to my mother's horror, a glossy mynah bird that woke me up every morning by reciting 'I love you' in a broad Irish accent. It was here, to my mother's even greater horror, that I had taken possession of Tiki, my cunning and swift Indian mongoose that nearly gave an elderly lady a heart attack in an Italian restaurant by climbing up her stockinged leg on to her lap, on to the table, to help her open the clams in her spaghetti alle vongole. And it was here, perhaps, that a passion to discover the mysteries of those distant places had been awakened in a child's mind.

But the Harrods of today was a very different place. Only a few pink-eyed white rabbits, a cluster of bored hamsters spinning round on little wheels, and a whelp of miniature, fluffy puppies now filled those cages which had once dazzled and deafened me with colour and cries. It had become, quite rightly – for the animals anyway – more politically correct.

I entered the accessories department and headed for the dog section.

'I'd like to see some dog leashes, please,' I asked the matronly salesperson politely. 'Strong dog leashes.'

'We have just got in a new range, sir,' she replied grandly. 'These are perfect for taking your little friend for walkies in the park. We have found them very popular. They have detachable collars which come in thirty different colours, made from the finest crocodile skin. For an extra fifty pounds, we can engrave your little poppet's name in gold plate on the collar.'

'No, you don't quite understand,' I answered, discarding the selection of fabulously expensive and fabulously fragile filigree leads that she was offering me, all of them just about strong enough to hold a mouse. 'You see, I want a proper chain lead, a really strong one. You know, one of those choke chains, the ones that pulls my little poppet up short if he gets a bit mischievous.'

Her eyes, heavily mascaraed in a shade of bright indigo blue, rounded in indignation behind her bifocal lenses. She pursed her scarlet lips, as if sucking a lemon, and seemed to grow in front of me as she thrust out her immense bosom. 'Well, sir,' she replied snootily, 'we do not sell such items at Harrods.'

I wasn't going to be intimidated. 'Well, do you know where I can get one?'

'Nowhere, I would imagine,' she replied disdainfully, thrusting out her bosom even farther. 'I believe they are illegal. Will there be anything else I can help you with?'

Purely by chance, on my way to have lunch with my nephew in Soho, I passed a sex shop. Its window displayed the usual scanty, supposedly seductive undergarments, a few videos, their fleshy covers advertising contents of uncensored steamy sex with special offers of a free vibrator, and an exhibit of what I can only describe as instruments of torture: a black executioner's hood, a collection of leather metal-spiked straitjackets, whips, some strange sharp objects attached to some chains, and a much thicker chain connected by a loop to an even thicker chain collar. Looking to my left and right, I scuttled quickly inside. A bored young man wearing a fan of peacock feathers, which I soon realised was his own hair, was slumped over a desk reading a comic.

'Um, um, how much is that er, that er, that chain thing in the window?'

'Wot won?' he replied, too bored to look up from his comic. 'The nipple piercer, the penis padlock, the clit ring, the crutch constrictor, the nut crusher . . . ?'

'No, no, no, the large chain,' I interrupted, 'the one with a collar.'

'Oh,' he replied, still not looking up from his comic, 'the throat choke. Thirty-nine ninety-nine plus VAT. Yours for thirty quid. Popular little number. Cuts the blood supply right off.'

'Actually, it's for a dog,' I replied weakly.

'That's wot they all say, mate.'

A few minutes later, after checking that the coast was clear, I put my head down and scuttled out of the shop, clutching my throat choke in a brown paper bag.

The evening before I left, with the cooler October nights drawing in, I packed for warmer climes. I thought about taking my GPS, my global positioning system, which Charles had disdainfully rejected. But I decided to leave it behind. How could I possibly be stupid enough to get lost? I just had to follow my river. However, I did add a few doggy items to my luggage: balls, plastic bones, a squeaky mouse and, of course, the throat choke. I was very excited. I was soon to meet my dog Pie and I wanted to make a good first impression.

I also packed a collection of useful dog manuals and a few old canine reference books. In one, I had found the wise words of an ancient Greek philosopher, who said that if you wanted to distinguish a dog from a man you should find out first whether he is faithful or not. If faithful, know him to be a dog; if not, know him to be a man.

In another, I found some more disturbing information: dog meat is a dish among certain Assamese gypsy tribes and, during special occasions, dog stuffed with rice is a traditional delicacy. I was, I realised, going to have to keep a careful eye on my dog. I reckoned he would be regarded with relish – a bit of a speciality. But if anybody was going to eat him, it was going to be me.

The best, however, was a slim little volume, called *Indian Notes about Dogs: Their Diseases and Treatment* compiled by a Major Chambers in 1881. In its section under Practical Rules, I learnt how to give a pill to an ordinary dog; how to give one to a big or savage dog; how to give enemas to a dog; how to muzzle a dog for operations; and, alarmingly, how to bleed a dog. It also contained a useful paragraph on how to manage a dog on board ship, which, considering my journey, would be most useful. I also had a splendid, concise Hindustani vocabulary book concerning dogs by the same author, which would be convenient for persons imperfectly acquainted with Hindustani and save the trouble of reference to dictionaries on emergencies.

From it, I learnt such useful words as *ganr* – the anus; *bhaunkhna* – to bark; *paitmenmarora lugga* or *koolinj* – colic; *dust lugga* or *paichulta* – diarrhoea; *pissoo* – a flea; *kuf* or *phen* – to foam; *hart* or *ugla hart* – the foreleg; *bhoonbhun kurna* – to growl; *gurm hona* or *mustee* – to be on heat (bitches); *chartna* – to lick; *keera* – maggots; *nur* – a male; *moonh bund kurna ka chumra* – a muzzle for dogs; *kutkutana* or *cheecheeyana* – to yelp; and finally, *bachadena* – to pup.

I felt I was as prepared as I possibly could be to meet and, hopefully, befriend a strange dog and take it down a river.

At a little farewell lunch on the day of my departure, my brother-in-law – a practical sort of fellow and a bit of a dog connoisseur – slipped a package into my hand.

'This,' he announced authoritatively 'is the key to a dog's heart. You can't go wrong. It never fails. But use it sparingly.' I was really intrigued. It seemed that I had been given some kind of magic dog talisman. I started to open the package.

'No, no, no,' he interrupted. 'Wait till you actually meet your dog. Trust me.'

That evening I flew east, into the warm embrace of Mother India.

Autumn in northern India: my favourite time of year, that fresh, transient period between the passing of the monsoons and the coming of winter. Days were hot and still slightly humid. Nights were cooler but still warm enough not to need a jersey.

Aditya met me at Delhi airport.

'Where's Pie?' I demanded.

'First things first,' he said, handing me a piece of paper. 'This is from Tiger Mountain. Read it. It's urgent.'

I read it impatiently. Aditya was right. It was urgent. I was booked to fly out of Delhi the morning after next. That left less than forty-eight hours to meet and bond with Pie, somehow get him on the same flight as me, meet the man who was going to act as my guide, pick up my final permission, which I'd been told was ready – though one could never trust bureaucracy – and tie up any last-minute loose ends. It was going to be a hell of a rush.

From Delhi, I was faced with a zig-zag journey – directed by a mixture of geographic and bureaucratic hurdles – to the north-east of India. The plane was going to take us to Guwahati, the capital of Assam, where I was going to try to sort out a suitable boat for the lower part of the river. That done, I was to take a helicopter to Itanagar, the new capital of Arunachal Pradesh. Here I was to check in officially – access to the state was closely monitored, but my permission gave me unique access to its most restricted areas. Perhaps more importantly, there was a chance of meeting there Arunachal's Chief Minister, who might be able to help arrange another helicopter. This one would take me right up to the top of the river, to a village called Gelling, close to the McMahon Line. Otherwise I was going to have to walk the whole way *up* the river as well as down it: the only track, which stopped thirty miles short of the border, had been blocked by landslides and was impassable to vehicles.

If I did manage to get a chopper, it would leave from Pasighat, the small border town between Arunachal Pradesh and Assam, where the Brahmaputra thunders from the mountains on to the plains of Assam. Pasighat was a day's drive from Itanagar. There we would pick up the final members of the team: our local guide – an Adi tribal familiar with the restricted areas – and our cook.

Delhi–Guwahati–Itanagar–Pasighat–the McMahon Line: it was about a thousand miles as the crow flies. The way I was going was about twice that, but hopefully it would get me to the top as quickly as physically possible. Just like Tibet, my visa for Arunachal Pradesh was valid for one month only.

Right now, though, I just wanted to meet Pie. 'What's he like? How's the training going? Will he like me? Is he in good health . . . ?' Anxiously I bombarded Aditya with a hundred questions.

'Wait and see, my friend,' he said ominously. My luggage was quickly loaded into the dicky of an ancient, but highly polished Ambassador taxi. Here another familiar face greeted me – Ajit, the taxi's owner. I had met Ajit a few years before and employed him to drive me whenever I was in Delhi. Driving is a hazard in Delhi, and drivers even more so. Good, reliable drivers are difficult, almost impossible, to find. Ajit was a gem. He never let me down – he was always on time and knew everything one needed to know about the country's capital city. He was also a disciple, like myself, of Ganesh, the all-powerful, elephant-headed God of Protection, the Lord of Beginnings. A plastic effigy sat proudly on his dashboard. It lit up prettily in a kaleidoscope of coloured lights when he applied the brakes. I noticed he had some brand new seat covers – bright blue spongy seat covers.

'Nice new seats,' I remarked.

'Thank you, sir,' he grinned happily. 'Next time you come, new car.'

This was possible: I overpaid Ajit ridiculously, but it was worth it. He was irreplaceable.

'Have you got the chain, the lead?' Aditya asked me as we sped into Delhi.

I pulled out the choke chain.

'Jesus Christ!' he exclaimed, as he studied with interest this sado-maschochist's instrument of pleasure. 'It's a bit big, and bloody heavy. I mean, it's a dog, not an elephant, you need to control this time. Are you sure it's for a dog?'

'Absolutely,' I lied.

'Well, it's going to be too big and heavy for Pie. I mean, he's a fair size but not that big. I tell you what, we'll stop quickly at a pet shop. We'll see if we can find something more suitable up there.'

The pet shop, grandly called the Windsor Pet Shop, turned out to be infinitely superior, infinitely less expensive, and its salespeople infinitely less snooty, than the establishment in Knightsbridge. I purchased a couple of suitable chain leads with leather collars, some more toys, and a lovely soft dog rug, designed in a fashionable tiger skin motif. I could see Aditya was getting impatient, particularly when I began to discuss with the helpful salesperson the pros and cons of a metal versus a plastic food bowl.

'For God's sake, Mark, hurry up. It's only a pi-dog. Anybody would think you owned some pampered, pedigree pooch.'

But I wanted only the best for my Pie. If I had had my way I would have had a bowl specially commissioned, like Mme de Pompadour, who had Lazare Duvaux, the celebrated French *marchand-mercier*, make a complete service of dinner bowls of the finest white Vincennes porcelain for her dogs. In the end, I settled for a metal bowl. At least it looked smart. And important. And grand. To me, it glowed like some priceless solid silver soup tureen.

On our way to Aditya's flat, we made one more stop at the butcher's. I was slightly alarmed when he struggled out with a goat slung across his shoulder. Worry turned to extreme nervousness – and extreme jealousy – as we approached Aditya's flat. There was a deep barking which, as we neared the door, rapidly turned into a hysterical, excited whine. Pie was obviously deeply attached to Aditya, I thought, unhappily. How was I going to transfer that affection? Aditya opened the door. I caught just a glimpse – a blur – of black as something hurtled past me and disappeared behind a bush.

'Now, look at that,' he said proudly. 'You see, he's been dying to pee for the last four hours. But he waited. You'll find that about pi-dogs,' he continued authoritatively. 'They're naturally house-trained, and incredibly clean. It's in their blood.'

'How do you know?' I asked suspiciously, as we waited patiently for Pie to finish his long evacuation.

'It's in my blood,' he replied. 'Remember, we're dog worshippers. You told me that. Now, come and meet Pie, your new best friend.'

I need not have worried about that transfer of affection. Soon I found myself flat on my back, straddled by a large, black dog with long legs and sharp toenails who was giving my face a saliva bath.

I pushed him off and got to my feet, my chest and legs lacerated by his nails. He jumped up again. I grabbed his face in my hands and returning his affection planted a kiss on his long nose. Pie, my Pie. My dog.

He was delightful, a sort of cross between a labrador and a jackal. His hair – what was left of it, for large, bare, pink patches of skin decorated his flanks and back – was that soft, silky hair of a Labrador. He was also thick-set like a Labrador, but that was where the similarity ended. His face was long and pointed. He had powerful jaws, wicked teeth and foul breath. His tail, what was left of it – the top bit was missing – must have once been long and bushy. It was now threadbare and stringy. He wagged it continually. And he was certainly scarred – his muzzle was a criss-cross of deep white lines and he was missing part of one pointed ear. I was slightly concerned about those bare patches of pink flesh.

'What are those?' I asked Aditya.

'Mange.'

'Mange! Pie's got mange!' I exclaimed in horror. 'Isn't it contagious?'

'I'm not sure,' he replied casually, 'but he's got scabies as well. And that is. Highly contagious. But don't worry, I've started the treatment. We'll discuss that later on. Now, let's take him for a walk. I want to show you how well I've trained him. We'd better put his lead on, though. He has a slight habit of taking off.'

'I thought you said you'd trained him.'

'Look, I've only had him a few days. And he's half wild.'

That was an understatement, I thought, as Pie pulled me down the road, straining at the end of his leash. We reached a small, dusty park where a group of scrawny dogs lay basking in the sun. What was left of the hackle on Pie's neck rose up as he leapt forward, barking furiously. The pack of dogs beat a hasty retreat, their tails between their legs.

'Now look at that, my friend,' Aditya said proudly. 'They know who's boss around here. He's a real Maratha. Brave as a lion. He'll take on anything.'

Hmm, I thought. I could foresee trouble ahead.

'Right, I'll take over now, Mark. Now, just watch carefully and learn.'

'Why don't you let me try first?' I said. 'Pie has to get used to *me* and *my* voice. And I haven't much time.' I needed to stamp my authority on Pie quickly. And, I admit, I wanted to impress Aditya.

He thought about it for a moment. 'Fair enough,' he replied grudgingly. 'But keep him on the leash.'

Grasping the leash firmly, I set off across the park. Immediately Pie shot ahead, almost pulling me off my feet. I jerked the chain and yelled, '*Suckhna*! Pie, *suckhna*!' Nothing happened. He pulled even harder. '*Suckhna*, Pie!' I yelled again, '*suckhna*!' It was impossible to stop him, I was running to keep up. Gasping for breath, I tried again. '*Suckhna*, Pie!'

'Heel, Pie! Heel!' a deep voice boomed suddenly across the park. Pie slammed on his brakes, and stood panting quietly at my side.

Aditya came over. 'What on *earth* were you shouting?' he asked incredulously.

'*Suckhna*,' I panted defiantly. 'It's Hindi for "to heel". It's in my book on Hindi vocabulary for dogs.'

'*Suckhna*?' he replied, even more incredulously. 'What the hell is *suckhna*? I never heard of it. It's certainly not Hindi, and it certainly doesn't mean to heel.'

'It does,' I insisted. 'Here, I'll show you.' I pulled out of my pocket Major Chambers' slim volume *Indian Notes about Dogs*. 'Look at the vocabulary. It's got all sorts of other useful words. Here, look – *suckhna* – to heel.'

Aditya grabbed the book and then raised his eyebrows in despair. 'For a start,' he explained patiently, 'you pronounce it "sookhna", like the word "souk", not like "suck", and, more importantly, it does not mean "to *heel*", it means "to *heal*". So much for your English education, my friend,' he added sarcastically. 'And another thing, do you honestly think I'd risk teaching Pie Hindi, considering your last efforts to learn it – let alone pronounce it properly – for Tara?'

'What do you mean?' I replied crossly, 'She understood me perfectly.'

'Only after about eight hundred miles or so. Remember the chaos she caused on the way?'

He had a point. Tara's disobedience had cost me a small fortune in compensation to farmers whose crops she'd devoured on a daily basis.

'Now, forget about your Englishman's doggy books. We'll just concentrate on basics. We'll start with three commands.' He slipped off Pie's lead. 'Pie – heel,' he commanded. Obediently Pie fell into step alongside him. 'Pie – stay,' he commanded. Obediently Pie stood rooted to the spot, as Aditya walked ahead. 'Pie – sit,' he commanded. Obediently Pie sat down. 'There,' announced Aditya, 'that's all you need to know at the moment.'

I was deeply impressed. India's ace dog catcher really did, it seemed, have mystical canine powers.

'Right, Mark,' Aditya said, 'you stay here and practise with Pie. I'll go and get the car. Just the three commands: heel, stay and sit. Think you can remember that? You'd better,' he added ominously. 'It's important you have some control, considering where you're staying.'

He had a point. My hostess, Ayesha Jaipur, or Her Royal Highness, the Rajmata Gayatri Devi of Jaipur, is a living legend. Considered one of the most beautiful women in the world, she was widowed early from her charismatic, polo-playing husband, the famous Maharajah of Jaipur, and has led the sort of life movies are based on. Born into Indian royalty, she shot her first panther at the age of eight, jetsetted the world with her husband, was elected a Member of Parliament by one of the biggest majorities the world has ever seen, was thrown into jail by Mrs Gandhi, and went on to found one of the most successful schools for girls in India. She's the last of a breed; a truly great character, with an indomitable spirit and a wicked sense of humour. My wife and I named our daughter after her.

Ayesha, true to her nature, hadn't batted an eyelid when I had told her I would be bringing an extra guest to stay – a pi-dog, yet I was still a little nervous about how she would react to this large black beast over which I had, as yet, no control.

However, I had a secret weapon. Out of my pocket I pulled the brown paper bag given to me by my brother-in-law before I left – the magic dog talisman or, as he put it, the key to a dog's heart. I opened the packet excitedly. I didn't really know what to expect, but it certainly wasn't what I found. Inside the bag was another bag, a bag of chocolate Goodboys. What kind of dog, I wondered in amazement, did my brother-in-law think I was going to find in India? A Chihuahua? A Yorkie? A Cruft's champion? At that moment I could have killed him.

Still, I had nothing else and, more importantly, no time to lose. I decided to give the 'key to a dog's heart' a try. I opened the packet and took out one of the little cylindrical chocolate drops. Pie, I noticed, had strangely gone quiet. He'd stopped straining at his leash and was staring at me – or rather at my hand – with one ear cocked, his tongue hanging out. This might just work, I thought. Slowly I lowered my hand towards Pie and said 'Sit.' He immediately jumped up and I just managed to remove my hand before it was taken off at the wrist by a snap of those wicked jaws.

I tried again. 'Sit,' I said, and gently lowered the chocolate drop. To my delight, Pie relaxed back on to his haunches. I wasn't going to risk my hand, so I dropped the Goodboy, which he caught neatly. 'Got him,' I thought, happily.

Then I tried the next manoeuvre – bringing him to heel. He behaved beautifully. He was right on cue. As long as I had one of those magical chocolate drops in my hand he was putty in my hands. Each time I rewarded him.

Next I tried the ultimate test. I took him off the lead and made him sit. Again I rewarded him, before beginning to walk slowly backwards. He sat there watching me. I stopped a few metres away. 'Stay,' I said. Pie stayed. Then I took out another chocolate drop.

'Stay, Pie,' I warned. He started to tremble with excitement. 'Stay,' I warned him again. Then I chucked the Goodboy into the air. Pie exploded towards me, leapt up, caught the chocolate and sat down at my feet, looking expectantly at me. Easy, I thought. One trained dog.

By now Pie was as good as gold. As long as that magic packet was in my pocket, he never left my side. I sauntered casually across the park, his leash slung across my shoulder, to where Aditya was waiting with Ajit and the car.

Aditya looked at me and then at Pie, suspiciously. 'How did you manage that? You haven't drugged him, have you?'

'Of course not,' I lied. Well, it wasn't really a lie, just a sort of white lie. 'I simply followed your excellent instructions and practised them. Pie and I are like *that* now. You know I have a way with animals.'

'Mmmm,' Aditya muttered.

I could see he wasn't convinced, however, as he noticed Pie trying to tear off my pocket. It was time to change the subject. 'Shouldn't we feed him?' I asked innocently. 'He must be starving.'

'That's the last thing we should do, Mark,' Aditya said pointedly. 'Pie gets car sick, *very*, *very* car sick. I know. You hop in the back with him and get more acquainted. As you said, Pie and you are like *that* now. I'll sit in the front.'

Ajit, no doubt concerned about his new blue seat covers, had already spread the lovely soft tiger motif dog rug across the back seat. I climbed in with Pie firmly attached to my pocket, and we set off to introduce Pie to his hostess.

It didn't take long. First the hot nose, then the panting. And then – I can only assume in the absence of grass, which dogs often eat to try and make themselves better – Pie began to dig furiously, searching for a substitute with those long, sharp toenails. First he shredded the lovely soft tiger motif dog rug; and then, much to the alarm of an increasingly agitated Ajit, who was not making things any better by swerving the car alarmingly as he peered anxiously into the rear mirror, Pie dug through the brand new blue seat covers and began to wolf down the spongy underlining.

'I think he's going to be sick,' I yelled.

Ajit slammed on the brakes, but it was too late. Before I could bale us both out of the back door, Pie neatly regurgitated over me, over the back seat, over the back doors, across the back of the front seats, an interesting and foul-smelling mixture of half a pound of chocolate Goodboys and frayed tiger motif dog rug, peppered with blue spongy material.

It was in this *déshabillé* state that I arrived at Ayesha's Delhi residence. Fortunately for me, she wasn't there. But her old retainers, whom I had known for many years, eyed my arrival with barely suppressed amusement. Aditya quickly took control while I cleaned up in the spare bathroom. Ajit was dispatched, looking remarkably happy, clutching another huge wad of money, to replace his seat covers. Aditya took Pie for a walk around the garden where, after devouring some grass, he threw up a few more times and was soon back to his former happy self.

Aditya and I sat outside on the veranda. I couldn't risk taking Pie into the house. A deep-blue, spongy seat cover was one thing, Ayesha's chintz sofas were another. It was then I felt the itching, itching as if my leg were on fire. I pulled up my trousers to find a spreading weal of livid red spots.

'Jesus,' I said, 'that's all I need. I've got scabies.'

Aditya inspected my leg closely. 'Mmmm,' he muttered casually. 'No, looks more like flea bites to me.'

'Flea bites!' I exclaimed in horror. 'What am I going to do? We can't infest Ayesha's home with fleas.'

'Don't worry, we'll keep Pie outside. Anyway, we'll kill them off later. I'm going to have to show you how to Butox him.'

'Butox? What's that?'

'Deadly poison. Kills everything – scabies, mange, fleas – even the dog itself, if you don't muzzle him. Now, it's quite a tricky procedure. Let me explain.'

It was just as Dr Patankar, India's ace dog catcher turned India's ace vet, was about to launch into canine medical care, that an elegant apparition, draped in an emerald-green chiffon sari, drifted around the corner.

'Ah, there you are, you two. I wondered where you were hiding,' she said. 'And this is . . . ?'

'Pie,' I said. 'Pie, this is Ayesha.' It sounded ridiculous. It was as if I were making some formal introduction at a cocktail party. Pie obediently wagged his stumpy tail.

'Hello, Pie,' she greeted him, and patted him lightly on his head. 'What a strange-looking dog. Rather sweet, though. Where did you find him, Aditya?'

'Well, Ayesha, he sort of found me. He sort of walked into my home. I'd call it destiny, wouldn't you?'

'Mmmm,' she said, clearly not believing a word. 'Is he house-trained?'

'Absolutely,' we lied simultaneously.

'And he's been vaccinated?'

'Oh, against everything,' Aditya replied smoothly, pulling out Pie's vaccination certificate. 'Against canine distemper, hepatitis, parainfluenza, *leptospira bacterin*, rabies, worms – he's had the lot.'

'Any fleas?' she asked.

'Absolutely not,' I said, the right side of my leg burning.

She peered down at Pie a little more closely. 'Looks like he's got a bit of mange, possibly scabies. What are you treating him with, Aditya? Butox?'

'Yes, Ayesha. He's already had two baths.'

'Good. Make sure you muzzle him properly for at least two hours after the baths. It can be fatal for dogs if they lick their fur.'

I smiled inwardly. India's ace dog catcher and vet had clearly met his match. Ayesha turned to me.

'I hope you've been feeding him, Mark. The poor dog looks awfully thin.'

'Umm, he's had a sort of snack,' I mumbled, 'but we bought some meat.'

'Good, I'll get my cook to boil some up for him later. Now, I'm going for a rest. Why don't you take him for a walk in the Lodi Gardens? It's lovely there, he'll enjoy it. I'll see you later.' She turned to leave, and then turned back again, wrinkling her nose. 'Has someone been sick?'

'No,' we lied.

'Funny, I could have sworn . . . Oh, well – see you later.'

Leaving Aditya to relax, Pie and I set off for the Lodi Gardens. By the time we had got there it was late evening, that moment just before sunset – or, as it is known in India, *ghau dhauli*, the hour of the cattle dust – when everything is bathed in a soft, golden glow. Outside the entrance there was an odd sign. 'Dogs are forbidden to enter before 8 a.m. and after 5 a.m.' Perhaps they meant 5 *p.m.* However, as with queues, nobody in India pays any attention to signs, and we slipped in.

I was finally beginning to unwind. It had been a long day and tomorrow was going to be hectic – there was still so much to do before I left Delhi. For the moment, however, I put it all out of my head, and simply enjoyed the company of my new best friend. We slipped in and out of the shadows of the great sixteenth-century sandstone tombs, and listened to the screeches and chatter of the parakeets and sparrows jostling for space in the tall Ashoka trees that lined the manicured paths. Occasionally, we encountered podgy, puffing couples dressed in identical, usually plum-red, track suits and brand new white Nike trainers, taking a little evening exercise in the form of a brisk walk around the circuit of the gardens. The brisk walk soon turned into a brisk circuitous trot as they caught sight of the black beast, straining against his leash in the gathering gloom.

We reached the great Bara Gumbad, the square fifteenth-century tomb, crowned with the imposing dome from which it takes its name. Like most of these great medieval monuments, it had been defaced with graffiti. Pie, I am ashamed to admit, defaced it further by cocking his leg on its ornamental stuccoed entrance. On our return we met other proud owners taking their dogs for a little evening exercise.

'Good evening, lovely time of year. Lovely evening, isn't it? Splendid. Interesting dog you have there. What breed is he? Bit of Lab, I'd say. Or maybe alsatian. This is Rani – she's pure-bred Lab. And this is little Tilly – our Peke.'

Little Tilly didn't realise quite how close she was to becoming Pie's dinner, as I struggled to control him.

'Excitable young fellow you've got there, haven't you, eh? Well, good luck, and good evening to you.'

I felt like doffing my titfer. It really was an incongruous situation. I could have been in Hyde Park, as the snooty saleslady in Harrods said, 'taking your little friend for walkies in the park'. Except that I was in India, and my little friend – a wild pi-dog – was taking *me* for a walk.

Back at Ayesha's house I found a special dinner had been prepared for Pie. His silver bowl was filled to the brim with milk, bread and a couple of boiled chickens. I peered at the chicken suspiciously. 'Aditya, he can't eat this. The bones will get stuck in his throat. He'll choke.'

'Mark,' he explained wearily, 'we are not dealing with one of your English pedigree dogs here. This is a wild street dog. He will eat anything.'

Pie thrust his muzzle into the bowl, slurped up the milk and bread, and in two quick mouthfuls demolished the two chickens. Then he shot into the kitchen, searching for more food.

I decided that Pie should sleep with me. After all, we had to get to know one another. We would be sharing close quarters for the next few months. I chained him to the iron bed leg, spread out my towel as a rug, filled up his new metal bowl with water, placed some toys strategically around him so he wouldn't get lonely, and closed the door of my bedroom. Then I joined the others for dinner. I had hardly taken a mouthful when a terrible wailing echoed through the house, followed by four heavy thuds, and a sound like a chainsaw gone berserk.

'I think it might be wise to keep Pie outside,' Ayesha announced. 'I've just had that room repainted.'

Mortified, I shot back to my room and tried to open the door, but something was blocking it. I pushed harder and managed to squeeze in. Pie had pulled the bed against the door. He was standing there mournfully amongst the debris of shredded towels and savaged toys, and was covered in a fine white coat of chipped paintwork. He wagged his stumpy tail and jumped up and licked my face. I couldn't bring myself to reprimand him. Poor Pie – he was lonely and disorientated. Everything in his world had changed so quickly. He'd gone almost overnight from a rubbish dump to royalty. He was a bit like Eliza Dolittle. Then I saw the back of the door. Or what was left of it. It reminded me of the scarred and scratched face of Mount Kailash. I looked at Pie. He looked at me. 'Well, mate,' I said, 'looks like we're in the shit.' He wagged his tail happily.

'Everything all right?' Ayesha's voice floated through the house.

'Er, fine, Ayesha,' I answered. 'He just feels a bit lonely. I'll take him outside – he'll be happier there. Aditya,' I shouted, 'give me a hand, will you?' Grabbing a bundle of leashes and chains, I pulled Pie out of the room, locked the door and joined Aditya behind the kitchen. We soon found a perfect place for Pie, a little patio, at the back of the kitchen.

'We can chain him to this,' he said, pulling on a thick metal water pipe that ran down the side of the kitchen wall.

Grabbing Pie, I put two leashes around his neck, threaded the chains round the back of the pipe, and then tied them together. I pulled to tighten the knot.

'Are you sure that's strong enough? It's looks a bit of a muddle, that knot of yours,' Aditya remarked.

'Look, Pie's not an elephant,' I replied irritably. I was becoming exhausted. Jetlag was taking its toll. It had been a long day. 'He's a dog. He'd have to be Houdini to get out of this. Here, try.'

Aditya pulled the chain. 'Yup, that's firm,' he said.

We went back inside to join Ayesha for an after-dinner drink. I had hardly had my first mouthful of whisky when the whining started again. I began to get up.

'No, leave him,' Aditya said. 'He'll settle down. He used to do that with me when I first got him. Trust me – he'll sleep soon.'

Eventually the whining stopped. I felt really happy: I was in good company with good whisky and good conversation and best of all, I had a dog of my own. After an hour or so, Ayesha announced that she was going to bed. Aditya and I stayed up for a while, drinking.

'Well, we've done it again, my friend,' he said. '*Jaimata* – your good health. Here's to Pie and your journey.' We clinked our glasses together.

'I wish you were coming with me, though,' I replied nostalgically. 'It won't be the same.'

'Don't be too sure about that – I might just join you both somewhere. Anyway, let's go and say goodnight to Pie. I've got to get home.'

We wandered into the warm, jasmine-scented night air. Bats flitted overhead. Everything was so quiet and peaceful.

Aditya put his finger to his lips. 'Ssh,' he whispered, 'we don't want to wake him.'

We went around the kitchen and peered into the little patio. It was very dark. We peered closer.

'At least I won't be woken up by your snoring,' I whispered to Aditya. 'Pie's a very quiet sleeper.'

'He's not sleeping!' Aditya exclaimed. 'He's *gone*!'

'*What*? You're jok—'

'I'm not joking, my friend,' he interrupted. 'Look – he's pulled the drainpipe right off the wall. That's gone as well.'

He can't have, I told myself. This is not happening to me. This is a nightmare. Like a sleepwalker, I slowly entered the little patio. Aditya was right. It was empty except for a few rusty nuts and bolts on the ground and half a drainpipe hanging precariously from the wall.

Panic set in. 'We've got to find him!' I was trembling, in a state of shock. 'Shit, shit, shit, *shit*!'

'Now, calm down,' Aditya said firmly, grabbing my arm. 'He can't have gone far. He's got a drainpipe around his neck.'

Slowly, the panic subsided. I began to think more clearly. 'Yes. But he's got a hell of a start on us. At least two hours. I bet he took off when the whining stopped. It's all your fault,' I accused Aditya unfairly. 'So much for your canine powers.'

By now the lights had come on in the house, and the servants came tumbling outside. Aditya explained the predicament. Torches were soon produced.

Then an imperious voice echoed through the still night. 'Who is there?'

'Christ,' I said to Aditya, 'it's Ayesha – we've woken her up. Now we're for it.'

Ayesha appeared out of the gloom. 'What on *earth* is going on?'

'Umm – Pie's gone, Ayesha,' I said.

'Gone? Gone where?'

'He's, er, escaped – er, with your drainpipe.'

'I thought you said you'd tied him up.'

'Well, I did. But he, um, pulled the drainpipe off.'

'Really, Mark – and Aditya – first you lose an elephant and now a dog.'

We stood in front of her, like a couple of sheepish schoolboys.

'We found the elephant,' I pointed out, weakly.

'Yes, I know that,' she answered witheringly, 'but an elephant, as you well know, is considerably larger. Pi-dogs are not exactly an endangered species. There must be about five million of them in Delhi alone.'

'Not attached to drainpipes,' I said, clutching at straws. At that moment one of the servants appeared out of the gloom. He was carrying something long and heavy. The broken drainpipe. He'd found it by the gate.

'Not any longer,' Ayesha observed unnecessarily. 'Now, look, I'll contact the local police and ask them to put out an alert. Not that it will do much good,' she added. 'I doubt a pi-dog is top of their priority list. I suggest you two, and you can take my staff, start searching. *Try* not to make too much noise. I do not want the whole neighbourhood woken up. I'll see you in the morning. Good night.'

'Good night, Ayesha.'

Aditya immediately assumed command. 'Right,' he said authoritatively, already seeming to relish the action ahead, 'we'll split up. We'll employ the old Maratha sweeping technique. Mark, you retrace our walk in the Lodi Gardens. The boys and I will check out the surrounding houses and gardens. We'll meet back here in an hour. Synchronise watches. It's now midnight. OK?'

In the daytime Lodi Gardens is green and welcoming, full of life. At night, it's downright spooky. It was closed. I climbed over the wall and started to walk up the long, empty avenue. 'Pie,' I yelled, 'Pie, Pie, come here. Heel, Pie!' There was nothing – just silence. I jumped as something moved in the bushes. I quickly shone my torch, catching a glitter like rubies as a mongoose stared back at me and then disappeared silently into the undergrowth. I walked on and on, calling his name, my voice echoing eerily as it rebounded off the dark and silent tombs.

I crossed the Athpula, the sixteenth-century ornamental bridge in the north-west corner of the park, and then started sadly back. How could this have happened? I just couldn't believe it. I felt a cad. I felt so guilty. Poor Pie. Where in the hell was he?

Unhappily, I climbed over the wall, out of the park. I knew, deep in my heart, that I'd lost him. On the way back I stopped every late-night stroller, who either quickly avoided this madman as he attempted to relate his tale of woe, or wasted valuable time by asking me my age, my marital status, about my job, my good country and the deplorable state of English cricket. I even consulted an old sadhu who was sitting stoned under the wall. He nodded wisely, not understanding a word as I poured my heart out. He blessed me, and then relieved me of a hundred rupees.

Back at the house, I found a dejected and weary Aditya with Ayesha's staff. They'd had no luck either. Aditya had been insulted by every houseowner he had woken, and narrowly avoided serious injury from their chowkidars. But he had managed to find Ajit at the local taxi rank. Now, at least, we had wheels. Ajit's back seat, I noticed, was covered in an even plusher set of seat covers – thick, furry, bright red velour.

In what was left of the night we trawled the city, stopping cars, policemen, politicians, beggars; we even went to the police station where we wasted more time filling in an endless report for a very bewildered officer. He couldn't understand why we wanted to find a pi-dog.

It was practically daylight by the time we reached Ayesha's house. Pale light streaked the eastern sky. I climbed out of the car.

'Look, Mark, get some sleep,' Aditya said kindly. 'We'll check the dog pounds tomorrow. We'll find him, don't worry. I'll pick you up first thing.'

I crept into my bedroom. Pie's earlier tantrum lay around me, a painful reminder of what might have been. Clutching a chewed squeaky mouse tightly to my chest, I fell into a troubled sleep.

I woke a couple of hours later feeling like hell – a combination of lack of sleep, jetlag, a hangover, anxiety and guilt. Serpents writhed in my belly. I made myself as presentable as possible and joined Ayesha for breakfast on the veranda.

She looked up from her newspaper. 'You must feel awful,' she consoled me kindly.

'I do, Ayesha. I've got jetlag. I've had no slee—'

'I'm not talking about how *you* feel, but about how you feel about *Pie*. Poor little thing. He's probably been run over.'

My belly churned as the serpents began a mating dance. Fortunately, Aditya arrived just in time to whisk me away, before guilt and anxiety necessitated further redecoration of the Rajmata's residence. I had to try and put Pie out of my mind. Today was going to be full enough as it was. My first appointment was to collect the vital permit that would allow me to enter the forbidden territory of the McMahon Line: a permit that people had said would be impossible to obtain.

Aditya dropped me off, having nobly volunteered to check out Delhi's dog pounds, and, with spinning head and churning belly, I entered the seething chaos of India's Olympus of bureaucracy, the Lok Nayak Bhavan: the vast and labyrinthine headquarters of the Ministry of Home Affairs, Foreigner's Division.

You fall foul of bureaucracy in many countries, but in India it's a work of art, an institution, an out-of-date colossus that, many of my Indian friends have told me, has really impeded their great and innovative nation's leap into the twenty-first century. Another friend of mine once told me that if you placed all the files in all the ministries in India end to end, they would encircle the world eight times. But it's not India's fault. It's our fault – the good old British. We invented bureaucracy. India just perfected it.

The long odyssey of my file had started two years ago and developed into an epic paper journey of gargantuan proportions. If I could have claimed air miles for my file as it whizzed backwards and forwards from east to west and west to east, I'd have been flying first-class for the rest of my life. Eventually, as all foreigners' files do, it ended up in the Ministry of Home Affairs.

This is where the traffic jam really starts: an inch-by-inch journey from one office to the next. It's called 'passing the buck'. No bureaucrat wants to take the responsibility of possibly making a mistake, or reaching the wrong decision. So the file is passed on, and on, and on, until it sometimes actually returns to its original source. It can be a maddeningly frustrating business. It can in fact drive you completely insane. Unless you know somebody.

Fortunately, I had a secret weapon: the unflappable and ingenious Dinesh Kumar of the British High Commission in India.

Dinesh had been monitoring daily the journey of my file through the maze of the Ministry of Home Affairs, giving it just the right amount of push when it started to gather dust, to ensure that it ended its long passage in the Ministry's *sanctum sanctorum* – the office of the Director. Here, in this small incongruous room on the third floor, a simple signature could either make or break you.

It was into this office that a covey of agitated and nervous peons ushered us. It was bedlam inside. Besides the Director, his secretary, Dinesh and I, there were eight people. The Director was hardly visible behind a stack of files piled on his desk, over which these eight were talking to him simultaneously: a group of sweating suits from a Dutch dredging company, a bearded Muslim, and a skeleton of a girl from Argentina, her skin the colour of a buttercup, dressed in a long, floating cheesecloth dress. I positioned myself as far as possible from her. She looked highly contagious. They all wanted the same thing – visa extensions. They were all standing up. And they were all shouting.

The Director took the madness in his stride. He was leaning back in his chair with his hands behind his back, an amused twinkle in those intelligent eyes, magnified by a large pair of tortoiseshell bifocals. He had seen and heard it all before. For years. Nobody could pull the wool over his eyes. Suddenly he raised his arms. There was dead silence. You could have heard a pin drop. It was unwise to cross swords with the Director. He looked up at Dinesh and me and smiled, and gestured us to sit down. Eight sets of furious eyes bored into me accusingly.

'If you would all be kind enough to come back, let's see,' he said, consulting his diary, 'next Tuesday, I would be most grateful. I do have an important meeting now.'

The six Dutch dredgers, the bearded Muslim and the bright-yellow Argentinian hippy filed silently past me. I didn't dare look up, but I could feel the rage. The door closed. The Director sighed – a tired sigh of relief. He stood up and shook our hands, sat back down again, rummaged around amongst the myriad manila files, selected a particularly thick one, and from that pulled out a two-page document.

'Well, Mr Shand,' he said, 'this is indeed an historical moment, not only for you, but for me. I have never signed such a permit. Nor, to my knowledge has anyone else, ever.'

He unscrewed the cap off a thick, black fountain pen: an important-looking pen, the kind used for signing important documents. Then he paused for a moment. My heart stopped.

'Please check it, Mr Shand,' he warned. 'There are certain rules which you must adhere to. Please read it very carefully.'

With shaking hands, I accepted the document that had taken two years to obtain. It had a wonderfully exciting title – 'Protected Area Permit' – and it listed all the places I was allowed to visit. Magical places, with names to dream about – names like Tuting, Korba, Gelling, Jidu, Bomda, and the upper reaches of the Yamne Valley. I devoured each one like forbidden fruit.

Next I checked the conditions:

a) He will report to the State Government Authorities at Itanagar. He will strictly adhere to the places and routes specified.

b) He should be self-sufficient and should not depend on the army to provide any assistance except for casualty evacuation on humanitarian grounds.

c) He will liaise with GSO 1 (Intelligence), HQ Eastern Command, Fort William, Calcutta on arrival and departure of the subject journey.

I gulped with relief as I read:

d) No maps, imageries or Global Positioning Systems other than the route chart will be carried during the journey.

Another useless gadget, I thought to myself happily, that would end up on the old Christmas list.

e) He will not film, photograph, video, prepare sketches of any unit, installation, equipment, nor interact with locally deployed army personnel in a casual manner.

f) Restrictions, if any, imposed by central Government and state Government will be strictly adhered to.

'I will adhere strictly to all these conditions, sir,' I answered gravely, and returned the precious permit to the Director. With a sweeping flourish my destiny was sealed, as he signed the permit with the important-looking pen.

I should have been over the moon as I walked out of the Ministry clutching that document. After all, I had made history. I had achieved what was thought to have been impossible. I'd negotiated the maze. But I wasn't that happy, not really. I'd lost my dog.

Perhaps there was some hope, I thought. Perhaps Aditya had struck lucky in one of the dog pounds. With my heart in my mouth, I returned to Ayesha's house to find an exhausted Aditya, sitting quietly on the veranda. I could see by the look on his face that he'd been unsuccessful.

'I'm sorry, my friend,' he said sadly. 'I've checked every pound in Delhi – no luck.'

'What do you think happened to him?' I asked anxiously. 'God, I hope he didn't get run over.'

'If I know Pie, Mark, he's fine. Remember, he's a survivor. He's a pi-dog.'

'I don't understand why he wanted to escape. I thought he was rather fond of me – of both of us.'

'There is no answer,' Aditya explained. 'It was just not meant to be. You know that. This is India. There are no coincidences.'

'But where on earth am I going to find another dog?' I whined. 'I'm leaving tomorrow.' I realised I sounded like a spoilt boy in a toy shop. Broke that one, so I'll get the newer model. But I did feel that somewhere out there, in that vast continent, there was a dog waiting for me. Perhaps Pie wasn't the one. Perhaps there was another one. Perhaps, as Aditya said, it was not meant to be.

Aditya had to get back home. 'I have a present for you,' he said, handing me a slim, square brown packet. I opened it up. It was a book by Miriam Fields-Babineau. It was called *Dog Training* and in huge bold yellow letters below the title was the word 'BASICS'. 'I thought you might find it helpful.'

'Very kind of you,' I thanked him, exasperated, 'but as you're very well aware, I haven't actually got a dog.'

'You will soon. Remember the old Hindu saying.'

'What's that?' I asked suspiciously.

'Dog finds dog.' And with a cheerful wave, India's ace dog catcher, ace dog trainer, ace dog vet and now ace dog loser, climbed into the car and drove off.

However difficult it was, I had to stop thinking about Pie. My next appointment was at the Tiger Mountain office. On the way, I stopped off quickly at the Windsor Pet Shop. I decided against any luxury dog toys, or soft dog rugs. It was clear to me now that pi-dogs, if I ever found one, didn't really get their point. Instead, I bought two new identical leads. The polite young salesman, although delighted to see me, was bewildered.

'You are having *more* dogs, sir?'

Not at this rate, I thought miserably. 'Yes,' I said firmly, crossing my fingers.

'Of what gender?' he asked politely.

'Female,' I replied. Well, why not? Anything was possible.

'And what is her good name?'

This flummoxed me, but only for a moment. First I thought of Tara. Except Tara would, I knew, be insulted. She was not, like most elephants, fond of dogs. She'd also be extremely jealous. Anyway, it would all become far too confusing. But thinking of Tara made me think of Kipling Camp, her home. Which then made me think of my friend Bob Wright, Tara's keeper and the owner of Kipling Camp. And thinking of Bob made me think of Tara's arch-enemy, the other pampered princess of Kipling Camp – Vicky, Bob's extremely fat and extremely spoilt golden Labrador.

'Vicky,' I answered.

'That's a fine name, sir.'

At Tiger Mountain, I was introduced to my guide. Yatish was a short, thickset man sporting a heavy black moustache, powerfully built, and a little overweight, like me. And, like me, a little past his prime. Unlike me, however, he seemed very quiet and reticent, almost introverted: the sort who kept things to himself. Exactly the opposite of me, in fact. I never stop talking. It sometimes drives people mad. When Yatish spoke, which was hardly at all, he mumbled. I wondered, rather uneasily, how we would get on, considering we'd be spending a lot of time in close proximity.

However, the moment maps and logistics were discussed, he seemed to come alive. Maps for where we were going were difficult to find, but good maps were almost impossible. If there were any, because of the sensitivity of the area, they were not for public eyes. Fortunately, I had managed to get my hands on a series of American satellite maps. These were on a huge scale, almost too bulky to carry. Unfortunately, section d in my permit stated, 'No maps, imageries or Global Positioning Systems other than the route chart will be carried during the journey.'

We decided to snip out the relevant part only and conceal it. Then it turned out that Yatish had an ace up his sleeve. He was well connected with the military. And what was almost better, Yatish, being Indian, *could* 'interact with locally deployed army personnel in a casual manner', which I was forbidden to do, as section e of my permit stated.

We'd be setting out in the morning for Guwahati, and then on to Itanagar, where I needed to report to the State Government authorities and liaise with Tiger Mountain's north-eastern representative. From there we'd travel to Pasighat, where I was to meet up with the other two members of my team: Topgay, our Ladakhi cook, and my Adi guide Jaro, something of a legend in the 'land of the dawn-lit clouds' for his knowledge of jungle lore and his skills as a great hunter. At least, I thought with some relief, that one part of my journey – through Arunachal Pradesh – was under control.

I still had to sort out how I was going to get down the river through Assam and Bangladesh. I rang Guwahati and spoke to a friend of mine, Manju Barua. Manju owned a beautiful wildlife camp in Assam on the banks of the Brahmaputra, called Wild Grass. I hoped to be visiting it in the later stages of my journey. In the meantime, he was supposed to be finding me a boat to get me down the river through Assam. The first vessel he'd hired for me, I was told through the hiss and static of a bad line, had sunk. He'd apparently managed to find a replacement – a government boat. But there was one problem. It had what he described as 'a very smelly convenience'. I assured him that this was the least of my worries. I enquired about the size of the boat. It was 'sort of big' came the vague reply.

Then came the warnings. Assam, Manju reminded me firmly, was not like some jolly ride on an elephant across India. Although officially open to foreigners, there was always a danger of insurgency, particularly on the river. Piracy and kidnapping were not out of the question. And a 'white sahib', as he described me, was a pretty tempting target. He didn't want to waste valuable time and money in negotiations to bale me out. I was glad he was even thinking about it. No one else would. I assured him I would behave impeccably. I could tell he didn't believe me. It didn't matter. With Assam more or less organised, I was now pretty well set. I could leave the logistics of Bangladesh until later on. I had enough on my plate already.

The real problem was that I still hadn't found a bloody dog. I obviously wasn't going to find one in my last few hours in Delhi. That left Guwahati. And there, it suddenly struck me, I might just get lucky. Another friend of mine, Reeta Dev Verma, lived there. She was, I knew, an avid dog lover. And Reeta had a brother,

Ranesh Roy, who was the manager of Manju's camp, Wild Grass. We'd never met, but Ranesh was due to be in Guwahati in case I needed any help. I did. I needed a dog.

When at last I got back to Ayesha's house, exhausted and depressed, I tumbled into bed and started to read Aditya's gift to me, *Dog Training: BASICS*. I fell asleep at the beginning of the first chapter entitled 'Why Train?'.

Early the next morning, loaded up with rucksacks, two new leashes and a large shiny bowl – but still dogless – Yatish and I boarded the plane for Guwahati, or, as it was known in the ancient Hindu texts of the *Kalik Purana*, Pragiyotishpura – the 'city of eastern lights' – where the great God Brahma first created the stars.

FIVE

I always forget quite how far north Delhi is. As the aeroplane banked sharply right, heading south-east and climbing through the haze of pollution and broken cloud into the clear blue sky above, I could see the Himalayan chain through the window to my left. I shivered as I looked at that cold, icy and seemingly impenetrable fortress. Yet, I remembered, I had found a chink in its armour just a few months ago with Charles – and not just once, but twice. In a few more months I could be doing it all again. Only about six thousand metres below me, on the other side of those mighty white mountains, an icy river swept inexorably eastwards. As we flew swiftly past the lofty peaks of Annapurna, Everest and Kanchenjunga, I thought of the brave men and women who had clawed their way up those sheer icy flanks, some of them even without the aid of oxygen.

The aeroplane began to descend. Below, the sun reflected off a glittering patchwork of green and brilliant white, as if some great mountain god had stepped down from his lofty abode and unfurled a priceless carpet of emeralds and diamonds. As we descended farther, the emeralds became brighter but smaller, the diamonds bigger, yet duller. We were flying now above what seemed to be a sea – a caramel-coloured sea. These were the great reaches of the Brahmaputra or, as it was known by the Ahoms, the great Shan invaders who had ruled Assam for over six hundred years, 'Nam-Dao-Phi' – 'the river of the Star God'.

Pragiyotishpura, the 'city of eastern lights', did not live up to its name – its shining brilliance had decidedly dulled over the centuries. Its current name, Guwahati or 'the market of betel nuts', seemed eminently more suitable as Yatish and I rattled, at alarming speed, along a potholed road in the back of an Ambassador taxi towards the city. Endless neat plantations of tall, elegant betel nut palms lined the road, like soldiers on a parade ground.

Guwahati was a seething, polluted, chaotic metropolis, northeast India's fastest-growing and most important city – the service centre for the country's vast oil and tea industries. Only as we neared our hotel could I begin to picture how delightful it must once have been, lining the banks of the Brahmaputra that ran through it like a great watery artery.

As we sped along, I caught enticing glimpses of my river through a blurred palm-lined esplanade of crumbling old mansions with gardens running down to the water: a placid brown carpet stretching, it seemed, into infinity. But appearances can be deceptive. Beneath that unruffled surface, across which a myriad different craft chugged, puffed, glided and sailed, there writhed a terrible labyrinth of treacherous cross-currents, whirlpools, eddies and ever-shifting sandbanks. The river not only gave life – it took it away. Nothing in this magical country is simply what it seems. The poignant truth of this became apparent when I asked the driver about a large crowd of people who were gathering on its banks.

He explained that only yesterday a *bhut-bhuthi* – the local Assamese name (derived from the ear-splitting sound of its engine) for the long, elegant type of canoe that is used as a ferry – had sunk. There were sixty people on board, and no survivors. The crowd were relatives and mourners, who had come back to the very place that had taken their loved ones away, to bid them farewell on a journey to another life by spreading their ashes on the river's sacred surface. The Brahmaputra was both an end and a new beginning.

I noticed something else as well. Nothing complex, mystical, mysterious, tragic, poignant or wonderful, just deeply worrying: I had not seen a single dog on the entire two-hour drive. I remembered my dictionary's definition of a pi- or pariah dog – an ownerless cur of eastern towns. Guwahati was India's *largest* eastern town.

I recognised Ranesh Roy immediately we entered the lobby. I had known his sister Reeta for years and the family resemblance was obvious. Reeta enjoyed the typical beauty of Assamese women. With their slightly slanting eyes, high cheekbones, long limbs and beautiful skin inherited from their great Shan ancestors, they represent the real essence of this hot, tropical, almost oriental eastern state. Even the ascetic Mahatma Gandhi was bowled over by their beauty. He simply called them 'lovely'.

In the Roy family these genes had blessed the men as well. Ranesh was elegant, tall and best of all, wonderfully irreverent. And coincidentally – if there is such a thing in India – he turned out to have been a school contemporary of the Maratha, Aditya Patankar, although he had not seen him for over thirty years.

I was intrigued. 'What was he like when he was young?' I asked Ranesh.

'Just like you,' he replied with an amused twinkle in his eye. 'A mischievous rogue, always up to no good. But he was one hell of a sportsman – the best in the school.'

This was true. I remembered practically crying with frustration as Aditya had taken me apart on the tennis court, prior to our journey with Tara. And, over the years, even after his hip operation, I'd yet to master his devastating, deceptive and slow looping off-spin. The Maratha could turn a cricket ball at right angles.

'I just want to make one thing clear, Mark,' Ranesh announced suddenly.

'What?' I replied, mystified.

'You can't have one of mine.'

'One of your what?' I said, even more mystified.

'One of my dogs.'

Dogs, I found out as Ranesh and I settled down in the bar to try out the different brands of Assamese beer, ran in the family. He was potty about them. A wistful look clouded his eyes as he described in great detail all the dogs he had owned. Now he had just one – a little bitch called Sumo who lived with him at Wild Grass which he ran for Manju.

'By the way,' I asked, 'where is Manju?'

'Manju's out of station,' Ranesh said. 'Which is probably a good thing for you. You're not exactly popular at the moment. He's spent the last few weeks searching for a boat for you.'

'A boat's the last thing I need at the moment,' I replied mournfully, downing my beer in one gulp. 'What I need is a dog.' I glanced at my watch. Time had just flown. 'Shit!' I exclaimed. 'I've clean forgotten to call Reeta.'

At precisely that moment, the receptionist walked up. There was a telephone call for Ranesh. He picked up the extension at the bar and then held it at arm's length, his eyebrows lifted in amusement. A tinny, shrill staccato echoed around the marble-walled room.

'It's for you,' Ranesh announced happily. 'My sister wants a word.'

'Hi, Reeta! I was—'

'Don't you dare try to make excuses,' she yelled down the line.

'But—'

The volume rose, so, like Ranesh, I held the telephone at arm's length.

'Why haven't you bloody well called me?' she interrupted. 'I'm one of your oldest friends. I've known you for thirty years, and you *knew* I was here. Instead, you've been hanging around with that brother of mine – probably drinking.'

'Reeta, Reeta,' I yelled. I had to yell to get a word in edgeways. 'I *was* going to call you. I've only just arrived,' I lied. 'I'm trying to find a dog. My other dog in Delhi was unfortunately not suitable—'

'Don't you dare lie to me,' she interrupted again. 'Your aeroplane got in hours ago. I checked. And I know what happened to your dog. It's a national scandal. You lost him. Typical.'

'Well—'

'Get in a car right now and come and see me. I've got dogs. If you're very nice to me, I *might* lend you one. And bring that brother of mine.'

Yatish decided not to accompany us, mumbling something about helicopter arrangements. Ranesh and I set off through the heavy traffic for the outskirts of Guwahati. An hour later, we reached Reeta's house, Beltola, named, no doubt, after the large bel, or wood apple tree that stood in her garden. Bel trees have a religious significance – significant to my old friend, the great Lord Shiva. He never seemed to be very far away from me during this journey. It was rather comforting. The leaves of the bel trees were offered to the great Lord of Dance to cool and reduce the heat of his body when he drank the poison of the 'churning seas' to save the world. I thought I could use a few of those leaves now, to cool and reduce her anger.

Fortunately, Reeta had calmed down by the time we arrived and was soon showing me round Assam's first Aids clinic, which she had started here in her house. However, Aids was not really on my mind. Dogs were. I could hear them, endlessly barking – a high hysterical bark – one more loudly than the others. Reeta introduced me to its owner as we went inside. Or rather, she tried to. Rani, admittedly a sweet-looking little mongrel was, I could see, highly neurotic. Reeta explained that she'd had puppies. I was not a canine expert – not yet anyway – but there was something about Rani that didn't turn me on. I knew she would not enjoy, or benefit from, a journey such as mine. And, more importantly, she clearly didn't like me. I tried to soften her up by offering her a chain of biscuits, but she refused to take them. In fact, she refused to come anywhere near me. It was an awkward situation that needed a lot of diplomacy. After all, I was not in a particularly strong position. I was actually being offered a dog. I needed one desperately as I was off tomorrow. Reeta was a very old friend of mine and I didn't want to offend her. Rani was being offered to me on a plate. But I did not want her.

'Wow!' I said. 'She's so beautiful, Reeta. How can you possibly want to part with her? And she clearly adores you.'

Reeta purred with pleasure.

'As much as I'd like to,' I went on, 'I feel it would be wrong to take her. She belongs here with her pups – her family – and with you.'

Out of the corner of my eye I could see Ranesh smirking. He knew what I was up to.

'Also,' I continued smoothly, 'the poor thing's bound to get banged up. There are plenty of wild dogs where I'm going; and then we'd have *more* stray dogs running around. And being a female she could easily get attacked . . . '

Suddenly I had this weird sensation that somebody or something was watching me intently. As if by some invisible, powerful force, my eyes were drawn to my left, to the dark shadows beneath the stairwell, straight into another pair of eyes – fathomless, slightly slanted eyes that were coolly appraising me.

'Who . . . ? What is that?' I heard myself say, my voice an echo.

Reeta turned round. 'Oh,' she said, almost dismissively, 'that's Vikki.'

'Vikki?' The hair on my back rose up. I found I was covered in goose bumps. Was there really such a thing as a coincidence?

'I only took him in a couple of weeks ago,' Reeta carried on. 'He was hanging around the house. He had such bad mange there was hardly a hair left on his body – he's made a remarkable recovery. But you can't have him. My servant adores him. He's a strange dog – very independent.'

But I wasn't listening. Whatever was sitting quietly, independently underneath the stairwell, was mesmerising me with those cool, hypnotic eyes.

'Vikki,' I said softly. 'Come, come here.'

'Forget it,' Reeta interrupted, 'he won't listen. Goodness – that's strange . . . '

Suddenly, from the dark shadows of the stairwell, Vikki headed slowly, cautiously across the marble floor, straight towards me. He walked so softly he seemed to be floating on air. If I hadn't known about his past history and that he had a large scar over his left eye – perhaps the souvenir of a street scrap – I would never have guessed he was a pi-dog. He was more like a pure-breed, like a small Husky, a kind of little sleigh-dog, with short, thick golden hair, almost russet, like the colour of autumn leaves, and a beautiful creamy chest. He was just under two feet high with a compact muscular body ending in a lovely bushy tail which curled back on itself, a few hairs of the tip jet black as if he had accidentally flicked it against a freshly painted door. He had small pointed ears, and a coal-black, slightly blunted muzzle; his whole demeanour radiated brightness and intelligence. He stopped for a moment to scratch. I noticed that three of his nails on the paw of his left hind leg were a delicate shade of pale pink, like mother of pearl. He got up and slowly moved towards me again, those extraordinary eyes, two deep pools the colour of liquid chocolate, never leaving mine. He sat at my feet and sniffed my knees as if checking me out. I offered him a biscuit: he didn't grab it, but took it gently, revealing small, white, sharp teeth. He had, quite unlike Pie's wicked halitosis, the sweetest breath. It was almost as if he had just cleaned his teeth. My heart was pounding. I would do anything to get this dog. He looked up at me as if reading my mind and then, quite suddenly, jumped up on to my lap, curled up, sighed and closed those cool, hypnotic eyes. He had taken possession of me.

I knew I needed to look no further. I knew it with the same certainty as when I first encountered Tara – this was the dog for me. Every other dog would pale in comparison – even, without wishing to be callous, my Pie. I understood now, as Aditya had said, that Pie was just not meant to be. Pie had been a moment – albeit an intense, meteoric moment. His escape showed that Aditya had trapped him against his will. But this was different. This dog, I knew, had been waiting for me.

'Good boy,' I said, as nonchalantly as possible, trying to conceal my own amazement and running my fingers through his soft hair. He smelled deliciously of shampoo and freshly mown grass.

Reeta was impressed – it was hard not to be – but I could sense she still hadn't made up her mind. Vikki's destiny lay in a precarious balance. Ranesh came to my rescue.

'That's remarkable,' he exclaimed. 'It's almost as if he's known you all his life.'

I felt the same way. I felt I'd known him all *my* life. We looked at Reeta expectantly – all three of us. Vikki had opened those extraordinary eyes. He was hard to resist.

'All right, Mark,' she said at last, after pondering it for what seemed like an eternity. 'You can take him. But on one condition.'

'What?' I asked warily.

'Vikki is your dog now. I will always consider him to be your dog. But when you've finished your journey, he is to return home here.'

'Of course, Reeta,' I lied smoothly. There was no way, even over my dead body, that he was going to return here. Vikki belonged to the great outdoors, not to the streets. I would find him a suitable home, a wonderful home, just as I had for Tara.

There was just one other thing I had to sort out: Vikki's name. Vikki was a male, and although Vikki was probably short for Vikram – a common enough Indian name – I just couldn't handle it. It was a bit like that song *A Boy Named Sue*. I couldn't imagine shouting 'Vikki, Vikki, stop that!' as he rogered silly yet another tribal bitch. I knew I was being pedantic, but if Vikki remained Vikki, in my mind he would always be a girl.

I explained this to Reeta as tastefully as I could. I actually doubted whether Vikki knew he had a name at all, of any kind. And even if he did, it didn't matter. Tara, my elephant, I told Reeta, had been called Toofan Champa. I'd changed her name as soon as I'd bought her, I pointed out, and unlike Vikki she'd been with the same owner for several years.

Reeta sighed wearily. 'OK. But what are you going to call him?'

'Why not name him after me?' Ranesh said suddenly.

Reeta was appalled. 'After *you*? Ranesh is an appalling name for a dog.'

Even I agreed.

'No, no, no,' he said. 'Not Ranesh. Bhaiti. Bhaiti, Mark, means "little brother" in Assamese. After all, I am Reeta's little brother. What do you think?'

Bhaiti, I thought. Bhaiti (pronounced 'Bitey'). I liked it. It rolled off the tongue nicely. And what was even better, it meant I finally had some male company in my family. I had always been outnumbered by the fairer sex – a wife, a daughter and a large female elephant. Now I had a little brother to play with: it redressed the balance a little. I'd found my dog.

I had believed it before, but now I was really sure: there were *no* coincidences. Not in India, anyway. Everything that happened was meant to be. Even before I had met Aditya, years before our elephant trip, his father-in-law had owned a Labrador bitch called Tara. Tara had pups. Among them was a rather aggressive little fellow who was always getting into fights. He had a scar above his left eye. Bhaiti had a scar above his left eye. I have a scar above my left eye. Aditya's father-in-law named that aggressive little fellow 'Mark'.

I took Bhaiti for a trial spin around Reeta's garden, on a lead. I was already confident that he was not the kind of dog to take off, but I wasn't going to take any chances, considering my last experience. He had put up a little resistance, not surprisingly, when I attached the strange, alien object – the leather collar – around his neck. But he immediately relaxed and trotted obediently beside me. Then, suddenly, he stopped and started to quiver with excitement. He was staring at something intently, like a pointer. I followed his gaze. Hovering a few feet above the lawn was a kind of dragonfly. Bhaiti, I was to find out, was the ultimate insectocutor. If it flew, he zapped it.

I let him off the lead and watched as he raced silently across the grass, jumped into the air and, with a single snap of those small, sharp teeth, swallowed his victim. Then he returned and sat down beside me. I felt very proud, but now also deeply possessive and perhaps neurotically protective. Although he clearly had strong hunting genes and was going to have the most wonderful time in the vast, unexplored forests of Arunachal Pradesh, there was no way he was going to end up stuffed with rice and laid out on a banana leaf as a delicacy at a tribal ceremony. Nobody was going to eat Bhaiti – particularly me. I would rather die first.

After a spot more insectocution, we took a breather and stretched out together in the shade of the bel tree. It felt so cosy. I already imagined us curled up together in my sleeping bag in our tent, sharing secrets late into the night. It was just as Ranesh had said. It really did feel that he had known me all his life, as he snuggled in the crook of my arm, resting his head on my chest. But there was something more than that. It was as if I *knew* this dog, or had read about a dog that looked like this. Suddenly it came to me. It was in a book, a book I had recently: Mr Soman's book, the greatest authority on the pi-dog. He had, if I remembered correctly, described a dog just like Bhaiti – a hunting dog. And, if I wasn't mistaken, the dog originated from somewhere in these parts. I couldn't wait to get back to the hotel to check it out.

But first I had something else to do. I had finally been granted a dog. The gods had smiled on me in spite of my failed devotions at Kailash and Manasarovar. Now I would repay them, and seek blessings for my journey. I would pay a visit to the great Shakti temple of the Mother Goddess, Khamakya.

Going to Khamakya was itself something of a ritual for me. I had visited the temple twice before on my trips to India: once as a young backpacker, and again with my friend and elephant guru, Parbati Baruah, the 'queen of the elephants'. Apparently to gain the full power of the Mother Goddess, one has to visit Khamakya three times. It boded well: this was my third visit. Ranesh kindly offered me the services of his family *panda* or priest to guide me in my obeisance. Leaving Reeta to say her goodbyes to Bhaiti, I set off.

The temple was magnificently positioned on a steep hillock, locally named Nilacha, the Blue Mountain, with stunning views of the Brahmaputra and, on a clear day, way beyond to the peaks of the eastern Himalayan range of Bhutan. It is a powerful, ancient place – of pre-Aryan origin – and its rituals are soaked in blood. According to Hindu mythology, it was created in an epic tale of love, lust and woe.

The great Lord Shiva (yes, the same god whom I had failed to honour on the roof of the world in western Tibet a few months before, the god who lived on top of the Crystal Mountain) once fell in love with a beautiful girl called Sati. Sati's father Daksha, obviously a strict, traditional and unimaginative sort of gentleman, was horrified that his daughter was to marry this weird and wonderful god, who had matted dreadlocks and hung out with his cronies on a tiger skin rug on top of the Crystal Mountain, getting stoned. Daksha refused to come to their wedding. Such was Sati's shame that she died of grief. Such was the great Lord Shiva's grief and anger that he roamed the world, hither and thither, carrying her dead body on his head as a penance.

The other great gods became concerned about Shiva's state of mind because, in another reincarnation, he was the Lord of Dance. There was a danger that he would begin the dangerous, whirling dance of destruction, that he had the power to destroy the world. If he started it, he would open his third eye – the great all-seeing eye – and incinerate everything.

It was agreed that Lord Vishnu would tackle the problem. Mounting his eagle – his fabled Garuda bird – he flew up to where Lord Shiva was sulking in his snowy abode, and threw his chakra – his razor-sharp discus – at the body of Sati. The body fell to earth in fifty-one different pieces, in fifty-one different places. Wherever the pieces fell the ground was considered sacred. Sati's vagina fell on the hillock, marking the beginnings of female Shakti worship at the temple of the great Mother Goddess, Khamakya.

After the original temple was sacked by the Mohammedans in the early fifteenth century, its restoration a hundred years later was celebrated with a huge sacrifical ceremony in which, it is said, a whole 'hecatombe' of victims, including 140 humans, were decapitated, their heads presented to the Mother Goddess on bronze salvers.

Khamakya has always been a sacrificial temple. Still today sacrifice is at the heart of its ritual: by decapitation only of males of all species. The ancient Sanskrit text, the *Kalika Purana*, states that birds, tortoises, alligators, fish, buffaloes, bulls, billy goats, mongooses, wild boars, rhinoceros, antelopes, iguanas, reindeer, lions and tigers were sacrificed here. The list of species goes on and on, and, of course, it includes humans. But not, curiously, I discovered, elephants or dogs. I had come to the right place.

Endangered species and humans have now been struck off the sacrificial list but the temple feels no less powerful for that. People still come from all over India, carrying pigeons and chickens and pulling goats, to offer them to the great Mother Goddess. On my last visit here, I met a family who had made a four-month, two-thousand-mile journey from the south, hauling a young buffalo all the way.

But with power comes money. And with money come the *pandas*, the priests. They were sitting in a long line, hunched like vultures waiting patiently for the remains of a kill, on a wall outside the temple. And exactly like vultures, when they saw me – the easy pickings of the rich firingee – they all hopped off the wall and, spreading their vermilion wings, surrounded me. I was only saved from being stripped to the bone by Ranesh's *panda*, who literally had to tear me away from their greedy claws.

We removed our shoes and walked up a little path lined with booths selling every kind of religious offering. You name it, they had it. I wasn't into sacrifice, so I settled for bundles of incense sticks, garlands of marigolds and sweetly scented pink frangipani, bunches of red lotuses and a basket of coconuts. I also carried lots of five and ten rupee notes. Ranesh had warned me about the venality of the *pandas*, and I had changed all my high denomination bills before coming.

Staggering under the weight of my horticultural arrangement, I stumbled into the main temple complex. It was pandemonium inside – lots of *pandas* moaning. And chanting. And ringing bells. Goats bleated in terror. Chickens squawked and clucked. Doves and pigeons flapped and cooed. The air was heavy with the smell

of incense. But there was another smell. It enveloped me. It seemed
to seep into my very pores. It was more of a taste: that sharp metallic taste of fresh blood.

Guided by my vermilion-clad *panda*, we followed a colourful
ribbon of devotees around the complex. We stopped at the large
stone effigy of an elephant – a blood-red elephant, covered in a glistening slick of vermilion paste. Beside it hung a brass bell.
Memories came flooding back of my last visit here as a devotee of
my elephant guru, Parbati Barua, of the special elephant mantra
she had finally given me when she considered me worthy enough,
and of the metal elephant-headed bracelet that she had blessed
here and then presented to me.

Bowing my head, I quietly recited my mantra, removed a dab of
bright red vermilion from the statue with my thumb, and anointed
my forehead. Then I rang the bell three times. I was both surprised
and apprehensive as my *panda* led me by the hand to the entrance
of the domed temple. On my previous visits here, I had been barred
entry to the hallowed, subterranean inner sanctum. On my last
visit Parbati had taken my offerings and presented them to the
Goddess on my behalf. Now – perhaps because of my persistence,
the great Goddess had finally recognised me as a true devotee – I
was to be allowed in. Just outside the entrance, we passed the sacrificial slab. A beefy *panda* was cleaning his long, sharp sword,
while a chela removed the headless carcass of a goat and another
threw water across the slab. The smooth stone floor was slick with
blood and water beneath my bare feet. I was relieved to see that the
devotees did not actually carry their offerings into the temple itself.
I had imagined a chamber of horrors, a kind of dark and ghoulish
abattoir.

Panda power clearly ruled here. Mine led me straight to the
front of the long queue and in, from bright sunlight, to total
darkness. For a moment, I was completely blind. Then, illuminated only by flickering candles in little earthen pots, we were

swept along with the other devotees, down a long tunnel. It was hot and the air was heavy with the overpowering scent of incense.

Deeper and deeper, we approached the core of the temple: a prehistoric cave, a powerful and ancient pre-Aryan shrine of tribal worship. Here in the crush of eager devotees the silence was broken only by the soft patter of bare feet on smooth stone, the occasional intake of breath, and the murmurings of a group of sloe-eyed *pandas*.

My *panda* managed to pull me through the crowd to the centre and the shrine itself, the sheer weight of people pushing me off balance. Carved from a large black granite slab, covered by a pure white muslin cloth and garlanded by mounds of crimson flowers, lay an ancient yoni – Sati's mythological pudenda. Over it oozed a steady trickle of water from a natural spring in the rocks above. Once a month, it is said, like the menstrual cycle of a woman, the spring turns red, staining the muslin like blood.

I could hardly breathe in the tiny, shadowy, claustrophobic chamber. The air was not only choking and heady, it also seemed charged with erotic energy. The colour red – the colour of sacrifice – was omnipotent, staining the ancient walls crimson. They seemed to be closing in on me. It was like being enveloped in a vast womb. I felt I was going to pass out. I quickly muttered my prayers, presented my offerings, cracked a coconut, gave a large donation, and in return had a holy thread tied around my right wrist and received another vermilion mark on my forehead – a blessing from the Mother Goddess herself, transferred by the spiritual hands of the chief *panda*. Gasping for air, I literally fought my way through the melée, up the underground passage and stumbled out into fresh air and sunlight.

Blessed and painted like an Apache, I made my way back to Reeta's house and to Bhaiti – my little brother. He bounded up to me. I bent down, and taking a little vermilion paste from my forehead with my thumb, I dabbed it between his eyes. Now we were both blessed for our jouney together. I gave a huge sigh of relief and pleasure, and hugged him tightly. Finally, I thought, I could relax.

Not for long, however. Our reverie was interrupted by Reeta shouting from the house. Yatish was on the telephone. And it was urgent, very urgent. Reluctantly, Bhaiti and I went in to take the call. Relaxation, it seemed, was out of the question. We had to leave now – right now – for the airport, we needed to get to Itanagar urgently. The Chief Minister was in residence, but was leaving early the following morning on a tour of the state. The only way to get there fast was by the twice-weekly helicopter, which was leaving in two-and-a-half hours.

I told Yatish that I had now found a dog. Could my dog go on the helicopter? Absolutely not. Dogs were not allowed on board, he insisted. He had only just managed to get *us* on, by some devious means. I was appalled. I had just got my little brother, and now it seemed I had to leave him behind.

'So how's Bhaiti going to get there?' I asked.

'Leave that to me, Mark,' replied Yatish. 'I've got someone who will drive him.'

'He'd better be bloody good,' I said. It was about ten hours by road from Guwahati to Itanagar and I didn't want Bhaiti in the hands of a total stranger. How soon would they get there? I asked. In a couple of days came the reply. A couple of days, I thought. A couple of days without Bhaiti. I was miserable. Yatish was panicking now. He implored me to hurry up. I explained the situation to Reeta and Ranesh.

'Well, I'm coming with you,' Reeta said. 'Bhaiti has never been in a car. Also, I've got to tell you all about his medical care.'

Under the dark and threatening looks of Reeta's servant, and to the sound of Rani's hysterical barking, we all climbed into a taxi and sped towards the hotel.

'Now, listen,' Reeta said, as we bounced around in the back of the car. She started furiously dictating detailed instructions about hygiene, diet and medicine. I wasn't paying much attention. It was hard enough to concentrate in the back of a speeding taxi with no suspension, let alone take notes. I had my hands full looking after Bhaiti. The poor dog, clearly traumatised by this strange and new method of transport, had crawled, whimpering, inside my shirt. I hated to imagine how he'd manage on the drive to Itanagar; or how he was going to cope with the other kinds of transport on our journey.

The dictation only ended as we screeched into the courtyard of the hotel. Another taxi was waiting with its engine running and the boot open, into which Yatish was piling our bags with the help of another younger man. Yatish introduced us: this was Neeraj, who was going to look after Bhaiti for a couple of days and then drive him to Itanagar.

Neeraj was another Tiger Mountain guide. I liked him immediately. He emanated good vibes. I could feel them. He was more gregarious than Yatish, and although younger and less experienced I almost wished he was coming with me. Here, I knew, was somebody I could travel with.

More importantly, he clearly liked Bhaiti and Bhaiti, who had quickly recovered from the taxi ride, clearly liked him. He stayed close to Neeraj, almost avoiding Yatish who had greeted him rather dismissively with a little condescending pat. I watched the scenario with interest. Always trust an animal's instincts: they are rarely wrong. I took him aside.

'Neeraj,' I said seriously – very seriously. 'If anything happens to Bhaiti while he's in your care, I'll kill you.'

His eyes widened in alarm. Then I laughed.

'Sir,' he said.

I interrupted him. '*Please* don't call me sir.'

'OK, sir,' he replied. 'Bhaiti is my responsibility. Nothing will happen to your good dog.' He put his hand on his heart. 'On Bolenath – the great Lord Shiva.'

'You're a devotee of Lord Shiva?' I enquired delightedly. 'So am I. Well, sort of.'

'Of course, sir. He will protect you, and Bhaiti.' He took a little bracelet of carved wooden beads off his wrist. 'Please take this sir, It has been blessed by Bolenath. At my home temple.'

I was deeply touched by this spontaneous gesture. I thanked him, and then did my best to pass on Reeta's instructions on Bhaiti's medical and culinary care.

'Do not worry yourself, sir,' he said solemnly. 'I am experienced in dog. Myself, I have two. All the needful will be done. I will see you in Itanagar. I will come quickly.'

It was time to say goodbye to Ranesh and Reeta. I could never thank Reeta enough. She had given me something special – another member to add to my growing family of Indian animals. I bent down to Bhaiti and whispered in his soft, pricked ear, 'I'll see you soon, little brother. Be good.' He licked me gently – a soft, gentle lick under my chin. Then I climbed into the taxi and Yatish and I drove at a dash for the airport. Like a child going back to school, saying goodbye to his parents, I waved continuously out of the back window until Bhaiti, my new best friend who was going to share lots of adventures with me, was out of sight.

SIX

For once, every traveller's essential companions, those two great rivals, the *Lonely Planet* and the *Rough Guide*, agreed. Itanagar, they stated, was 'not especially interesting' and 'holds little of interest to visitors'. I had extracted this valuable information from these two immense volumes on India (I wish they would design them smaller and lighter), as I sat squeezed into the back of a helicopter, taking us the 250 miles north-east from Guwahati, along the course of the Brahmaputra. How we managed to actually get on to the helicopter is a mystery, and one that the enigmatic Yatish was not going to share with me. He did mumble something about having two important officials removed from the passenger list, relations of the Chief Minister, which I thought boded well for my imminent meeting with the great man.

I gazed down at the vast expanse of water below. Only a few hundred miles north-west of here, over the Himalayan ranges, were its beginnings – a tiny glacial trickle. Even at eighteen hundred metres, its banks were barely visible. Every year this mighty artery unleashes its fury during the monsoons, spreading like a virus to

wreak terror, havoc, misery and death. But this year, it had surpassed itself. Assam and Bangladesh had suffered the worst floods
in history.

Itanagar, the capital of Arunachal Pradesh – 'the land where the
sun kisses Mother India first', a verdant state the size of Portugal –
nestles in the foothills of the eastern Himalayas, almost totally
camouflaged by the dense canopy of the surrounding forests.

'A network of beautifully surfaced roads connect all the sections of the capital which, with its newly constructed buildings
and residential quarters, illuminated with electric lights at night,
looks extremely wonderful,' wrote Mr S. Dutta Choudhury in the
'Arunachal Pradesh District Gazetteers', Subsansiri Division, in
1981.

It was up one of these steep, beautifully surfaced roads that we
were now travelling towards the capital, a few miles from the
helipad. I didn't feel I was in India. I could almost have been in
the Alps in summertime, with its cool, fresh air scented by the
pine forests, and its quietness. A drop-a-pin kind of quietness.
Mr Dutta Choudhury hadn't lied. The roads were beautifully
surfaced. They had been developed hurriedly by the Indians to
link up military bases to protect this sensitive state, bordering
Bhutan to the west, Burma to the east and Chinese-occupied
Tibet to the north, after the Chinese had swept into India as far
south as the city of Tezpur, on the banks of the Brahmaputra in
1962.

But Mr Dutta Choudhury was wrong about the 'electric lights at
night looking extremely wonderful'. As we crested the top of a hill,
somewhere below us lay Itanagar. It had been plunged into darkness by a power cut. The anonymous Hotel Arun Subansiri, named
after the river that runs through Itanagar, a feeder for the
Brahmaputra, was empty. Yatish and I were the only guests. Up
until a year ago, Itanagar's hotels had done good business with the
timber merchants. A year ago the Supreme Court had introduced a

total ban on logging. Now the hotels rely on sporadic tourism – a lesser, maybe, of two evils.

Arunachal Pradesh is the last remaining lung of this great continent, a continent that has already lost 90 per cent (although the Government's official figures are considerably lower) of its forests. It has 32,050 square miles of virgin, rugged, undulating terrain, with a population of just over a million. If the Government were to lift the ban, which it is under considerable pressure to do, India would not only lose its last great area of forest, but also destroy the indigenous tribal peoples Nehru fought so hard to protect.

Guided by a room boy, carrying our bags and a flickering candle, we climbed the marble stairs to our rooms. As we entered mine, the candle was blown out – and so were we, literally, by the hurricane whirl of the ceiling fan, given a sudden jolt of power as the hotel's generator started up.

'You have number one luxury room, sir. Full air-conditioning,' shouted the boy happily, as we battled back into the room against a force ten gale.

I thanked and tipped him, and quickly turned the fan off as Yatish announced that we had to get going once again. A car had arrived to take us to dinner with Tiger Mountain's representative in north-east India, a gentleman by the splendid name of Ozing Dai. It was already 8 p.m. After dinner we were supposed to go and meet the Chief Minister. I was beginning to worry about whether we'd manage it, given the time. Itanagar didn't seem to me like a late night, swinging city.

I found Ozing Dai irresistible. I was already prepared to like him simply because of his name and, even more endearing, what Tiger Mountain had told me about him in Delhi – that he was undoubtedly the most disorganised man they had ever encountered. But what really clinched it for me was that Ozing suffered from an appalling stutter. At the concentration camp that masqueraded as my public school, stutterers and bed-wetters were considered outcasts. We'd all been made to share a dormitory. Ozing would have fitted right in. A high-born Adi of a wealthy family, his stutter, if anything, just added to his laid-back charm, and his inability to take anything seriously.

'Oh, g-g-good g-g-god,' he welcomed me. 'Another b-b-bloody Englishman to drive me m-m-mad. I th-th-thought we'd got r-r-rid of you all.' Sporting a wispy kind of Chinese emperor moustache, his face had a look of perpetual surprise. With his Beatle-mop haircut, he reminded me a little of Peter Sellers playing Fu Manchu, and he was, if anything, funnier. 'An Englishman and his d-d-dog,' he giggled. 'W-w-well, what next? B-b-by the way, w-w-where *is* your d-d-dog?'

'My dog, Ozing,' I replied, trying to sound pissed off, 'should have been with me, but because *you* told Yatish to get me here as soon as possible to meet the Chief Minister, I couldn't get him on the helicopter.'

He giggled again. 'The Ch-ch-chief Minister is n-n-not here.'

'Not here,' I gasped incredulously.

'I th-th-thought he was here,' he gestured around, 'b-b-but he's not. Here today, gone t-t-tomorrow. Wh-wh-who knows?'

I could actually have killed him. I could have been spending valuable time 'bonding' with little Bhaiti. 'Christ, Ozing,' I said. 'So all this rush has been a waste of time?'

'W-w-wasting time, Mark,' he said, 'is an old Adi c-c-custom, you'll s-s-soon find out. As we don't have anything to d-d-do, we f-f-find wasting t-t-time gives us something t-t-to do. But you can,' he continued, 'check in officially with the S-s-state Authorities.'

'When?' I asked suspiciously.

'N-n-now,' he smiled, and introduced me to his dinner guest, Arunachal Pradesh's Chief Secretary, a relaxed-looking man, clearly from his more North Indian looks not a local. The Chief Secretary had been posted here from Delhi.

'I'm told I have to report to you, sir.'

He raised his glass,' he replied, 'you've reported.'

That was easy, I thought. It might have been a mad rush to get here, but I was beginning to realise that if you have to take things slowly in India you have to take them even more slowly in Arunachal Pradesh. It had a wonderful informality about it.

'I think we can trust you, Mark,' the Chief Secretary continued with a twinkle in his eye. 'Anyway, we'll always know where you are. Ozing's in charge,' and he laughed uproariously.

It turned out to be an entertaining and unbelievably noisy evening. Not only was Ozing having his house refurbished outside, but his wife, a charming and hospitable lady, never stopped talking. I think I now understood why Ozing had developed his stutter. He had been trying for years to get a word in edgeways, but never could. He was clearly terrified of her.

'Ozing, Ozing,' she yelled every few minutes. 'Come and help me in the kitchen. Fill up people's drinks.' There was an endless stream of domestic demands. I could see who wore the trousers around here. Between her requests, and the constant banging, I managed to ask Ozing what they were actually constructing out the back. It sounded like a skyscraper.

'A d-d-dog kennel,' he explained. 'But in fact, it's just a w-w-way t-t-to remind us that we are p-p-part of this great c-c-country. We have to be seen to be keeping up with the rest of India by making some n-n-noise.'

As I bid him goodnight, I asked him again about my meeting with the Chief Minister.

'P-p-possibly tomorrow, or the n-n-next day,' he announced. 'Re-re-remember, as he's h-h-head of the s-s-state, he has to s-s-set an example. He has to w-w-waste more time than anybody.'

And so it proved. Over the next couple of days I waited, trying hard to cultivate the Adi way of doing nothing – the Adi kind of patience. It was difficult. I rang Ozing repeatedly, desperate for some kind of news. Ozing was always out, doing god knows what. Yatish and I had a few sporadic attempts at conversation, and then he left for a day to see his brother, the Colonel of the Assam Rifles, who was making a tour of Arunachal, inspecting military bases. When he came back, Yatish reported that military choppers were supplying relief to the areas that had been cut off during the monsoons. There might be a chance of our cadging a lift on one of them if the Chief Minister didn't come through. Yatish, I realised, was a man of more resource than I'd given him credit for. He was good at choppers.

Meanwhile, I sulked and worried about Bhaiti in my room, not daring to move, in the unlikely event of a telephone call from Ozing about my meeting with the Chief Minister. It felt strange, though, being the *only* foreigner in a capital city, however small – Itanagar had a population of just 17,000 people. I was beginning to go stir-crazy.

To fill my time, I lay on my bed watching what every bored hotel prisoner in the world watches – CNN. As usual, there was only bad news. In fact it was disastrous. A terrible hurricane, Hurricane Mitch, had struck El Salvador, Nicaragua and Guatemala. It was the storm of the century. So far two million people were homeless and over eight thousand dead.

I knew that the area I was in was prone to natural disasters too – huge ones. On 12 June 1897, the biggest earthquake in modern history hit Assam. It reached magnitude 8.8 on the Richter scale, leaving over 1500 people dead. A week later, on a tea estate in Assam, a glass of water left on a table was reported not to have stopped trembling since the quake. And then another in 1950, whose aftershock was felt over 650,000 square miles, wiped out the little market town of Sadiya, where Charles Allen had spent his childhood.

Disasters. God, I hoped Bhaiti would be okay. Suddenly I remembered that, buried in my bag, was Mr Soman's book on the

Indian dog. I'd completely forgotten it in the dash from Guwahati. I opened it eagerly at the chapter on the pariah and the mongrel, mentally stroking Bhaiti's short, thick russet hair. It confirmed just what I'd suspected the minute we'd met: Bhaiti was from the Pomeranian breed, like a Husky or a Samoyed, or a Finnish Spitz. In fact, he could be a pure breed. And, as I'd guessed, he had originated from Assam – or, more precisely, from Tripura, the state that was formerly part of Assam. He came from the Lushai Hills. He was a Tripuri dog.

Tripuri dogs, I discovered from the authoritative Mr Soman, are about forty to fifty centimetres high and have muscular, compact bodies. That described Bhaiti exactly. The muzzle is usually foxy, the ears small and pricked, and the whole expression is bright and intelligent. Just like Bhaiti. The nose is black, the eyes are light brown and slightly slanted. Bhaiti had lovely, slightly slanted eyes that were light brown like pools of liquid chocolate. Drop-dead sexy eyes – Assamese eyes. The feet, Mr Soman went on, are small, and they stand well on their toes. Bhaiti had exquisite feet and poise to die for. The coat is usually short but thick, and the tail bushy and tightly curled over the back. I thought of Bhaiti's lovely, bushy, tightly curled tail, with its little splash of black at the end. The colours are usually black or light brown, but with some white patches. That was Bhaiti's beautiful, creamy chest. And then came the bombshell. Tripuri dogs are wonderful hunters, and tribesmen often use them for hunting wild boar and deer. They are extremely rare and not at all suited to urban areas. Unfortunately, they're becoming almost extinct, due to crossbreeding in cities. No wonder Bhaiti had been waiting for me. He had to get out of town. I knew he belonged to the outdoors. There was no way he'd be going back to Reeta, that was a promise. Where we were going, he'd be free. But he had to get here first. Where the hell was he? Why was Neeraj taking so long?

And at that moment I thought I was being hit by another

earthquake as the door was almost blown off its hinges and Bhaiti, hotly pursued by Neeraj, burst into my room.

I could not have dreamt of a more affectionate reunion. I was bowled over – literally – as Bhaiti leapt on the spare bed, bounced off it, landed like a missile on my chest, and knocked me backwards on to my bed, covering my face with a thousand little licks. Worryingly, I noticed his nose was hot and dry, and his coat seemed to lack the silky lustre I remembered.

Neeraj explained that this was just due to the vaccinations he had been given and would soon wear off. Bhaiti, he told me proudly, had not even flinched at the needles, and produced his brand new medical certificate as if to prove it. I was furious when I noticed the vet had scribbled 'local cross' under the section headed 'Breed'. Evidently, he wasn't a canine expert. I crossed out 'local cross' and proudly entered 'Tripuri hound from the Lushai Hills'.

We tried to feed him a thick soup of milk, eggs and vegetables, prepared with loving care by the kitchen staff, who had also fallen under Bhaiti's spell and were clearly pleased to have something to do. They now had four guests in the hotel. But Bhaiti turned his nose up at it and yawned. Neeraj and I ate it instead.

Neeraj crashed out and I prepared a bed for Bhaiti next to mine, using most of the hotel's bath towels, and lay down on it to check that it was soft enough. I was sure a good night's sleep would restore him. Now we were together again, I wanted to get going as soon as possible. I made one more call to Ozing. This time, miraculously, he answered, but there was still no sign of the Chief Minister. I told him it didn't matter. I'd had enough of hanging around in Itanagar. Bhaiti was here and the Chief Minister might never turn up. I'd take my chances on finding a chopper in Pasighat through Yatish's contacts.

'Come and pick us up nice and early, Ozing,' I said. I knew it would be a long drive.

'Of c-c-course, Mark,' he promised. 'W-w-with the sunrise.'

I'll believe it when I see it, I thought. There was no chance of Ozing arriving anywhere early.

Then I settled Bhaiti down. 'Sleep tight, little brother,' I whispered, climbing beneath my sheets, and soon I was asleep with Bhaiti beside me, curled up on his bed of towels. In the middle of the night, I felt something warm and soft snuggling up to my side. Bhaiti had felt lonely.

I was woken the next morning by Bhaiti licking my face. He was hungry. In the dining room he wolfed down a huge breakfast. It must be the only restaurant in the world that not only lets a dog in, but feeds it before the other guests.

Naturally Ozing hadn't arrived, so after breakfast Neeraj and I decided to give Bhaiti a bath. He needed one. His coat was all matted and he stank – not the way a Tripuri hound should be. We climbed the stairs to the top of the hotel and on to the roof. It was a beautiful, hot day. We doused him down with buckets of water, but before we had a chance to lather him with my shampoo he wriggled free of Neeraj's grasp and scarpered across the roof. Most dogs don't like baths, but this was ridiculous. It seemed I owned a dog with a pathological hatred of water. It took us five attempts to get him clean – not, I thought, a good sign, considering our future journey together, where rivers would play a big part. But the end result was worth it. Bhaiti's once lacklustre coat, dried by the hot sun and softened by the conditioner, now positively gleamed, contrasting beautifully with his creamy white chest. I felt I could have entered him for Crufts.

Ozing eventually turned up four hours late to drive Yatish, Bhaiti and me to Pasighat. I was seething with impatience and started to give him a bollocking, but soon gave up. Ozing was Ozing. He was never going to change. That was his charm.

I bid farewell to Neeraj. He had arranged a comfortable bed for Bhaiti in the back of Ozing's jeep alongside Yatish. It was about time Yatish got to know Bhaiti better. Then finally we set off on the seven-hour drive for Pasighat – the next stage on my journey to the river.

Our route took us in a large loop: first a gradual descent south back into Assam; then a long ride north-east following the great alluvial plain of the Brahmaputra; and finally a turn back to the north and once more into the hills of Arunachal Pradesh. Unfortunately, Arunachal Pradesh's network of beautifully surfaced roads ended abruptly soon after we left Itanagar and crossed the border into Assam. Assam is not renowned for the quality of its roads at the best of times, but after the worst monsoons in history they were almost impassable – a crater-ridden, spine-jarring trail from hell – the surrounding countryside scarred as though it had suffered some great battle. The local people walked slowly and listlessly, like bomb victims, picking their way through the debris of their homes. Trucks lay upended, like bloated metal corpses. Groups of little boys and girls paddled on lengths of timber – perhaps the bones of their homes – on slimy, lotus-clogged ponds, their laughter a light relief from the terrible tragedy that filled the air. Most bridges had been washed away and we waited in long lines of trucks and vehicles before we inched across bouncy, hastily constructed bamboo substitutes. On the outskirts of a little town, we passed the Hotel Raj, a concrete survivor of the holocaust, the waterline clearly visible just below its top windows, its sign accurately describing its facilities – 'Sleeping and Flooding'.

It wasn't just the roads that had changed, but the climate too. Here on the alluvial plains it was warmer and stickier, with palm and banana trees instead of the pine forest of Arunachal Pradesh. It was more like India altogether – a return to chaos after order.

It was on this long and uncomfortable journey that I discovered another side of Ozing. He started to relax more, and even his stutter diminished. Ozing, I soon realised, was incredibly well read. He

JOHN BULMER

The north face of Mount Kailash.

ANONYMOUS PILGRIM

JOHN BULMER

Bad karma – beaten by the mountain.

Mark and Charles Allen in Tibet.

YATISH B

Mark and Bhaiti looking into Tibet on the McMahon line.

The Tripuri Dog from the Lushai Hills of Assam.

The Siang River in the morning, from Gelling, Arunachal Pradesh.

The Siang River in the evening, from Gelling, Arunachal Pradesh.

Girl Power – the porters in the Siang Valley.

MARK SHAND

MARK SHAND

That first cane bridge.

Whoops!

Relaxing after the narrow escape.

Moods of the Siang: the spitting serpent.

The seductress.

Those cool hypnotic eyes . . .

The legendary Adi hunter, Jaro Dai,
capturing poisonous beetles.

The Dream Team – left to right – Neeraj and Bhaiti, Corporal
Shortcut, Corporal Classic, Topguy, Jaro and guest.

The head *gam* of Pugging village,
Arunachal Pradesh.

A male monk from Majuli Island.

The crew of the *Kailash* – left to right – Laxman, Gamma,
Topguy, Pandit, Vijay, and Neeraj and Bhaiti.

was an accomplished historian, not only of his own country's history, but of early English history – of its poets and writers, and in
particular, William Shakespeare. He gleefully regaled me with stories about his ancestors, the fierce Abors, now known as the Adis,
who had made a mockery of the British, and he punctuated his narrative with the sonnets of our great writer and poet.

Meanwhile, in the back, life wasn't so much fun. On the best of
roads, the front seats of an Indian Maruti jeep are the only place to
sit. Due to a flaw in design, the vehicle is almost devoid of suspension. It's like being locked in a tin trunk and chucked over the
Niagara Falls. The top of Yatish's head was being continually
slammed into the roof. Bhaiti had given up altogether. He had
buried himself in the bed that Neeraj had prepared for him, and
wedged himself in between the back seat and the back of Ozing's
seat. I changed places with Yatish and did my best to comfort my
dog.

About halfway, we stopped in a small town for tea. Next door
was a chemist. Being a hypochondriac, I couldn't resist. I love
chemists, particularly Indian ones. They're full of the most sur-
prising things. I purchased an Ayurvedic balm for bruises, a new
toothbrush and some anti-tick powder for Bhaiti, made by a gentleman called Dr Khan. Dr Khan it seemed, as I studied the label,
was remarkably well qualified. He had trained in London, New
York, Calcutta, Delhi and Moscow. The instructions were a little
confusing: 'Daily put the powder liberally over the body of the
animal, and then after ten minutes brush off.' This I could follow.
But the next line? 'Make sure you apply the powder to all creaks
and corries of the kennies.' There was even a telephone number for
Dr Khan, in Calcutta. I thought about giving him a call.

It was early evening when we reached the Assam–Arunachal
Pradesh border. My passport and permit were scrutinised thoroughly by the border police, and then we were waved through. It
was, in the space of literally a few yards, like entering another

world. The road suddenly became smooth-surfaced again, and we seemed to glide through a Garden of Eden. It was so green and empty. I wound down the window. The air was deliciously pure, scented by the foliage that surrounded us as we sped down a long, green tunnel under a canopy of soaring bamboo groves.

The change in Bhaiti was equally extraordinary. He put his head beside mine out of the window, his eyes bright, his ears pricked, pointing his little black muzzle into the air. Then he barked. It was a bark of happiness. Bhaiti, I realised, was coming back to life – shedding the mantle of his early life as a scavenging street dog to become what his genes had designed him for – a happy hunting dog. Bhaiti was coming home – home to the hills.

We were back in Adi territory now, their villages stockaded, the traditional houses simple rectangular or square bamboo constructions built on stilts, with intricately woven thatched roofs made from palm leaves. And by contrast here and there on the way we also passed a few traditional Assamese houses, like British mock-Tudor cottages, criss-crossed by black beams. But mainly we just saw forest, the towering trees impenetrably massed on either side of the road, ancient, silent and forbidding.

It was nearly dark by the time we reached Pasighat, perched on a hill, cradled in the great curved arm of the Brahmaputra. Here the river was majestic and calm, having spread out on the plains after its turbulent, twisting three-hundred-mile downhill journey through the Himalayan ranges to the north.

Pasighat, the regional headquarters for East Siang, was like a miniature British market town, with leafy promenades and lines of little houses surrounding neat postcard-shaped parks. It had an air of genteel tranquillity. It used to be an administrative centre for the British and with its sister town, Sadiya, a little farther south-east, which was destroyed in the great earthquake of 1950, was one of the two easternmost outposts of British India.

Here, at the beginning of the nineteenth century, when the East

India Company had decided to maintain its hold on this newly lib-
erated land, Pasighat and Sadiya became bases for British efforts to
unravel the mysteries of the course of the Brahmaputra. They were
also great trading centres, where the hillmen, the Abors, traded
with the plains people of Assam – cloths, yarns, salt, utensils, agri-
cultural equipment, deerskins, wax, madder, ginger, ivory and tiger
skins.

In the summer the Tibetans came to trade from beyond Gelling,
through the Kebang La Pass, bringing rock salt, iron, warm material, hand-woven cloth, swords, turquoise necklaces, blue porcelain
beads, yarns of different colours, snuff, musk, amber, china, silver
and large bronze pots. In exchange they carried back raw hides,
deer horns, white and red rice.

Today, Pasighat still boasts a small market selling produce, spices
and clothes. It really hasn't changed that much – a little piece of
British India preserved in a time warp.

Ozing dropped us off at the Government Circuit House where
accommodation had been arranged, and went off on his own mysterious business. A new, grand, three-storied stone construction, the
Circuit House had east- and south-facing rooms benefiting from
balustraded balconies. It was empty. Bhaiti and I chose the suite,
with its magnificent view of the Brahmaputra from the balcony. I
checked out the bathroom. It was like something out of *House &
Garden*, a vast marble atrium with a bewildering number of old
fashioned chrome taps. Twenty of them. I turned them on – all of
them. A dribble of water wetted my neck from the vast, overhead
chrome shower, and a bewildered cockroach scuttled out of
another spout.

But the Circuit House deserved at least one, if not two stars for
its cuisine, prepared by a cook who was as every cook should be –
fat, jolly and immensely helpful. Cookie, as I called him, prepared
a sumptuous meal for Yatish, Bhaiti and me. Hot, doughy chapattis, lovingly moulded in his soft podgy hands, three different kinds

of curry – fish, chicken and some kind of meat, fluffy basmati rice and bowls of steaming, fresh vegetables.

Yatish, clearly exhausted and battered from his journey, took his food to his room, leaving Bhaiti and me to dine, à deux, by candlelight, served by the splendid Cookie. We went for a short walk to digest our dinner. It was a beautiful night, the eastern sky ablaze with stars, a dark blue velvet cape studded with diamonds. We could hear the murmur of the river to our right as it started its journey westwards.

I looked northwards, towards that series of undulating hills, and wondered what adventures lay beyond for Bhaiti and me. Tomorrow, with any luck, we would find out. And tomorrow, I remembered as Bhaiti sniffed the clean, crisp air contentedly, we would also meet the last two members of our small team: our Adi guide, and our cook.

I had arranged for tea and biscuits for Bhaiti and me to be brought to us in the morning, at what I thought was a reasonable hour – 7 a.m. We both needed a bit of a lie-in. All too soon, though, there was a frantic banging on my bedroom door. Groggily I looked at my watch. It was only 6 a.m. Maybe there was a time change in Arunachal Pradesh, I thought, as I climbed out of bed and opened the door. Instead of a smiling houseboy bearing our tea and biscuits, I was greeted by a fully dressed, frantic Yatish.

'We've got to go, Mark. Now!'

'W-why? W-where?' I was still half asleep.

'To the helipad. To get on a chopper.'

'What bloody chopper?' I asked irritably. Yatish seemed to be obsessed by them. He thought of nothing else.

He interrupted impatiently. 'Indian Air Force, Mark. As I told you, they're ferrying supplies up to the villages. Look, there's one leaving now.'

I looked out of the window. Below I could see it taking off. It hovered for a moment, then banked right, climbing quickly to clear the surrounding ranges to the east.

'I checked.' Yatish continued urgently, 'There's one leaving for Gelling. But I don't know when – they're going everywhere. It all depends on the weather. We've got to get down there. Now.'

'How are we going to get on it?' I asked.

'You're going to have to use all your charm. Particularly with a dog. You know the rules.'

I didn't even bother to reply. Fuck the rules. Nobody was going anywhere without Bhaiti. 'What about the rest of the team?' I asked. 'Where are they?'

'Waiting at the helipad. And Ozing's waiting downstairs to take us there.'

I dressed quickly, stuffed all my kit into a bag, attached Bhaiti to his lead and shot downstairs. A smiling, fat, familiar figure was standing by the door holding a package. It was the indomitable Cookie.

'Omelettes and chapattis for you, sir. And two eggs. Full boiled – six minutes – for Bhaiti,' he said, handing me the package. I could have hugged him.

'Want to come, Cookie?' I asked. I would have taken him anywhere.

He laughed, his whole body shaking like a child's bouncy castle.

'No, sir. No food up there. Cookie will die. I'll be waiting for you with full meal. You will need it.'

We thanked him and climbed into Ozing's jeep.

'G-g-good morning, Mark, and g-g-good m-m-morning, Bhaiti. L-l-lovely day for flying,' he giggled as he drove us off.

'Thank you, Ozing. By the way, where did you get to last night?'

'I was at my c-c-camp.'

'Your camp? You've got a camp?' I was intrigued.

'V-v-very luxurious camp,' he replied. 'For Tiger M-m-mountain clients. V-v-very expensive, though. You c-c-couldn't afford it. But

I m-m-might give you a d-d-discount,' he giggled. 'You could s-s-stay there on your r-r-return. If you r-r-return.' Ozing had a camp, I thought. Now *that* was something I had to see.

We reached the perimeter of the field that served as a helipad and unloaded our bags.

'I p-p-probably won't see you again,' Ozing said, trying to keep a straight face. 'I've b-b-been sending smoke signals all morning to my p-p-people up there. I've t-t-told them that another b-b-bloody Englishman is coming to plunder their lands again, like your b-b-bloody predecessors. They'll p-p-probably k-k-kill you,' he said. 'If y-y-you behave, my U-u-uncle Jaro might keep y-y-you alive.'

I felt a light tap on my shoulder and whirled round. I don't know what I expected but it certainly wasn't the small, strong, casually dressed, smiling man with kind eyes, gold glints in his hair and a gap in his front teeth, who stood in front of me. Jaro was my Adi guide. From his reputation I'd expected, well, someone more tribal, carrying at least a gun or possibly a bow and a quiver of arrows. Or maybe even barefoot. Instead, Jaro was wearing a pink polo shirt, a pair of smart trousers and brown lace-up shoes. He carried on his back the only giveaway that he was a legendary Adi tribal guide, a beautifully woven rattan backpack. In it was a small, collapsible pink umbrella. He took my hand and shook it in a very firm grip.

'Mmmm,' he murmured, a sound I was to find out that he always made before saying anything, as if he were thinking about what it was he was going to say. 'I am Jaro. And you are Mark. Welcome.' He smiled. 'Mmm. How old are you?'

'Forty,' I lied.

'Mmmmm,' he said, studying me carefully. 'I think you are older. Maybe 48?' I nodded reluctantly. 'Mmmmm. Good,' he said. 'I am younger – 43. Between us we have 91 years. We are old men. We will walk slowly.'

I was delighted by this news. I had already imagined puffing up those sheer hills, trying to keep up with some lithe, young, fast-moving Adi hunter. Jaro knelt down and whistled – a curious low whistle. Bhaiti cocked his head and then whimpered, a little whimper of pleasure. He sidled over to Jaro and sat down at his feet.

'Mmmmm, good hunting dog,' he said, caressing Bhaiti's ears. 'He will enjoy our journey.'

It takes one to know one, I thought happily.

Yatish seemed happy as well, no doubt as relieved as me that we were going to move slowly. But there was one member – the last member of our little team – who wouldn't, or couldn't possibly move slowly: Topgay, our Ladakhi cook. Rather like my first impression of Jaro, he wasn't at all what I imagined a cook should look like – nothing like Cookie, for instance.

Topgay certainly wasn't fat; nor was he tall, or big, or muscled. He was rangy. There was not an inch of excess flesh on him. He was wearing shorts. His legs were long and sinewy, the legs of a greyhound. Topgay came from the steep, cold terrain of Ladakh. He was a true mountain man – quiet, gentle, unassuming, and shy. And, I was to find out later, nothing was too much for him. As a happily married man with a large family, he certainly didn't fit his name. So I called him 'Topguy', which was far more appropriate. What a team! I couldn't have hoped for better.

We bid farewell to Ozing. He was clearly overjoyed to hand the responsibility of another b-b-bloody Englishman over to Jaro. Topguy picked up all our bags as if they were feathers, slung them over his back and we headed towards the helipad.

There we waited, and waited, and waited, all day, watching as helicopters landed and then, almost immediately, took off again re-supplied, on another sortie to places like Anini and Along – but not to Gelling. Gelling, Yatish had found out, was experiencing bad weather – low clouds. He had also found out from the dispatcher that a bad weather pattern was moving in, which meant the choppers probably wouldn't be flying for the next few days. That explained the early start. It was either today, or a long wait in Pasighat.

I'm not naturally a patient person. It usually takes me at least a couple of weeks on arrival in India just to slow down to the rhythm of the country. But this time it had been crazy, almost surreal. Since I'd arrived in Delhi, we had been either in a mad rush or at a complete standstill, like now. What was it about getting to this river? And poor Bhaiti. I felt terrible. What was I dragging him into? He was having yet another miserable day. He was traumatised by the sounds of the choppers, burying his head in my shirt again. I carried him into a little wooden hut, where everybody was waiting. He curled up under a table on which Jaro, with the inbred patience and skill of a hunter was playing chess, annihilating, one by one, the helicopter ground crews. Jaro, I found out, was the Gary Kasparov of north-east India. He had represented his state in many national championships all over India.

I felt the room closing in on me. I had to get out. I asked Jaro to look after Bhaiti and tried to burn off my frustration by running maniacally up and down the field.

At around 3 p.m. Yatish finally came over to put me out of my misery. The next chopper, he told me, was for Gelling. The weather had cleared. A few minutes later the now all-too-familiar sound echoed across the field. I ran out to the helipad and waited, soon blinded by the whirling dust as the chopper settled gently like a huge black fly. The engine shut down and the rotors slowly stopped turning.

Two dashing young men climbed out of the cockpit, sporting aviator Raybans and wearing form-fitting orange flying overalls over highly polished boots. They looked so intimidating, so official and so, well, commanding that, although I had never been in the services, I found myself saluting. They both started laughing, and taking off their shades, introduced themselves.

'I'm Shantunu Basu, and this is my flight officer, Prakash.' I shook their hands. 'Well, Mr Shand, what are we carrying for you today? Another elephant?' Shantunu noticed my amazement.

'I recognise you from your books,' he laughed. 'But you look older.'

Fame at last. But it couldn't have come at a better time.

'Not an elephant this time, but a dog,' I replied. 'And four other people, including me.'

'Pity,' he said. 'I've always wanted to airlift an elephant. We can carry over four tons. It would have been quite a challenge. Anyway, it'll be a pleasure. Get your boys and your dog on board as quickly as possible. We've got to move fast. The weather's a little unpredictable around here. Might be a bit of a rough ride. But,' he added with a grin, 'we'll give it a go.'

And give it a go he did. For these pilots were the 'top guns' of the Helicopter Unit of the Indian Air Force – the cream of the bunch – the ones that flew by the seat of their pants. Their squadron was named the First of the Ranas – and their motto described them aptly – 'Undaunted, undeterred'.

We quickly piled into the cargo hold, where two narrow wooden benches secured to each side served as seats. The rest of the space was taken up by the cargo, piled on a trolley on runners in the centre of the hold. There was no back to the helicopter. It was wide open.

Shantunu invited me up front. He told me I would get a superb view of the river. I declined. I had to look after my dog, who for obvious reasons was banned from the cockpit. Yatish took my place, while Topguy, Jaro, the loaders and I squeezed into the back. As the rotors started to spin, Bhaiti started to howl and tried desperately to escape. I didn't blame him. The noise was deafening. I managed to get a grip on him, and held him tightly against my chest. He stuck his head down my shirt and, apart from shaking constantly, didn't move from that position for the entire journey.

Shantunu and Prakash lived up to the motto of their squadron, 'Undaunted, undeterred', for we were soon descending rapidly, almost clipping the trees on the top of the hill, which I could see out of the back of the chopper. We crested a rise, and then swooped down. A few minutes later, we landed perfectly on a broad field – the combined helipad and football pitch of one of India's most remote outposts – the village of Gelling.

I looked out of the window. It seemed we had a welcome committee, composed not only of the lines of villagers squatting on their hunkers around the edge of the football field but also, alarmingly, of three soldiers, dressed in camouflage fatigues. They were standing rigidly to attention by a small wooden table with two wooden chairs. I carried Bhaiti out of the cargo hold into the cool, fresh air, and let him off his lead. He went berserk. He rolled over and over on the grass, shook his head from side to side as if to rid himself of the noise of the helicopter, deftly assassinated a fly that had dared to try and land on his head, and then ran at full speed three times around the football field. He was happy again.

Jaro and Topguy unloaded our gear, while Yatish went to meet the military. I bid farewell to my intrepid pilots. They had to get off immediately – the weather was closing in. Shantunu ripped off a little triangular badge that was velcroed to his uniform. He turned it over, wrote on it and then presented it to me. It was the emblem of his squadron – the 127 Helicopter Unit, the First of the Ranas. On the front was a little image of a chopper with the words 'Undaunted, undeterred'. On the back, he had written 'Mark – all the best, Shantunu, Gelling, 2 November.'

'At least you can now prove you got this far,' he said.

I shook his hand, and thanked him.

'Good luck,' he said, climbing back into the cockpit. 'If you get into trouble, send up a smoke signal. We'll come and find you.'

I waved as they lifted off, and watched the chopper bank right and head south until it was invisible, its dark green body blending in against the sheer sides of the forested valleys that rose up from the river bed. As I dropped my hand, a strange feeling of loneliness suddenly enveloped me. It had taken all this time to get here and now I had arrived, I missed my family. But then I felt a reassuring warmth pressing against my leg. I wasn't alone.

I wandered over to the wooden table. The three soldiers snapped to attention and saluted. I saluted back. Still, I was keeping strictly to the instructions of my permit, section e. I was *not* interacting with locally deployed army personnel in a casual manner. The Subedar Major, in command in the absence of the Captain of the Assam Rifles, who was away on leave for a few days, asked if I would like some refreshments. This put me in a bit of a quandary. According to section b of my permit, I should be self-sufficient and not depend upon the army to provide any assistance, except for casualty evacuation on humanitarian grounds. There was no casualty evacuation. Not yet anyway. But I *was* being offered assistance – admittedly only food. What the hell, I thought, let's live dangerously, and I gratefully accepted.

In minutes, Yatish, Bhaiti and I were tucking into tea – lemonade and ginger biscuits – while the three soldiers stood to attention behind us, only moving to fill up our glasses. It really was the most incongruous situation. I asked Yatish where Jaro and Topguy had gone. He mumbled something incoherent. I asked again.

'They're staying in the village,' he replied, implying that *we* weren't.

'Well, aren't we all staying together?' I asked.

'No, this is a military zone. You and I are staying up at the army base, about a mile farther up. No outsiders, not even the villagers, are allowed there. It's a restricted area.'

I was appalled. 'Well, you and I are outsiders,' I argued. I wanted us all to be together. We were a team.

'Orders, Mark,' Yatish replied, ominously and finally.

I felt like arguing further, but thought better of it. Yatish, with his military connections, obviously knew something I didn't. But I was still unhappy, and abruptly I got up and left the table.

Yatish hurried after me and tried to make amends. 'Look,' he said, 'we'll be sleeping right below the McMahon Line. And I've already asked for clearance to see if we can go even farther, right up on to it, to the last Indian checkpoint overlooking Tibet.'

I looked at him in surprise. This was an unexpected initiative – Yatish must have been quietly pulling his connections again. I did feel excited, even if I couldn't share this adventure with Jaro and Topguy.

'And Bhaiti?' I asked, innocently.

'I don't think the military regard dogs as security risks,' he replied.

'What about me?' I said. 'I could be James Bond.'

'You're being closely monitored.'

I began to wonder if old Yatish was not being a bit paranoid. After all, although I was in a restricted area, I had been given clearance by the Government of India. They obviously didn't consider me particularly threatening, and certainly not a spy. And anyway, if I were one – which I wasn't – my loyalties would be firmly with Mother India.

We started the steep climb up to the military base. I noticed a long line of tall, elegant, fluttering prayer flags surrounding the little stone *gompa*, or monastery, more reminiscent of Tibet than India. It made me realise suddenly just how far north I was. The villagers, too, had much more Tibetan features. They were ruddy-cheeked, and the women wore shiny silk Chinese waistcoats over long woollen skirts. Yatish explained that these people, and the surrounding villages, were Buddhists from the Monpa and Memba tribes – the last survivors of a Buddhist culture from farther north, over the McMahon Line, in Tibet.

Just as we were leaving the village, an old man with Tibetan features wearing a bright red woollen coat, his neck encircled by a necklace of turquoise stones and puffing on a bamboo pipe with a silver bowl, blocked my way and bowed to me quickly three or four times. Slightly taken aback, I bowed back. He then bowed back again. And so it went on. It was ridiculous – we were bobbing up and down like two old cock pheasants disputing territory.

'He thinks you're Japanese,' Yatish said.

'Japanese?!' I asked incredulously. I've often been mistaken for an Australian, but Japanese – this was pushing it. I was outraged.

Yatish told me that in 1992 a joint Indo-Japanese army rafting expedition had started their journey here at Gelling, riding the massive and uncharted rapids of the Siang to Pasighat, and then down the Brahmaputra to the India–Bangladesh border. The old man, who'd never seen any other foreigners in his life, assumed that all outsiders were Japanese.

As politely as I could, I bowed swiftly once more and moved on. At least, Yatish told me, the Japs hadn't been allowed to go where we were going. That made me feel better. In fact, in over half a century, only one foreigner, as far as I knew, had been where we were going.

His name was Verrier Elwin, the great English philanthropist and champion of tribal peoples. Born in Dover in 1902, the son of an Anglican bishop, Elwin arrived in India in 1927 and immediately fell under its spell. He met Mahatma Gandhi and under his influence became so enthusiastic for India's independence that he severed his connection with his church and country, and went to live in a remote tribal village in the middle of India. Increasingly, he devoted himself to the tribal world, opening schools and a leper home, travelling and photographing, writing tirelessly about tribe after tribe. He had, I knew, visited Gelling – and probably farther – in 1954, when Nehru appointed him Adviser for Tribal

Affairs for the North-East Frontier Agency. I was proud to follow in his footsteps.

But first I had to get to the army base. We were exhausted by the time we reached it – it was over two miles, all uphill, from the village. We arrived at a large gate, surrounded by a tall fence of barbed wire. Inside, I noticed a volleyball court, a few wooden shacks with corrugated roofs, a couple of bunkers, a long line of drying washing, and a smaller hut, fortified by sandbags, with aerials and a satellite dish on its roof. This was clearly the communications centre, from which echoed the tinny beat of a popular Bollywood disco song.

I was rather disappointed. I was expecting, well, a massive defence line with ack-ack guns, mortar emplacements and squadrons of soldiers on full alert. After all, this was India's last line of defence against the might of China.

I suddenly realised that by writing this *now* – which I had written *then* in my diary – I might be suspected of intending to give away secrets – valuable information – to the Chinese. I might be considered a spy. But I was just being paranoid, because such was the sophistication of modern technology nowadays that Indians, Chinese, Americans, anybody with the right equipment, were probably watching my stumbling progress on screens in hidden bunkers, in hidden places, beamed down from the satellites that were passing regularly overhead, somewhere in space above me.

However, I was *not* going to be allowed into the main part of the cantonment. I was firmly ushered by my military escort up a steep hill to the left of the base. We arrived at a wooden shack surrounded by a herbaceous border of flowering shrubs. Beyond that was a sheer drop – and beyond that – nothing. Except paradise. An astonishing panorama of the entire Siang Valley. Far below I could see the Siang – my river – a slender silver serpent twisting and turning through the green valley, its murmur just audible, music to my ears.

This was our new home – the officers' billet. The kind but absent commander of the base, whom for security reasons I shall call Captain K, had obviously vacated the billet in order to put us up. It seems we were expected. Our accommodation was simple but comfortable. Captain K had gone out of his way to make us feel at home. A rug was thrown across the earthen floor. Two charpoys lay side by side, their mattresses covered in clean sheets, decorated with pink roses. And even a blanket had been put down for Bhaiti.

We dined immediately on *chung* – Indian military rations made from buffalo meat, washed down with Contessa rum, another thoughtful gesture from the Captain. Yatish soon crashed out, exhausted.

Bhaiti and I went outside. It was still light. I sat down on a little wooden chair on the square patch and just enjoyed the incredible view of the river that lay below me. I wondered if perhaps Verrier Elwin had sat right here, where I was sitting. In his autobiography he had written,

> If all the pens that ever poets held were to get to work on it, I doubt if they could digest into words the fascination of this wonderful river. So exquisite, so mysterious, so varied in its charms. At one point flowing through gently sloping woods, at another forcing its way through high gorges. Its colour is always changing, and when you see it shrouded in gentle mist against a background of snowy mountains towering in the distance, it is one of the loveliest sights that can meet the eye of man. The Siang is a hard mistress, and sometimes exhausted me so completely that I came to think of it as the river of no return. Indeed, I would be happy one day to lay my body beside its waters.

The river of no return, I thought as I lay my body six hundred metres above its waters, a little later, in the warm confines of my sleeping bag. Bhaiti, clearly lonely and cold on his rug on the earthen floor, soon joined me.

Next morning, it seemed that the 'river of no return' had already cast its spell. It turned out that I was going nowhere – up or down the river. I was, to the great embarrassment of Captain K, who had arrived late last night after a forced march of thirty miles from the village of Tuting, farther down the river from Gelling, under arrest. Not arrest exactly, more like house arrest – temporary detention. It seemed we had jumped the gun. Although we were expected, we had arrived at Gelling *earlier* than we were expected. I argued vehemently with the unfortunate Captain, waving my permit under his nose like a spoilt boy. But he was adamant. He had not received any *official* orders from headquarters – from GSO 1 (Intelligence) HQ Eastern Command, Fort William, Calcutta. It was ironic, I thought. India had finally rid herself of the British after over two hundred years of rule. Now she couldn't seem to get rid of one impatient Englishman.

The problem lay, we finally ascertained after hours of discussion between myself, Yatish and the Captain, with communication – or the lack of it. It seemed that GSO 1 Headquarters (Intelligence) HQ Eastern Command, Fort William, Calcutta were under the impression that I had not liaised with them before my departure, as per section c of my permit. 'He will liaise . . . on arrival and departure of the subject journey'. But I had liaised – admittedly not in person. A written message had been sent, or was supposed to have been sent, from the relevant ministry in Delhi to Calcutta on the day that I got my permit. That message, it seemed, had never arrived. Perhaps, I thought, they wanted me to liaise in person. But as far as I was concerned, and as far as any dictionary was concerned, the word 'liaise' means 'to form a link', or 'to be, or get in touch with'. I had hardly thought it necessary to make the long detour to headquarters in Calcutta.

What was driving me mad, and what I couldn't understand, was why they couldn't radio from here to headquarters in Calcutta. Headquarters could then contact the ministry in Delhi, who could then quickly assure Calcutta of my liaison. Then the confirmation could be radioed back here. It all seemed very simple to me, considering the sophistication of communications technology.

An embarrassed Captain K explained that was actually what he had been trying to do. But Gelling could not contact Calcutta directly. Instead they relayed radio messages via Along, a town to the south-west of Gelling which was the regional headquarters of the Assam Rifles. Also, the radio link between Gelling and Along was kept open only at a specific time each day – in the evening. Unless there was an emergency. Captain K would try again that evening.

I pointed out that this was an emergency. He rightly suggested that it was not. He had a point. A Chinese invasion was hardly imminent, or an emergency evacuation – just a bolshie Englishman and his dog trying to go either up or down a river. I wondered if boredom qualified as an emergency evacuation on humanitarian grounds, *re* section b of my permit.

Unbelievably, this charade dragged on for a further three days. The blameless Captain K became desperate as he relayed the latest news to me each evening. On the first attempt the relevant military authority at the end of the radio in Along was out at a party. The following day, when he returned from his party, the relevant authorities in Calcutta and Delhi were unavailable. It was a Sunday. Captain K went out of his way to make our detention as comfortable as possible. He endlessly worried about us – if our food was up to standard, or if our accommodation was comfortable enough. Every evening, he produced another bottle of Contessa rum from the army stores to, hopefully, I imagined, calm me down. He was in fact possibly disobeying orders, *re* section e of my permit – ' . . . nor interact with locally deployed army personnel in a casual manner'. But this was clearly an emergency. The commanding officer, when cut off from headquarters, had the authority to do what he felt best. He had to make the executive decision.

Meanwhile, I was going stir-crazy. Yatish simply gave up and retired to his bed. I felt like a prisoner of war. I was not allowed on the base – my entire world was a two-metre-square patch of ground, perched on top of a hill, admittedly with a stunning view. And that was what was driving me even more mad. To the south, far below, the river murmured enticingly. To the north, even more enticing, lay an impenetrable forested ridge – the McMahon Line.

It was Bhaiti who came to my rescue. He sensed my frustration. He stopped me from going completely mad and throwing myself off the ridge. Bhaiti, being a dog – but no ordinary dog, a super-sleuth of a dog – was not considered a security risk. Every day, he would sneak into the base where, judging from the size of his stomach when he returned, he had not only befriended every soldier, but in particular the cook.

It was from him that I learnt interesting and vital information. We would huddle, side by side, whispering to each other, much to Yatish's astonishment (he clearly was travelling with not only a madman but also a talking dog), as Bhaiti fed me salacious titbits of dog gossip: of the three other dogs on the base, and in particular of the saucy tan bitch he fancied; of the secret dump behind the canteen where the leftovers were deposited; and of the amazing variety of wildlife that abounded in this area. These specimens would be proudly presented to me as if he were worried I hadn't enough to eat – a collection of large, winged insects, a few different species of rodents, and a lizard or two.

And it was Bhaiti who also discovered and led me to our secret hiding place. A slippery path led down from my prison to an old, disused bunker. There, out of sight, in the dark confines of this man-made tunnel, we whiled away the long hours, playing hide and seek, sharing the ginger biscuits that were both our favourites, and wondering about the journey ahead and what secrets the river had in store for us. It was then I really got to know Bhaiti. He and I were very similar: on the exterior, reasonably resourceful and independent, but underneath soft, craving affection. It was vital to always have someone to come back to. We were a perfect match.

It was late on the fourth evening, when I had just finished debriefing Bhaiti on his last secret mission, that a beaming Captain K entered his own quarters. A radio link had been established. Headquarters had cleared us – not only cleared us, but cleared us to go up to the McMahon Line. At last – the green light. I was about to make history.

At the crack of dawn the next morning, carrying day packs and plenty of water, and under the vigilance of a veteran Border Security Force scout, dressed not in uniform but in jeans and a tee-shirt, we set off north around the perimeter of the camp, towards the steep hills that lay ahead. Before we left, Captain K had given us strict orders. Under no circumstances, in the very unlikely situation that we were to bump into a Chinese patrol, were we to make contact of any kind. We were to sit tight. Apparently this was standard drill, even amongst the patrols that swept the McMahon Line every day. I now understood why our scout, whom for security reasons I will call S, was dressed in mufti. If a Chinese patrol happened to catch sight of us, no connection could be made to the military. But I then wondered about the logic of this subterfuge. I could understand Yatish, S, or even Bhaiti causing no interest or concern to a hidden Chinese patrol – but a foreigner, an Englishman? This was hardly a well-trampled trail, advertised in the glossy pamphlets of some mountain trekking outfit.

We climbed higher until we reached the tree line, and then entered a silent, dark world. S whispered to me that we were now in the midst of the McMahon Line – the buffer zone between Tibet and India. I couldn't believe it. In my mind, because there was so little, actually no geographical information available about the

McMahon Line, I had imagined an actual line – the kind of line that you step over – in fact, the kind of line where you can have one foot in India and one foot in Tibet.

But the McMahon Line is a very grey area – a large, grey area drawn up all those years ago at the Simla Conference of 1911 by General Sir Henry McMahon, the then Governor-General of British India – running hundreds of miles west to east, along the eastern Himalayas from Bhutan to Burma. In fact, on a Chinese map, the McMahon Line does not exist at all; instead red territory stretches a hundred miles or so farther south, right to the borders of the Brahmaputra, north of Guwahati.

It was through this disputed land that myself, Yatish and Bhaiti, whom I had attached to my waist, struggled up behind S, who cut a path for us through the thick bamboo forest. Occasionally, he would stop and listen, which considering how much noise Yatish and I were making as we gasped for breath, seemed unnecessary. Any Chinese patrol within five miles could have heard us.

I was buzzing with excitement. Each falling leaf or sudden rustle I imagined was a Chinese patrol, squatting silently, camouflaged, a few metres to my left or right in the thick jungle. We took a breather in a cave. Clearly, by the debris that covered the ground – cigarette packets and the remains of a burnt-out fire – it was a reg-ular bivouac for patrols. Indian patrols it turned out, disappointingly, as I carefully studied each crumpled pack of ciga-rettes, butt end and scrap of paper for Chinese signs.

We pushed on, climbing higher. The canopy of jungle and bamboo was beginning to thin out. Trees soared above us, through which shafts of sunlight pierced the high foliage like lasers, turning the forest floor into a carpet strewn with gold coins. It was silent, except for the chatter of bird song far above us and the odd buzz of an insect, which drove Bhaiti mad and drove me off my feet as he whirled around me, tangling my legs in his leash. We reached a giant of a tree, its girth almost four metres in circumference. S pointed out deep scour marks, oozing fresh sap where a black Himalayan bear had recently been sharpening his claws.

The path became much easier now. Through the chinks of daylight in the forest to my left, I caught glimpses of a valley. It seemed that we were travelling along the edge of a bluff. The bluff ended suddenly as we entered a clearing. Below, there was nothing – just a sheer drop of a thousand metres to the river below which, even at this height, we could hear faintly murmuring as it thundered through the gorge. In front of us a series of undulating hills rose higher and higher, either side of a deep chasm. Through that deep chasm ran the river – not the Siang, or the Brahmaputra, but the Tsangpo. We were looking into Tibet. We had reached the extremity of India's north-eastern border. I could go no farther. I checked my watch. It was precisely 1.16 p.m.

In the distance, up that valley, something flashed. I pulled out my binoculars (which I had hidden carefully in my rucksack, although according to my permit I wasn't breaking any laws) and through the high-powered lens could make out a small township, the sun reflecting off its corrugated roofs. This, I realised excitedly, might be Metok, the last destination that my Tibetan permit allowed me down the northern part of the river. In a few months, I could be there, looking south instead of north, at this Indian outpost. Perhaps S might even be here.

I started to wave. I was convinced that somewhere, deep in a bunker in Beijing, a huddle of confused Chinese, their narrow eyes rounding in disbelief, were staring at a screen on which an enlarged image, beamed down from a satellite, clearly highlighted the colour of my hair. It was a foreigner waving maniacally at them. I could imagine the confusion, then the worry, then the panic, as an urgent call was made to the President for an executive decision.

S and Yatish clearly thought I was insane. On the other hand, Bhaiti was just as excited as I was, and started barking loudly. I picked him up and we both waved. I could now imagine the gasps of heightened astonishment of the spooks around that screen – 'foreigner has dog' – and further frantic messages being sent up to High Command, to make more executive decisions. Eventually, exhausted by my fantasy, Yatish, S and I celebrated this historic moment with a toast of rum and a packet of ginger biscuits for Bhaiti.

But I felt I needed to actually christen the moment with something more permanent. I noticed a large tree overhanging the clearing. Borrowing S's machete, I cut a slice of bark out of its trunk. I took a black indelible pen from my rucksack and wrote my name, the date, my citizenship, and underneath added, childishly, 'Rule Britannia'. This was to remind the Chinese that although we didn't own the land now, we once had. And they bloody well should have signed that agreement in Simla, over ninety years ago. To rub salt into the wound, I flattened out a gold packet of Benson & Hedges cigarettes and pinned it to a tree. That would confuse them, I thought. Bond would have approved.

S indicated that we must head back. Night-time fell early in this easternmost region. Perched on that high bluff, looking back again on to the roof of the world, I paused for a moment to think of all the long journeys that had brought me here – from the pages of Charles' book so many years ago, through sex shops and pet shops to the heart of the bureaucratic labyrinth; from a holy mountain to a temple of sacrifice; from finding and losing a dog in the streets of a capital city, to finding one again across an entire continent at the house of a friend in the 'city of eastern lights'; and finally, farther north-east, across my great river again and up to its Indian fountainhead. These were not separate journeys, I realised, as we turned back. They were all part of my river journey. And tomorrow, twelve rollercoaster days after arriving in India, the next stage would begin: we would head down to meet the river itself.

Early the next morning we bid farewell to Captain K. He was going on leave in a few days. He deserved it. However, although we had been released from our confinement, we were still in military hands – in the hands of an armed escort that was, according to Captain K, going on leave to Tuting. Replacements were already on their way up. I wondered about this. I think it was probably more likely that orders had been received from HQ Eastern Command, Calcutta to keep an eye on a certain Englishman and his dog, and keep them out of trouble.

We made our way down the hill to Gelling. Jaro and Topguy were waiting with a posse of porters, their backs bent by large bamboo baskets filled with provisions, tents and all kinds of other paraphernalia. It was embarrassing – they were all young girls, in bare feet. It was great to see Jaro and Topguy again. It had been far too long. With great pride and purpose, Bhaiti and I set out down the sheer incline to the river bed, followed by what had now turned into a small army.

Disaster struck almost immediately.

SEVEN

It was probably my fault, or bad karma, or a combination of both. Keen to set an example, or perhaps to show off to Yatish, Jaro, Topguy, the porters and the army just how fit and sure-footed I was, I set off at far too fast a pace down the twisting 300-metre incline, my speed increasing as Bhaiti towed me like a water-skier at the end of his long leash. We hurtled around a corner. The path divided around a small, grey stone stupa marking a little Buddhist shrine to our right. Bhaiti took the left fork, circumambulating the stupa clockwise. I took the right fork, circumambulating the stupa anti-clockwise. The lead took the middle path, smack into the stupa. We impacted in a jarring collision on the far side. Fortunately, Bhaiti and I were undamaged. But the stupa was not. I watched in horror as the stupa's little finial, shaped like a lotus bud, wobbled for a second and then fell to the ground. Bhaiti and I looked at each other. Trouble, we thought.

Realising I only had a few seconds before my act of sacred demolition was discovered, I picked up the finial, climbed on to the stupa and placed it carefully back into position. Short of an earthquake, I reckoned I'd got away with it.

I held my breath as the soldiers filed silently past, followed by the posse of chattering girl porters, a heavily laden Topguy, and a slow-moving Yatish. I breathed a sigh of relief, and waited for Jaro. He joined me by the stupa.

'Hi, Jaro,' I greeted him innocently.

'Mmmm, Mark,' he said, staring at me thoughtfully. 'Better to move slowly. Remember, we are old men. Easy to have accident on these paths.' He disappeared into the bushes and returned with a handful of wet mud and pebbles, climbed up the stupa, removed the finial, studied it for a moment, and then replaced it, securing it with the paste of pebbles and mud. He admired his handiwork and then climbed down. He smiled at me. I smiled back ruefully, suitably chastened.

However, bad karma is bad karma, even if you do repair the damage. Minutes later a worried-looking Topguy, who had sprinted up the hill, still, I noticed, carrying his immense load, relayed to us that Yatish had fallen, injuring his right knee. Yatish was in a bad way. He was lying on a tree trunk, his face ashen-white with pain. Jaro carefully pulled up his trouser leg. His knee was swollen and already turning purple. Jaro probed gently with his fingers, and announced it wasn't broken, more likely a torn or twisted ligament.

Yatish knew it, I knew it. We all knew it. His trip was over. But he wasn't going to give up, spurning my offer to return to the army base to seek assistance. After all, this was a genuine emergency, meriting evacuation on humanitarian grounds *re* section b of my permit. He could make it to Tuting, he told me. It was only fifteen miles. If his leg hadn't recovered by then, he would reconsider the situation. I wondered about the wisdom of this. But Yatish was tough, and it didn't seem the right moment to argue with him. I gave him a couple of strong painkillers, rubbed arnica into his knee and, supported by Jaro on one side and my Leki Trekki on the other, he hobbled slowly down the path. Topguy had already sprinted off to catch up with the porters and to prepare our camp for the night. I'll never know how Yatish made it through that long day, over the treacherous, steep terrain.

As Bhaiti and I moved on ahead, Jaro warned me to walk carefully and slowly, since at one point the track would divide. I must not, he told me, take the left-hand fork. This would lead to a long cane bridge that crosses the Siang. Take the right fork and continue along the right bank of the river. I think he noticed my excitement when he mentioned the cane bridge. I had read about what Verrier Elwin had described as 'those marvels of untutored engineering skill'. He reiterated again not to cross the bridge. It may not be safe.

Bhaiti and I crossed a tributary, a feeder of the Siang, by jumping from boulder to boulder and traipsing tipsily across fallen trees. We then began to climb again, out of the mist and into the hot sunshine. It was very humid. To my left, down a 300-metre drop, I caught an occasional glimpse of the river through the thick foliage. But I could always hear it as it roared through a narrow chasm over a labyrinth of rapids, and then settled into calmer water.

I thought about the bravery of the Indo-Japanese rafting team when I heard that roar – of their terror, and then their relief at having survived the rapids, and then the fear again as they hit the calm water, always a sign of a further explosion just ahead. I almost envied them. At least they had been on the river. I couldn't seem to get near it. It was frustrating, so close – yet so far. But I couldn't risk a descent of the vertical drop to my left. Like Verrier Elwin, I wanted to lay *my* body beside its waters. But, unlike him, alive and kicking.

The humidity was becoming unbearable. I stopped every half an hour to rehydrate myself from the two large water containers filled with sachets of Electrol that I was carrying. Uphill, Bhaiti was a godsend – he would literally pull me up. Downhill, I needed all my balance and concentration as he continually tried to dart into the thick undergrowth either side of the track. I longed to set him free. I felt almost cruel. After all, he was a hunting dog and, having released him from the prison of urban life, I was now imprisoning him again. But I couldn't risk it. Apart from the abundance of lizards, birds, rodents and winged insects, there were other much more dangerous predators around – predators that would consider a small dog a delicious snack. For a start, four kinds of big cat – tiger, leopard, clouded leopard, and perhaps even the rare and elusive snow leopard – not to mention Himalayan black bears, wild boar and, of course, snakes. And – certain dog-eating tribes . . .

Occasionally the forest would thin out and we'd cross sunlit clearings where every inch had been transformed by the traditional *jhoom* or slash-and-burn cultivation, patchworks of yellow, green and purple fields of maize, millet and rice, tobacco, opium, red pepper and ginger. Then we would plunge back into darkness, sucked in by the greedy green maw of that hot and fetid forest – a forest so thick, so ancient, so impenetrable, that nothing it seemed, apart from mankind, could destroy it.

But I was wrong. The very nutrient that had created it had also destroyed it – rain. No ordinary rain, but the torrential and devastating downpour of the monsoons. At one point it was like leaving heaven and entering hell in one step, as angry brown scars – swathes of destruction – had cut through this once rich landscape. Bhaiti and I inched our way across these treacherous landslides, littered like the aftermath of some great battle with the corpses of thousands of trees, convinced that at any moment our movement would cause the earth to move once again and carry us into the river far below.

A couple of hours farther on, as Jaro had warned, the track divided. I stopped for a moment, my mind echoing with his words. What the hell, I thought, I've got plenty of time. I'll just pop down and take a look. No harm in that. Bhaiti and I set off down the steep little track.

The forest ended in an almost perfect circle of light. It was like looking down the wrong end of a telescope. In front of me stretched what seemed to be a giant cobweb, extending about 275 metres, and suspended about thirty metres above a calm stretch of the Siang, still partly camouflaged by the morning mist. It was a long, impossibly fragile-looking bridge. I hesitated again. But not for long. It was irresistible – it was just too exciting – it was like something out of a James Bond movie. And at that moment I felt like James Bond. I *had* to give it a go.

So, being impulsive and carried away by my new James Bond fantasy, I ignored Jaro's words of warning. I was also hindered by a further impediment – a dog. A dog that was determined not to cross the bridge. Bhaiti might have been spooked not only by this long, swaying bamboo tube, but also by the ghosts of his predecessors. In some of those dog-eating tribes, I knew that before the construction of a bridge, they used to sacrifice a dog to the Spirit of the Mountain. It was, therefore, understandable that the moment I tried to pull Bhaiti, he would not budge – not even to put one paw on the first of the bamboo slats that were placed about thirty centimetres apart to form the walkway of the cane bridge. In the end, I picked him up.

To complicate matters further, there was our own combined weight to think about: myself – ninety kilos or so – a fifteen-kilo backpack, a few kilos of cameras, plus eight kilos of struggling dog. And to complicate matters even further, I had only one hand free to hang on to the side rails.

Evoking all the names of the gods that I knew, and determined to outdo Bond, I set out resolutely. It took me well over half an hour just to negotiate the first fifty or sixty yards. The bridge didn't start swinging in the middle, it started swinging immediately. I was thrown from side to side as Bhaiti struggled in my arms, necessitating me to change hands constantly in order to grab the relative safety of the left and right handrails. I inched forward, placing my feet carefully on the bamboo slats, convinced that at any moment they would break.

I was beginning to regret my foolhardiness. But to turn around, I thought, would be even more of a danger. A smooth current of milky-green water was flowing thirty metres or so below me. I had finally reached the river. Nearly, anyway. I wasn't going to let such a moment pass. I decided to take some photographs. Very slowly, I lowered Bhaiti on to the cane walkway, caressing and reassuring him. He struggled for a moment and then stood stock-still, trembling, while I attached his lead to my belt.

Swaying on the bridge, I watched the mist evaporate, revealing the river as an opalescent ribbon of melted ice uncurling beneath me. I now did not regret my decision. For me there was no better way to finally see this legend – a legend that had haunted me for so many years. Hovering above her, I found myself wanting to join her, enticed by the soft murmur of her siren song. Then I turned my head. A few hundred metres farther downstream, the siren was transforming into an angry, spitting, twisting white serpent as she entered the narrow confines of a rocky chasm.

I was now halfway across the bridge. I was about to move on when something stopped me in my tracks. It was another cobweb, but not a cane one – a real cobweb – an old and sticky cobweb. Jaro had been right. It seemed this bridge had not been used for some time.

I turned round. Bhaiti was standing stock-still, quivering, but not from fear – from excitement. His ears were pricked and he was staring at something intently a few metres farther along the bridge. I followed his gaze. Sitting quietly on one of the bamboo slats, enjoying the morning sun, was a bee.

'Bhaiti, noooooo!!' I yelled, at the same time fumbling desperately with one hand to grab the leash that was attached to my belt, and with the other to grab the handrail. But it was too late. Bhaiti lunged forward like a tiger, and I was jerked off my feet. There was a sound of cracking wood. And then nothing.

I dropped straight down, my legs scissoring through the air. Then I jerked to a halt. Something banged hard under my chin, and my neck felt as if it had been separated from my head. I felt like I was being hanged. 'Fuck a duck,' I gasped. 'This is not funny.' I took stock of the situation. I was suspended some twenty-five metres above the river. The entire lower part of my body up to my shoulders, including my left arm, was hanging below the bridge. My head, backpack, cameras and my right arm were above the bridge. It was my backpack that had saved me. It had wedged itself behind my head on some slats that had not given way.

Quickly, I reached out my right arm and grabbed a strut connecting the handrail to the walkway. At that moment, a bundle of howling fur hit me in the face, and then, whirling and turning, it danced around my head, entwining me in the chain lead. The lead bit into my face as Bhaiti tried to pull away again.

I couldn't understand what had happened to Bhaiti. Through the chink in the chain that surrounded my head, I could see him frantically rubbing the side of his nose against the bamboo slats, and clawing at it with his paws. He was whining horribly. Then I realised that he had been stung by the bee.

'Bhaiti,' I whispered softly. 'Come here, come here. It's going to be all right.' Whimpering, he slid towards me. He rubbed his face against mine. I could see where the bee had stung him. His upper lip was beginning to swell.

'Calm down,' I whispered, 'calm down,' desperately trying to calm myself down. He understood and lowered himself against my face. I felt a sharp pain in my leg. I looked down, and saw that my right ankle was covered in blood. I watched mesmerised as it oozed out of my sock, on to my boot, and then dripped slowly into the river.

There was only one thing to do. I had to remove my right hand and rely on the backpack to support me. There was another agonising crack and I felt myself slipping farther down, and then another jarring, reassuring thud as the backpack held fast. I reached for the metal strut.

I took a deep breath and pulled with all my might. Bhaiti suddenly leapt up and shot away from me, forcing the coils of the chain lead deeper into my face, but actually pulling me up in the process. I wrenched my right arm through the hole and managed to grab hold of the bridge. Then I gave one large, final pull, and I was through. I lay gasping for breath and hanging on for dear life. I pulled up my trouser leg. My ankle was criss-crossed with deep, bloody lacerations. But I was okay – and so, just as importantly, was Bhaiti.

I started to laugh hysterically – not out of joy, out of sheer relief, hysterical relief. Bhaiti, whimpering with pain, sat in my lap. I stroked his swollen muzzle and we sat quietly recovering together enjoying the warm sun. Verrier Elwin was right, I thought, peering through the broken slats. She was a hard mistress indeed, his 'river of no return'.

We crawled back across the bridge. A familiar figure was waiting at the end. It was Jaro.

'Mmmm,' he said. 'Good bridge, Mark?'

'Absolutely, Jaro. Fantastic! Beautiful!' I noticed him looking at my torn and bloody trouser leg. 'Oh, that's nothing,' I said. 'I just cut myself on one of those struts.'

'Mmmm. This bridge is called Chitum Bridge. Remember name, Mark,' he added pointedly. 'I do not think you will forget it.' He then disappeared into the bushes and returned a few minutes later, clutching a handful of ferns. He rubbed them together to form a paste and, bending down, gently applied it to Bhaiti's upper lip. 'Mmmm, bee sting,' he said. 'Not serious.'

Bhaiti licked him gratefully.

'Where's Yatish?' I asked.

'Mmmm, maybe gone ahead,' he replied. 'Mmmm, Mark. Better we move on now.'

A few miles farther on, we reached the village of Bona. A small stone stupa and a line of tattered prayer flags indicated it was another Monpa settlement of small wooden houses on stilts. The village was empty. Everybody was at work in the surrounding fields. My Assam Rifles escorts welcomed me warmly into their small wooden bivouac. Topguy and the porters had already moved on to the village of Korba to set up camp for the night. Yatish was asleep on a bamboo bench.

Captain K's men had gone out of their way to make us feel at home. We lunched on coffee, *chung* and local spinach. Bhaiti was spoilt rotten and fed an endless supply of biscuits. Jaro's magical jungle remedy had already worked – the swelling on his lip had almost disappeared. I wished he had a magic remedy for me. The cuts on my ankle were beginning to throb. I bound up my leg and set off with Jaro and Bhaiti, leaving Yatish in the capable hands of the army.

Unhindered by Yatish we made good time. The track became easier and broader, dipping up and down like a rollercoaster, through the forest, clearings and across occasional landslides. Far below me to the left, the river still uncoiled seductively. I had nearly succumbed to her embrace once. Now I was determined to meet her on my terms.

In tactical positions we passed cleverly camouflaged foxholes – army bunkers – their hidden empty gunports facing north towards Tibet, built after the 1962 Chinese invasion. India had learnt her lesson then, and now this important strategic area was well prepared.

I thought back to when I had first arrived at the army base at Gelling, and of my disappointment at the lack of military muscle.

The Chinese would encounter a very different scenario here. The Border Security Force Assam Rifles were a formidable opponent, experts in jungle warfare, concealment and, above all, quick moving. As I struggled along the path, small platoons mysteriously seemed to appear from nowhere, heavily armed and carrying at least forty-kilo packs. They melted past me like phantoms, the only indication that they had been there at all was the smell of sweat and gun oil, and the occasional pungent odour of a *bidi* – the local Indian cigarette – left hanging in the hot, fetid air. Yatish had told me a story about this crack regiment – of a tough veteran colonel's idea of a little light exercise in between military manoeuvres. They had first rafted on a home-made bamboo craft right down the Siang from Tuting to Guwahati in Assam. Then, accompanied by the colonel's equally fit wife, they had run the three hundred miles alongside the river to the India–Bangladesh border at Dhubri.

The foxholes were driving Bhaiti mad. His hunting instincts had not been dented by the incident with the bee. He was desperate to explore them. I was determined he wouldn't and held him on a very tight, short leash. In the gathering gloom, we met a hunter. He was carrying a single-barrelled shotgun. Around his waist he wore an ammunition pouch made of fur – exactly the same colour as little Bhaiti's coat. He laughed and pointed to his pouch, and then at Bhaiti. In the darkness, my little Bhaiti could easily have been mistaken for the animal that now decorated his waist. I held his head tightly – I had already lost one dog. I wasn't going to risk losing another, especially to end up as an ammunition pouch.

We reached Kopu, another Monpa village, sitting prettily on a bluff above the Siang. Although it was almost dark and raining, we were, I realised, much lower and closer to the river. I could hear it thundering below me. Tomorrow, I thought, I was going to make my formal introduction to that hard mistress.

Topguy had performed a miracle. The inside of the little wooden army bivouac had been transformed. Our sleeping bags were neatly laid out on raised bamboo pallets. Mugs of tea were waiting for us, and the smell of cooking filled the air. Yatish soon arrived with the army escort. He was exhausted and in great pain. I gave him some more painkillers and arnica, and he crashed out. After a delicious supper of pork, lentils and spinach, followed by some first aid – disinfectant and plasters for me – Bhaiti and I climbed into my sleeping bag and crashed out as well.

Unfortunately, not for long. Jaro woke me to announce that the girls of the village were all gathered outside waiting to perform a traditional dance in our honour – to welcome strangers. Apart from a cut ankle – which admittedly was quite sore right now – I didn't have a valid excuse like Yatish. Bhaiti and I accompanied Jaro into another small wooden building. As I entered a little candlelit room, thirty women and children all bowed deeply, and then started giggling. I stood there amazed, and rather embarrassed. They all bowed again. Then the penny dropped. They thought I was Japanese too. The Japanese had stopped here for the night on their rafting expedition.

I was getting sick of being mistaken for a Japanese man – especially when I heard that they danced well. But I was damned if I was going to be outdone by them. Fortified by immense quantities of *chang*, the local millet beer served from plastic buckets, Bhaiti and I danced and howled the night away, and after joining in their strange, shuffling, clapping traditional dance, strutted our own stuff together – a bit of good old dog 'n' roll. We received rapturous applause.

'Mmm,' said Jaro. 'Not such old man. People tell me, better than Japanese. Do not want you to stop.'

It turned out to be a long evening. Eventually, dripping with sweat, I extracted myself and climbed into my sleeping bag. Bhaiti soon joined me.

Fifteen miles or so to Tuting would have been an easy day's walk in normal conditions. But imagine adding 80 per cent humidity,

treacherous tracks up and down 300-metre inclines, the constant
fear of new landslides and handing it to one middle-aged man with
an appalling knee injury. That is what Yatish had to face the next
morning. His knee had swollen even more during the night and
when he had swung himself off his sleeping pallet, his leg had
buckled under him and he had collapsed. We agreed that he would
travel with the army again: he was tough but he really needed support.

However, I too had a problem – nothing compared to the seri-
ousness of Yatish's, but a problem all the same. It wasn't just my
ankle that was hurting. I had blisters. Just one day's walk had
turned my soft feet, toes, soles, uppers and heels into a livid red
spongy mass – 'water bottles', as Aditya used to call them on our
elephant journeys. I taped them up like a geisha with one of what
I consider to be the six most essential items to carry on journeys –
'second skin' (the others are earplugs, a lunghi or sarong, a torch,
an endless supply of cigarettes and a tongue-scraper) – and hobbled
off towards the river with Jaro. It was still early when we reached
the ridge. Far below the river was again almost invisible, obscured
by the mist. But we could hear its distant roar.

'Mmmm. Rapids,' Jaro suddenly said, breaking the silence.
'When we are at bottom, Mark, you must be careful.'

But to reach the bottom of the precipice, one had to be even
more careful. Following Jaro, who had wisely taken care of Bhaiti
in one hand, and was cutting a path through the thick vegetation
with a machete in the other, I inched my way down a treacherous
morass of slippery roots and tangled, skin-ripping thorn lianas. It
was wet and the leeches were having a field day. I could feel them –
that familiar slight sting as they purchased a hold on one's skin and
then settled down happily to feed. They hit us from both ends,
from the overhanging trees down our backs, and then up over our
boots to our legs. It took us almost two hours to get down that
precipice. And there was another problem – Bhaiti. The nearer he

got to the river, either terrified by the increasing roar, or because of
a pathological hatred of water, the more he did his best to escape.
Jaro was permanently being pulled backwards as Bhaiti strained
against his leash, his ears flat and his tail down. In the end, Jaro
picked him up.

We were approaching the bottom. The towering trees and
bamboo had thinned out and we picked our way across a yellow,
white and purple carpet of fallen orchids. The river was deafening.
The mist had lifted to reveal a small, sandy beach littered with
boulders and fallen trees. Beyond was a thundering mass of water.
We had hit a point where the river was squeezed between two
narrow chasms, choked and littered with a labyrinth of huge boulders, over which four- to five-metre waves were crashing and then
dumping into deep, churning pools.

Jaro and I deleeched one another. He beat me by five. I picked
twenty-seven off him. Bhaiti didn't do too badly either – seventeen,
and one really tricky one attached to his eye. I was now standing
about twenty metres from the river bank, yet I was already being
soaked by the cloud of spray that whipped off the river like a high-
powered shower. Jaro yelled at me to be careful. The Adis have an
almost reverential respect for the Siang. But I had to get closer. Her
calling was, if anything, more bewitching than ever. Its sheer power
seemed to pull me closer.

But it was not easy. Like a movie star, her security was formidable. Now, sheets of water were smashing into my body, throwing
me off balance. On all fours, I crawled upwards over slippery-
smooth stones to the safety of a ledge, protected by a huge boulder,
directly above the river. With my back against the boulder, I held
out my left arm. It was immediately thrown back at me, whipping
me sideways. I had at last – and literally – experienced the power
of this mighty river first-hand. It was awesome.

I looked down the river. Half a mile or so farther downstream,
it shot out of the chasm to become wide and peaceful. I badly

wanted to bathe in that water but it was impossible to get around the rock face. I would have to wait to pay my full obeisance. I sat for a long time on that ledge. I needed to absorb the river that had haunted and fascinated me for so many years. I thought of the tiny stream nine hundred miles or so farther north-west, high on the Tibetan plateau, that I had so easily straddled a few months before. And I thought of what lay ahead – the Brahmaputra widening into a sea as it poured into the Bay of Bengal.

The sharp ping of a pebble hitting rock awoke me from my reverie. It was Jaro signalling me to return. I thrust my hand into the torrent and tightened my fist, trying to steal a little of that power and take it with me, only to have my arm catapulted back again.

I rejoined Jaro and Bhaiti, who were waiting for me well away from the river, in the safety of the tree line. I was soaking wet. Bhaiti looked at me – a smug kind of look. I took off my shirt and wrung it out over him, drenching his warm dry coat in an icy torrent. He howled in protest and shot off up the bank, jerking Jaro off his feet. Bhaiti too had now been introduced to the river and received her blessings.

My diary entry for that day reads: 'Would it be possible that I gained something from that river today? I feel at peace, and yet at the same time, curiously energised. I walk as if in a dream, not even feeling the agony of my feet. It seems that the river has somehow entered my soul, my very being. It has become part of me. Its power is running through my body, like the blood in my veins. I feel, as long as I am close to it, as long as I can hear its music, that nothing can go wrong.'

We caught up with the army on the outskirts of Tuting. Yatish was finished.

'I am sorry, Mark,' he said. 'I'm going to try and get a helicopter out of here. But I'm going to send someone up as a replacement to look after you.'

'No, no, Yatish,' I replied. 'You've no need to worry about that. I've got Jaro and Topguy. I don't need anybody else. And also,' I added with a grin, 'I've got Bhaiti.'

'That's what I'm worried about,' he replied, a rare smile stretching his pain-racked face. 'But I have my orders.'

While Topguy and Jaro went off to buy presents for the porters, Yatish and I were escorted to the Assam Rifles officers' billet. Considering that I was in the middle of nowhere, I was disappointed by Tuting. I almost felt I had re-entered civilisation. Tuting sits in a bowl-shaped valley where the Yangsang Cho River drains out from the north-east to join the Siang. The township of Tuting grew to prominence during the Indo-Chinese war of 1962. An airstrip and communications centre had been installed by the Indian Army. Basically a military cantonment, it now boasts Government offices, a healthcare centre, a couple of schools and plenty of lines of bamboo market stalls.

Just as Yatish and I were sitting down to lunch, a young soldier walked in, saluted politely and informed us that there was a helicopter leaving for Pasighat in five minutes. Grabbing Yatish's bags we jumped into a jeep. A familiar figure was standing by the helicopter. It was Prakash, Shantunu's First Officer, who had flown us up to Gelling. He looked at Yatish.

'One down, one to go,' he laughed. 'I'll be coming to pick you up next.'

I embraced Yatish. He pulled something out of his bag. It was a small dog-eared Indian book with a plain cloth cover.

'I've been meaning to give you this for some time,' he said. 'I think you'll find it interesting. I've marked the relevant passage for you.'

I was intrigued. As the helicopter lifted off, I realised with a touch of regret that I had never really got to know Yatish.

Bhaiti and I were escorted back to our sleeping quarters, the Inspection Bungalow. It was frightfully grand, and empty. Our bedroom was delightful – two four-poster beds draped with mosquito netting, a dresser, a desk, two chairs, an overhead fan, a Casa Pupo rug, chintzy Colefax & Fowler curtains, and a soft, black and white velveteen blanket to sleep under. Bhaiti immediately debugged the room, literally. In minutes every living insect had been executed – except for one – a large spider that was sitting smugly in its web in the corner of the ceiling. Being a perfectionist, Bhaiti went mad. He started barking loudly, and tried to climb up the wall. I could see I wasn't going to get any peace, so I extracted the poor thing with the tip of my Leki Trekki and to give it a fair chance, threw it out of the window. Bhaiti quickly followed and by the instant sound of snapping jaws, swallowed it. A little later Jaro and Topguy returned from their shopping spree. The girls had been delighted with their gifts and set off home happily.

'Mmmm, where Yatish?' Jaro asked.

'He's gone, Jaro. On a chopper. To Pasighat.'

'Gone,' he said incredulously.

'Yup. Evacuated out.'

'Mmmm. Now it is just three of us.'

'Just four of us.' I corrected him.

Topguy had soon magically conjured up a wonderful dinner of chicken, rice and a bottle of Contessa rum which he had commandeered from the officers' rations. And a little bowl of milk for Bhaiti. Jaro and I toasted one another. Topguy did not drink.

'*Agampe*,' Jaro said – Adi for cheers.

'Bottoms up,' I replied.

'To Siang,' he toasted again.

'To Siang,' I replied happily.

Later, snuggled up with Bhaiti under the black and white

velveteen cover, by the light of a sputtering candle, I began to read the book that Yatish had given me.

It was called *Indian Explorers of the Nineteenth Century* and it dealt exclusively with the extraordinary journeys and ingenuity of the pundits, the Indian secret agents who were trained and employed by the British Survey of India during a strange and shadowy conflict known as the 'Great Game'. Best of all, it told in detail the story of the man whose quiet heroism Charles Allen and I had celebrated the first day we met, and who had helped me believe I could do this journey: a sturdy, lion-hearted 'coolie' called Kinthup – the 'almighty one'. He wasn't even, strictly speaking, a pundit, but for my money he was greater than any of them.

The pundits were, essentially, local geographer-spies recruited by the British from the mid-nineteenth century to help provide accurate geographical information about the countries bordering India – particularly Tibet. Under Chinese imperial orders, virtually no one was allowed to enter the 'forbidden land'. But there were semi-Tibetans from the areas near the border who could, and it was from these people that the pundits were first enlisted, and then trained in a secret school in Dehra Dun by an experienced British surveyor.

Here, to prepare them for their risky ventures beyond the white fortress of the Himalayas, they were taught both conventional and clandestine methods of surveying. They learnt how to measure distances using specially adapted ritual beads, the number of beads on a string reduced for the purpose from the traditional 108 to a more computable 100. They learnt technical data by translating it into verse and mantras, which they repeated time and time again as they walked along. Ingenious instruments were designed for them – boxes, baskets and clothing with secret compartments, and prayer wheels specially adapted with a lid into which minute top secret data could be concealed. They learnt the arts of disguise, as pilgrims and traders, or whatever role suited the particular occasion. And, finally they donned new identities – *noms de guerre* – like Number One, GM, GK and AK. This was real James Bond stuff, I thought.

One of their first missions in the 'forbidden land' was to try and trace the course of the Tsangpo/Brahmaputra and mark it accurately on a map. It was a dangerous, difficult task, both physically and politically, and for their extraordinary bravery and ingenuity some received their just rewards. The pundit known as Number One, for instance, retired with a proper pension, was made a Companion of the New Order of the Indian Empire (CIE) by Queen Victoria, and received the highest honour of the geographical community, the Patron's Gold Medal of the Royal Geographical Society.

But others were neglected – in particular my hero Kinthup. For sheer devotion to duty, in my opinion, nothing can eclipse the story of his efforts to try and establish once and for all whether the Tsangpo flowed into the Brahmaputra after it disappeared into the Himalayas.

Kinthup was an illiterate, brawny young Buddhist who had worked as the servant to a number of pundits on their expeditions. He had developed a reputation for being reliable and intelligent, and in 1880 he was sent as the assistant on yet another attempt to establish the Tsangpo/Brahmaputra connection, this time posing as the pundit's servant. Under instructions from a Captain Harman of the British Survey of India, their job was to get into Tibet, follow the river as far as they could and then, starting on a given day, throw into it five hundred logs, each a foot long and marked with special tags, at the rate of fifty a day. Downstream, Harman's men would be waiting on the other side of the mountain gorges, on the Brahmaputra. If the logs appeared, it would prove the rivers were connected.

Unfortunately for Kinthup, his pundit turned out to be a wastrel, a bully and a drunkard with no commitment to either the work or his assistant. After several months of hard travelling, on reaching an isolated Tibetan village high above the river, the pundit simply jumped ship. Without a word to Kinthup, he sold his 'coolie' to the village headman as a slave, packed his bags and set off home.

Abandoned and betrayed, Kinthup was nonetheless determined to complete the mission. After working as a slave for seven months he managed to escape and headed immediately for the Tsangpo. But he was quickly recaptured and, desperate, he pleaded with the abbot of the local monastery that he was a poor pilgrim who'd been treacherously sold into slavery by his companion. The abbot took pity and bought him from the headman for fifty rupees, on the condition that Kinthup repaid the debt by working for him.

Fortunately, the abbot was a kind man and Kinthup began to see his opportunity. But it would take time and careful planning. First, he asked permission to make a pilgrimage to a sacred mountain farther down the Tsangpo. The abbot agreed and after many months Kinthup finally reached the remote spot where he and the pundit had been supposed to release the logs. Painstakingly he set to preparing them, somehow obtaining a saw, marking them with Harman's special tags – which, amazingly, he had managed to secrete all this time – and finally hiding them in a cave. There was no point in releasing them without alerting Harman in advance. But how to do so?

The only way was to send a letter from Lhasa. Kinthup returned to the monastery, where he worked patiently for two more months before getting permission to go on another pilgrimage to the Tibetan capital. There, being illiterate, he arranged for a letter to be written to a pundit now living in Darjeeling, with whom he had once worked, asking that it be passed at once to the Head of the British Survey of India. In its understated resolve, modest dignity and dedication in the face of suffering, it is entirely characteristic of its author:

> Sir, the lama who was sent with me sold me to a village head-man as a slave, then he himself fled away with Government instructions that were in his charge. On account of this the journey proved a bad one. I, Kinthup, have prepared five hun-dred logs according to the order of Captain Harman, and am ready to throw fifty a day into the Tsangpo from Bipung in Pemako, on the fifth of the fifteenth of the tenth Tibetan month of the year called Chhuluk.

Then Kinthup returned to the monastery for a further nine months. At last, as the date approached, he asked again for leave to visit the sacred mountain by the Tsangpo. This time, the abbot, impressed by the devotion of his servant, granted Kinthup his free-dom. He headed back to his secret spot on the river and there, finally, released the logs over ten successive days. Having success-fully completed his mission in the face of every conceivable obstacle, Kinthup made his way back to India – a journey which, almost inevitably, involved him in yet further trials, dangers and setbacks. By the time my hero reached home, he had been away for over four almost impossibly arduous years.

What he found was little comfort for his pains: indeed he found only further disappointment. His mother had died, believing him also to be dead. The pundit to whom his letter had been addressed had died as well, so the message had never reached the British Survey of India. And in any case, Captain Harman was himself dead, having long ago given up hope of catching sight of any logs. They had merely floated unnoticed down the Brahmaputra. All Kinthup's years of devotion to his British masters had been in vain.

Perhaps worse, hardly anyone believed his amazing story. He sank back into obscurity in Darjeeling where he barely eked out a living as a tailor, unrecognised, unthanked and unrewarded, with no offer of support or compensation for what he had endured. But there remained in the Survey files his dictated account of his travels, a mass of topographical detail.

It wasn't for nearly thirty years that anyone realised just how accurate Kinthup's account was. Colonel Eric Bailey, a British Frontier Officer whose journey in 1911 effectively settled the last doubts about the exact course of the Tsangpo, travelled extensively in the little-known area which Kinthup had described and compared his findings with Kinthup's files. Convinced that Kinthup had been telling the truth all along, Bailey tracked him down in Darjeeling and lobbied hard but unsuccessfully for him to be granted a pension. Instead the British Government gave him a lump sum of a thousand rupees. It was small enough recompense for all Kinthup had done, and in any case it was too little too late, for very shortly afterwards Kinthup died.

It was an extraordinary tale and I thought Kinthup had been treated outrageously. Not only should he have had a proper pension for his service; he should have been awarded the Gold Medal and all the other honours of the Royal Geographical Society. In fact, I would have had him knighted. And the story of those logs was so amazing. What had happened to them? Might some have been washed up on the banks of the river? And if so, was there a chance of finding one? To do so would be to own the greatest treasure I could imagine.

Most people would think it a childish fantasy, but the more I thought about it, the more possible it became – because the wonderful discovery I made that night from Yatish's book was that I was actually following exactly the same route as Kinthup. Not only was I walking in my hero's footsteps, but I had a pretty good idea where he had hidden the logs. It was right under my nose – down, somewhere on that forbidden stretch of river I had seen from the McMahon Line. So if he'd released them there, there really was, I thought excitedly, every chance of finding one washed up on the banks. After all, the odds weren't that bad, and there hadn't been many other souvenir hunters down this way in the last century.

Here was a great new quest, I decided: not only a river to follow but a log of historical significance to find. Before I fell asleep, I told Bhaiti and then reminded myself to inform Topguy and Jaro of the new venture first thing in the morning.

EIGHT

I was not too keen to stay in Tuting. I found it charmless, oppressive and over-populated. I wanted to get back on to the river. I was missing it, and I wanted to find those logs. However, there were certain duties I had to perform – military duties – to thank the Assam Rifles for my imprisonment, my release, and for their hospitality and their escort. My small army was deserting me. It seemed I was finally to be trusted. I spent a hectic morning visiting the Officers' Mess; taking tea with the Subedar Major's family, where Bhaiti disgraced himself by relieving himself on their nice new tapestry carpet, and where they kindly presented me with a little wooden sculpture of a Buddha; writing a formal letter of commendation to the Assam Rifles, and meeting the commander of the north-east region. I had found out he was a Maratha too, but unlike Aditya he was rather dour, and a little put out by my tales of his barbarous ancestors. Even Bhaiti met his match here, in the form of the commander's Tibetan mastiff who, remarkably for this ferocious breed, was a friendly giant. But, his size alone daunted Bhaiti, who sat quietly in the safety of my lap.

My duties finished, it was time to get going. We had another twenty kilometres to cover before the next village – Ningging. Our route, Jaro had told me, would be much easier that day, along an actual road, or, as I was to find out, more of a track, a track that linked Tuting to Pasighat, or usually did – it was now blocked by landslides. I was disappointed. I wanted to get down to the river as soon as possible, to start my treasure hunt.

Jaro explained to me that not even the Adis took the river route. There was no river route. One took tracks and then cut up and down away from the river wherever possible, such was the steepness of the terrain. He also told me that we were now entering tribal country, for Tuting was like a cultural crossroads, dissecting the Siang Valley between the northern Buddhist peoples of the Monpas and Membas, and the southern tribes of the Adis.

He had managed to secure some more porters – young boys this time – who had already set off with Topguy. He had no money to pay them so he informed me we would meet them on the road on their return. I still couldn't believe how fast these young people travelled, considering some of them were carrying up to thirty kilos. I was having enough trouble with just my ten-kilo backpack. It was pathetic.

However, it seemed I still wasn't out of the clutches of the military, because as we set off, south, in the boiling sun, we were joined by two elderly soldiers – big men in full camouflage combat kit, carrying huge backpacks. They had been seconded to Along, and I couldn't have wished for two better travelling companions. They were lifers in the army and had already served twenty-five years in the Assam Rifles. As soon as I had managed to put a stop to their military formality, the endless saluting, the endless 'sahibs', they relaxed into the very essence of the journey.

I called them Corporal Classic and Corporal Shortcut, the former because he kept nicking my fags – Classic is one of India's premier brands – and the latter because of his ability to find short cuts, albeit ones of unbelievable steepness. Being of a certain age, they enjoyed the leisurely pace that I had set with Jaro.

It was punishingly hot that day. Far below, at least three kilometres down, I could see the river, cool and inviting as we pushed along the road, following a high ridge. My feet were agony again and I had now discarded my Noddy boots in favour of trainers. Nor were the cuts on my ankle healing properly. Poor Bhaiti was suffering too. He stopped endlessly and lay down panting. There was no shade. Jaro came to the rescue by putting up his pretty, pink floral umbrella and sheltering Bhaiti from the hot sun, while I forced handfuls of water mixed with Electrol down his throat. His coat was so thick that he just couldn't cope with the heat.

On the road we passed groups of female labourers – Bihari and Oriya tribals – with baskets on their heads clearing the stone debris from the recent landslides. They were dressed in iridescent saris, contrasting brilliantly against the deep, dark green valleys that cut right down to the river, like precious stones on display on the green baize in a jeweller's window. An hour or two later, we met the young porters on their return home. They immediately started to barter furiously with Jaro. Jaro was determined to pay them the going wage – forty rupees each. They wanted a hundred and fifty. Jaro was furious when I undermined him and gave them each a hundred, telling me that I had now set a scandalously inflated standard for future foreigners. I pointed out that it was unlikely that there would be any future foreigners in this restricted area. Just then a supply aeroplane flew overhead on its way to Tuting.

'Mmmm,' he said, pointing at the aeroplane. 'Good aeroplane to fall from.'

'What?' I said incredulously. 'What do you mean, fall from?'

'Mmmm. Many times when young, Jaro fall from aeroplane. I have medal.'

I soon found out another astonishing facet to this extraordinary man. During his school and college days, he had taken part in all sorts of extra-curricular activities. He wanted, he told me, to be 'extra' ordinary. His speciality was the NCC, the National Cadet Corps, and he was selected from within the Corps to undergo preliminary paratrooper training at Agra in 1977. Having made the first five mandatory jumps successfully, he went on to free-fall and was awarded the Certificate of Merit, the first ever given to a tribal member from Arunachal Pradesh. However, his parents were not impressed or amused. To the Adis unnatural death is called 'dying in the sky' and here was their son, tempting his maker. It took Jaro years to explain to his father the art and skills of skydiving, but apparently he was never convinced.

'Mmm,' he announced with a knowing twinkle in his eye. 'Next time you go on bridge, Mark, better you take parachute.'

By the late afternoon we reached a narrow track that led almost vertically up off the road to the right. Corporal Shortcut announced it was a short cut, and we plodded up 6,840 little mud steps cut into the hillside, to the village of Ningging. Topguy was waiting. He had put up my tent – my first night under canvas. And what a campsite. Perched on a little patch of grass in front of the Inspection Bungalow, I looked directly south, east and west. I was above the cloud line, through which soared some of the higher parapets of the eastern Himalayas, their peaks dusted in snow, like magical citadels. Below me, beneath that cloud line, I could still hear the murmur of the river even at this height. It was very comforting.

Ningging was my first real Adi village. By the time we had set up camp and climbed another two thousand little mud steps, it was almost dark. Jaro introduced me to the headman, or the *gam*, as he is known in Adi language. I was disappointed. I had again, as when I first met Jaro, expected something more traditional, or tribal. The *gam* was wearing a pair of blue jeans, a tee-shirt and a nifty panama hat decorated with a logo of the World Cup. It seemed that even here, in this remote north-eastern part of India, Western influences had infiltrated.

When he heard I was English, he suddenly doubled up with laughter, slapped his thighs and then fell on the ground holding his stomach. I was astonished. The English, I admit, are a pretty curious race, but to cause this reaction? At least he didn't think I was Japanese. Was it something I was wearing, or the way I looked? Eventually the *gam* recovered from his fit and muttered something to Jaro. Jaro translated.

'Mmmm. *Gam* say he always wanted to meet Englishman.'

'Well, he has now,' I replied, rather tartly. 'But what's so funny about us?'

'Mmmm. *Gam* say that English are worst footballers in the world.'

I sighed. What an irony, I thought. I had travelled halfway around the world to this remote area to finally meet my first Adi tribal chieftain, who turned out to be a football fanatic. Football was like a virus – it ought to be obliterated.

'Jaro,' I said. 'Please ask the *gam* which country he thinks is best at football.'

'Mmmm. *Gam* say Germany number one.'

The *gam* and I were definitely not going to get on.

Still chuckling, he led us into a clean compound, up a narrow notched log just over a metre long that acted as a stairway, and on to a wide veranda. The floor was constructed from tightly woven split bamboo and bounced alarmingly as I stumbled in the darkness. I crashed my head into something as I bent double to enter the house. The *gam* again exploded into laughter – my clumsiness, no doubt, just reinforcing his opinion of English footballers. I shook my head and peered closely at what I had blundered into. It was an immense skull with long curved horns, a bit like a water buffalo.

The skull was the remains of the Adis' most prized possession, the mithun – or, as it is known in Latin and by naturalists, *bos frontalis*. The origins of the mithun are a mystery, even to the Adis. In all my travels in Arunachal Pradesh, I could never find out if they were originally a wild species, or a kind of semi-domesticated crossbreed, perhaps the result of a union between an indigenous Adi cow and a male water buffalo from the plains of Assam. I hadn't actually seen a live one as yet but research and a couple of photographs had revealed that they were large animals, not unlike the Indian buffalo but heavier in build with a sleek coat of either black, brown or a mixture of both. For the Adis they represent the ultimate in status and wealth, and are only sacrificed at the most important ceremonies. They can also be used as barter for the payment of debts, fines and marriage dowries.

When I stepped over that threshold into the little house, I left the western world behind. It was a long, low room, about twelve by six metres with walls made from rough-hewn timber, its bamboo rafters blackened by the central flat rectangular fire, or *merum*. The rafters were festooned with hunting trophies – skulls of bear, deer, squirrels, cats of different species – an array of cooking pots, and rows of drying shrubs and ferns. Hanging from another blackened bamboo beam was a selection of weapons – bows and arrows, long spears, and a couple of *daos*, the long, straight Adi cutting sword. Pride of place, though, was given to a modern, single-barrelled shotgun resting against the old, mouldy skin of a clouded leopard.

Around the fire squatted the *gam*'s family – three or four very young children and an older girl, wearing an exquisite turquoise stone necklace and pretty, flower-patterned metal earstuds. She was stoking the fire on which perched a battered, old tin kettle. Her smile of welcome lit up the gloomy interior like the morning sun. The *gam*, putting the politics of football aside for a moment, gestured me to sit by the fire. I squatted down next to Jaro and was soon enjoying a delicious tea made from ginger, served by the smiling young girl in little chipped Chinese bowls. My eyes were now smarting and tears running down my face from the smoke that sat like a fog in the gloomy interior.

'*Agampe*,' I said, raising my bowl. The whole family dissolved into laughter. The room vibrated alarmingly. They were clearly delighted by my limited knowledge of the Adi language, but not nearly as delighted as two other ancient members of the family – the *gam*'s mother and father who, veiled in smoke, I hadn't noticed before. They were really laughing – laughing so much that I wondered if I was going to bear the brunt of more derision about my country's footballing skills. But they were just extremely happy to meet me, and while the old mother joined the young woman to help with the tea, the old man came and squatted beside me and held my hand. I gave him a cigarette. He inhaled deeply and collapsed in a paroxysm of coughing. This caused more laughter. I had never met such a jolly family.

Traditions among the older generation, I was happy to see, were still observed, but less so among their offspring. The young girl, who I had found out was the unmarried daughter of the head *gam*, was wearing a simple, flower-patterned dress. If I had been here forty, or maybe even thirty years ago, I would have heard the clink of metal as she moved around, from the *beyop*, or petticoat, of round embossed plates of metal that signified chastity. However, both the old man and woman sported traditional Adi haircuts – black, Beatle mops, ending a good two inches above the top of the ear, fashioned by lifting the hair on a stick and chopping with a knife all the way round. Both also had distended lobes from which hung metal rings. And around the ankles of the old woman were broad bands of cane work, dyed a beautiful indigo blue. Around her neck she wore five or six necklaces of different coloured glass beads mixed with shells, and supporting her thick red and blue cotton lunghi was a magnificent belt of cane and cowry shells, some of them carved in the shape of animals.

The old man, clearly miffed by the attention I was paying to his wife, was not to be outdone. He scuttled into the back, to the dressing-up box, and reappeared a few minutes later in full Adi finery. His scruffy loincloth had been replaced by one of bark, made from the udal tree, and hung in strips about forty centimetres long, like one of those leather fringed skirts that were fashionable in the 1960s. His chest was naked except for a splendid fur cape of a black Himalayan bear. Around his waist he wore a cane sword belt supporting two magnificent *daos*, which in the past had no doubt regularly been tested on the soft white skin of the British. Across his back he carried a long bow and a quiver of poisoned arrows, their tips blackened with a deadly paste made from aconite. But it was the variety of hats that he proudly showed me that was truly astounding.

His ceremonial helmet was a cane skullcap adorned with bearskin, yak tails dyed red, boar tusks, feathers, and the curved beak of the great Indian hornbill. His war helmet was more simple – a masterpiece of practicality: rimless and oval it was made of successive rings of cane which were built up and bound together with strips of finer cane, woven vertically and so closely as to entirely cover the ringed foundation. It was both sword- and water-proof. The old man illustrated the strength of his war helmet by trying to place it on my head, which to his amusement I hastily declined, and then placing it on his son's, the head *gam*'s head. He then picked up a *dao* and, with a fearsome blow, cracked it down on the helmet. The head *gam* seemed unscathed, though I could only guess at the headache he must now be suffering. The helmet too was unmarked – the blade had simply skidded off.

Jaro told me that although they still used bows and arrows for hunting, they had generally been replaced by shotguns, which were supplied by the government. Arunachal Pradesh is one of the last areas in India where traditional hunting is still allowed. India still very much respects Nehru's old policy of protecting the autonomy and traditions of these tribal people. And, like all tribal people, the

Adis hunt in moderation – there is no overkill – and a perfect harmony with nature ensues. A strict policy is enforced by the head *gams* on when, where and what they can hunt, and even how many fish they can take from the rivers. It won't be the Adis that destroy the wildlife – it will be the timber contractors.

Back at the camp, Topguy had created a fairytale setting for Bhaiti and me to enjoy our dinner. The little porch of the tent, perched right on the edge of the bluff, had been opened, affording us a magnificent view of the night sky. A circle of candles had been stuck into the earth. Topguy had surpassed himself in his culinary skills that night. We dined alfresco, on mushroom soup, pork, rice, dhal and spinach. Afterwards, we stood together on the top of the world. A shooting star arced across the vast sky. I told Bhaiti that we must make a wish. I wished that I could let him off the lead – give him a day of freedom so that he could hunt to his heart's content. But I wondered what he was wishing. At night, I had begun to notice Bhaiti staring at me intently with those cool, hypnotic eyes. Perhaps he wished I were a dog. No, he couldn't have, I thought smugly. I was much better company than any dog.

Reveille was early next morning – 5.00 a.m. By the time Bhaiti and I eventually emerged from our quarters it was 6.00 a.m. A posse of young porters – all girls, all barefoot – were waiting patiently in a neat line. Hovering about them, and checking their baskets, almost drilling them, were Corporals Classic and Shortcut. The military, it seemed, had now taken over from Jaro in the organisation and recruitment of porters. The head *gam* was waiting to bid us farewell. He was still laughing. However, one of his children – a young boy I had met the night before, with a catapult hanging around his neck – shyly presented me with a basket filled with a variety of small, pretty birds, a squirrel, and a couple of rats. They were all dead.

We had a long walk that day – twenty miles, according to Topguy, to the village of Pango. We followed the trail up and down for a few hours, and then cut down a steep slope – another of Shortcut's short cuts – to a very rickety, overgrown cane bridge that crossed a feeder of the Siang, the Siyi River.

'Mmmm,' Jaro said. 'Old bridge. We must be careful – we go one at a time.'

I wasn't going to argue with him, considering my last experience. Jaro would go first with Bhaiti, then Classic, then Shortcut, then me. I asked Jaro the logic of this.

'Mmmmm. You are the heaviest.'

Jaro set off slowly across the bridge with Bhaiti secured to his belt. Halfway across Jaro yelled back and told us to be careful as some of the struts were rotten. The bridge creaked and swung ominously – even more so when Classic and Shortcut marched across. Clearly, they were experts.

The Siyi, really just a boulder-choked stream, gurgled about twelve metres below me as I made my way carefully across the bridge. I had now mastered the technique. It was all to do with the distribution of weight: one placed one's feet on the lines of wire that reinforced the slats from beneath, and, of course, kept two hands free to hold on to the side rails. I had almost made it. I only had a few feet to go. I was way over the river by now and could see the vegetation through the slats as the bridge ran up the steep bank. But yet again, I couldn't resist it – I had to show off. I increased my speed. There was a sharp crack and this time my left leg disappeared through the bridge, thankfully to meet solid ground. I pulled myself up quickly and lunged to safety.

Jaro was lying on the ground, cackling.

'Mmmm, Mark. When finish our journey, you can get new job in District Bridge Department – as safety officer.'

If I went on like this, I could see myself being pursued by heavily armed and enraged Adis, determined to chase me out of the country, like my British predecessors.

Up and over another hill, we cut down a steep escarpment to the

Siang. It was a beautiful place – a long, stony wedge of white sand fringed the river, today in a benevolent mood as she swept past like a silky carpet. Here was my chance to finally pay my obeisance. But there was work to do first. The sand was also littered with logs and broken trees. Operation Kinthup Log Search was to be put into immediate effect. I had only just begun explaining to Jaro about this strange new quest of mine before he interrupted me.

'Mmmm, Kinthup,' he said. 'Looking for logs, yes?'

I was astonished. Not that I'd imagined for a moment that Jaro was uneducated in any way, but his scholarly credentials – including a university degree – were truly impressive, considering the extraordinary conditions in which he had started his studies. There was no electricity in his village and no kerosene, or any other type of lamp. There were many times when he had had to do his homework by burning dry bamboo sticks, or even by moonlight.

Jaro didn't consider my quest totally off-the-wall, so we explained the game to Classic and Shortcut. They thought it was a splendid idea, particularly when I mentioned there was a prize of a case of rum. Then we all stripped to the waist and started combing the banks for a foot-long log with a metal tag. Even Bhaiti joined in – for different reasons. As we pulled up great tangles of rotting trees, a myriad of insects would try to escape to safety in different directions. He also had a new prey – butterflies – which enveloped us in white and yellow clouds. The insectocutor had his work cut out that day. As did we and it was hard work, but after a couple of hours we had swept every inch of that sandbank. No joy, but I was not disappointed or disillusioned – this was just the beginning.

The sun was now high and hot. It was time to take a bath, time for full immersion. I found a safe bathing spot – a kind of whirlpool trapped between two large boulders – and stripped off. I was reeking – I hadn't had a proper bath for about ten days, since Itanagar. I thought about giving Bhaiti one as well, but realised this would involve a major operation and in any case the current was too strong. I checked that nobody was watching. Jaro, the Corporals and Bhaiti had retired tactfully into the shade of the forest line. I pulled down my underpants and stepped in.

It was cold – but deliciously cold. My problem was not just to keep upright but to avoid getting swept away, as the current churned and pulled against my legs like a washing machine, immediately freezing the pain from the cuts on my injured ankle. With a certain amount of dexterity, I managed to wedge myself between the boulders, and using one hand, soaped my body thoroughly. I had even managed one application of shampoo before the bottle was swept away to join Kinthup's log somewhere down the river.

I felt like a new man when I climbed out, clean both physically and spiritually. I had finally paid full obeisance to the river. I stretched out to dry on a warm rock, and hoped that no unfortunate Adi would pass by to get the shock of his life on seeing this unknown river monster – plump, white and hairy – like a large harp seal. I was soon joined by other sun worshippers – butterflies, hundreds of them, who again covered me in a yellow and white blanket. I must have fallen asleep, for the next thing I knew I was being rudely awoken by another of Jaro's missiles zipping off the rock beside me. It was time to leave.

The climb to the village of Pango turned into one of the longest yet. Classic and Shortcut marched on ahead, leaving Jaro, Bhaiti and I to puff along together, stopping frequently for refreshment as Jaro cut sheaves of succulent sweet plants for us to suck on, and opened up little brown buds to reveal seeds that looked and tasted like lychees. I complained to Jaro that I was just too fat, too unfit, and too old for this sort of thing any longer. He consoled me by telling me that the Adis consider fat people to be potent and of substance, and age is always venerated. Anyone over forty is considered old.

As we climbed higher the track was lined with neat, tall, impenetrable bamboo groves, almost like the fortifications of some jungle citadel. The higher we got, the more the vegetation thinned out and the steeper and narrower the track became. We were now hemmed in. It was humid. Spanning the gully above us, I noticed little bamboo strips at regular intervals. They looked man-made. I was right. Jaro explained to me the ingenuity of these Adi traps. Mice and rats used the little bamboo strips as routes to the other side of the gully. At one end of the bamboo strip was a small cane spring trap that snapped shut when the victim knocked over the trigger, a tiny cane stick holding the jaws apart.

When we reached Pango it was dark. We found Topguy in a rage. All our chocolate, powdered milk, and most of our rice had been stolen by those naughty boys who had portered for us from Tuting to Ningging – the boys that I had overpaid. Jaro was outraged, muttering that this sort of thing would never happen in his village.

I was not in the best of moods, either. Not only was I exhausted, but the cuts on my leg were now swollen and infected. I badly wanted to rest but I was soon surrounded by a throng of curious children and a very loquacious gentleman, the local teacher, who wanted to practise his English with me. He didn't start off too well, by asking my 'sweet name'.

Feeling anything but sweet and not bothering to eat, I retired quickly with Bhaiti to the privacy of our tent. It wasn't private for long. For the next hour or two it was surrounded, and sometimes knocked into, by inquisitive children. Much later we were besieged again, this time by the local dogs. I wielded my Leki Trekkie like an Adi *dao* that night, defending one side and the back of the tent with sharp blows to the dogs' muzzles as they pushed against the soft folds, while Bhaiti defended the other side and the front by launching himself at them from within. All night, they sat outside and howled. 'Thank God,' I wrote in my diary, 'for earplugs.'

*

Wherever one is in the world, I've found, the advent of morning generally dissipates the memories of a bad night. It brings with it a sense of great relief, of comfort; it removes the panic, the nightmares. One almost feels gratitude that one is alive, and everything is normal – back, however mundane the situation, to reality. My situation, as I awoke groggily that morning, was far from mundane. Firstly, Bhaiti had decided to sleep on my face. God, he smelt. I was going to have to get him into that river. Secondly, I was surrounded – again. I could hear and see the children as they pushed up against the side of the tent, giggling, and then, as they heard me move, silent. I could feel the anticipation.

I thought I'd surprise them – really surprise them. I painted my nose and cheeks in sunblock, a white zinc paste, and crept very slowly to the entrance. I whipped up the zip and sprang out with a roar. It had the desired effect – a hundred little boys and girls fled, screaming across the field into the village. Now I felt guilty, and cruel. I noticed a little wooden object lying on the ground. It was a handmade cricket bat. Ah, I thought, this is my kind of village – a village that plays cricket, not football. A proper game.

I picked up the bat and practised a few deft strokes, a glance to mid-on, a fine cut past point, and a pull over mid-off. Slowly, groups of little boys filtered over, one by one – some braver than others. A little wooden ball was produced, a wicket set up. We had a game. Being the visiting team, they politely gestured that I should bat first. I took my guard, and thought I'd show them a thing or two. I felt a bit like Ian Botham.

With some alarm I noticed the bowler, a small boy of about seven, pacing his run out. He disappeared into the morning mist to reappear again at great speed. Something hard and travelling at great velocity zipped past my knee and whipped back the middle stump, made from a bamboo stick. There was a great roar of approval from the players, the crowd, and even a bark from Bhaiti. Turncoat, I thought. Embarrassingly, I was dismissed in exactly the

same way by the following two balls. There was great excitement –
a hat-trick. I then tried a bit of bowling, first trying to intimidate
these aspiring Sachin Tendulkars, by glaring at them in good old
Aussie fast bowler tradition, and then thundering in at quite a
pace. My over cost sixteen runs. I was dispatched to all corners of
the village. But I had made a lot of new friends.

The exercise had given me an appetite. Bhaiti and I entered the
moshup, or long house, where Topguy, Jaro, Classic and Shortcut
had spent the night. They were huddled around a fire on which
Topguy was cooking up rice and chillis for breakfast. It was dark,
draughty and filled with smoke. I could hardly see the other end.
We made our way across the bouncy bamboo floor. Overhead,
wooden beams were festooned with animal skulls and drying
herbs. The *moshup* is the hub of every Adi village. It acts both as a
bachelor dormitory for the young, unmarried men, and a place
where the *kebang*, the council of *gams*, meets to discuss the affairs
of the village. Here, around one of the many *merums*, or fire-
places – in this one there were seventeen, each representing the
different families of the village – in theory the *gams* decide everything from hunting to marriage, crime, repayment of debts,
punishment and personal problems. They are a bit like agony
aunts – something, I thought, the West could benefit from.
Community is almost a forgotten concept nowadays. One rarely
even knows one's neighbour.

On the other hand, it could work against you. You could get
into serious trouble. In the old days adultery was severely frowned
on by the *kebang* and bizarre punishments were dished out.
Women had a particularly rough deal. Men found guilty of the
offence were simply fined six or eight mithun and if they were too
poor to pay they were sold into slavery. Women on the other hand
were stripped naked, tied up in the *moshup* and had chillis stuffed
up their bums.

I sat down gingerly by the fire, and hoped the chillis were not as hot as the ones I was eating for breakfast. My eyes watered as I listened to a long statistical dissertation on Arunachal Pradesh from the gregarious teacher, eager to practice his English. I learnt that at the last census there were exactly 461,742 males and 397,150 females, and other such fascinating titbits. Fortunately, an hour or so later, his busy schedule ended my lesson, and I was left in peace with Jaro and Bhaiti. Topguy and the Corporals had disappeared on porter recruitment.

A few minutes later, an old man wearing a rattan bowler hat, a red woollen coat, a loin cloth and carrying a bow and a quiver of arrows, shuffled across the wooden floor and sat down beside me. He had a proud face – the skin pockmarked and stretched so tight that it reminded me of the leathery, lizard-like skin of a selak, an Indonesian fruit. Through Jaro's translation, I learnt he was the retired head *gam* of the village. He had heard I had arrived – a Britisher – and was determined to meet me.

He had met only one Britisher before – a man he had liked and respected enormously. He called him Megan Elwi. He was talking about Verrier Elwin! The old man remembered him well. He told me that Megan Elwi always carried a gramophone and tins of sweets. He had been a good, kind man, who had puffed and panted up and down the hills. As far as the ex-*gam* was concerned all British people were good.

He reached into his red, woollen coat and produced a leaf parcel, which he presented to me. Inside was a chicken's egg, cushioned by powder to stop it breaking. Jaro gave a sharp intake of breath. He explained to me that this was the highest honour an Adi could bestow upon somebody they considered a friend. I was deeply moved, but also embarrassed. What could I give this gentle old man in return as a gesture of my friendship? Jaro pointed at my cigarette. I pulled out two packets of Classic – hardly a gift of much substance. But the old man was pleased, and immediately fired one up, inhaling deeply.

I noticed that the old man had a tattoo – a small tattoo of a cross on his throat. It was a traditional tribal decoration, I knew, and not a sign of any alien Christian influence. Verrier would have liked that. He was the greatest defender of tribal life and staunchly, like me, anti-missionary. He considered them 'social uplifters'. For me too, the greatest bequest that the British left behind was their policy of banning missionaries from Arunachal Pradesh – a policy adopted by Nehru, and still pretty much intact today. Under the British a few 'social uplifters', convinced that the little tattooed crosses were of significant religious importance, had tried to infiltrate the tribe, without success. They were all French, and they were all killed.

Jaro took off to do some chores and left me and Bhaiti alone with the old man. We sat side by side in companionable silence, sometimes communicating by hand movements and gestures. He pulled out of the folds of his loin cloth a beautiful bamboo pipe with a long, slender stem, a little silver bowl and a sticky black lump the size of a golf ball. He pointed at my swollen leg and nodded. I nodded back eagerly. I knew what it was. It was opium. It would, of course, have been impolite to refuse, and after all, it was for medicinal purposes.

He carefully prepared the pipe, lit it, took a long pull, and passed it to me. I took a longer pull and curling Bhaiti into the crook of my arm stretched out on the floor and floated away.

My diary entry for that evening read, 'No pain in feet. Bhaiti's fur, toenails and eyes.' I remember vaguely getting back to my tent and lying down. The pain in my leg had vanished. Bhaiti's fur took on a strange orange glow, almost like a halo. His three pink toenails glittered as if they had been just varnished and his eyes . . .

I am not an expert on opium, but whatever the old man popped into that pipe the previous night was still working the next morning. When we were leaving he wanted to have a photograph taken of us together. I gave the camera to Jaro. Jaro was a hunter, and held the camera as true and steady as a bow. We posed for the photograph, soon joined by the rest of the village, including the young cricket team.

I was standing at the back, next to the old man. He had his arm around me. As Jaro clicked off a few frames, I felt a warm sensation running down my left leg. I looked down – it was a steady stream of urine emanating from somewhere in the folds of the old man's loin cloth. I looked at him. He looked at me and smiled. I smiled back. Thanks to the lingering effect of the opium, it didn't worry me at all. Perhaps, I thought, this was an old Adi custom to bid farewell to a good friend. Or perhaps the old man was overcome with sadness and the emotion had triggered his bladder. Or perhaps it was just incontinence. Whatever – strangely, I found it rather flattering. Before I left, he slipped something into my hand. It was a little bamboo pipe and a small ball of opium. He pointed at my leg, not the leg that he had pissed on, but my injured leg. He chuckled. I understood. It was, of course, to be used only for medicinal purposes.

Our journey for the next couple of days took us away from the river, mostly along a switchback of dusty, dirty roads. There fat babus sat comfortably on chairs in the shade, picking their noses and scratching their arses, monitoring the work of the unfortunate tribal labour, toiling all day in the hot sun as they cleared the blocked roads. We spent one freezing night in a *dhaba*, or roadside café, perched on the edge of a bluff, and fought a hundred battles with a hundred different mangy dogs (all of which we won). We eventually reached another Inspection Bungalow. The terrain was just too steep to pitch tents.

For once, the Inspection Bungalow had charm. It was built in that British mock-Tudor Assamese style that I had seen on my drive to Pasighat. It was a little raised concrete bungalow crisscrossed by black and white beams, surrounded by a wide veranda. I could have been in Weybridge. However, there was a problem –

the door was secured by a large padlock. We checked round the back for a way in. It was like Fort Knox. Corporal Shortcut handed me his rifle. For a moment, I thought he wanted me to blow off the padlock, until he gestured to the steel-plated butt. Destruction of Government property is an imprisonable offence. It was better that a foreigner take the rap. It needed just one blow and we were in. The room was small and musty, piled with old mattresses, with a large hole in the centre of the floor.

After a light dinner – rations were getting low – of rice and aubergines we settled in for the night. I had just finished dressing my injured leg, which now resembled one of those strap-on ankle weights in a shocking purple colour, when a head popped up from the hole in the floor. It was a dog, soon followed by another dog – Bhaiti. He disappeared in hot pursuit.

A short, vicious battle took place beneath the floorboards. My hero soon reappeared back through the hole, victorious and a little bloodied. It was not wise to mess with a dog that had been brought up on the battlefields of urban Guwahati.

The next morning I had a narrow escape – one of many on what turned out to be a long, extraordinary day. Outside the Inspection Bungalow, I found a perfect place for a wash. A forked stick supported a bamboo tube from which flowed a stream of ice cold water, like a little waterfall. I squatted down, dunked my head under the stream, and started scrubbing my face and hair with soap. As I pulled back, wiping the soap from my eyes, I noticed something swaying. It was really just a blur. I am long-sighted. I remembered thinking, how odd. It couldn't be the bamboo. It was securely fastened. It seemed I was sharing my ablutions with some-one else.

I slowly drew my head back, wiping the soap from my eyes. I found myself staring into the cold, obsidian eyes of a large snake. It was sitting on its coils, its black tongue flicking in and out, thirty centimetres away from my face. I moved back very slowly, very carefully. When I gauged I had enough distance between myself and the snake to avoid its strike, I shot to my feet and sprinted into the Inspection Bungalow, yelling my head off.

A posse of men was soon peering round the corner at the green-and-yellow-striped reptile that was enjoying its bath. Bhaiti, thank god, was chained up inside. I crouched nervously behind the door, watching as Topguy and Jaro approached the snake. They both carried sticks. The reptile turned, and then pulling its head back, struck at the stick that Topguy was holding in front of it. Quickly, Jaro, who had worked his way behind, managed to slip his stick into the lower snake's coils and, lifting it up, catapulted it into the bushes.

'Why didn't you kill it?' I asked Jaro incredulously, terrified that it was going to return. He was meant to be a hunter.

'Mmmm,' he replied. 'Why kill it? It has not harmed you. And it is not good snake to eat. But,' he added with a chuckle, 'mmmm. If snake bite Mark, Jaro bite Mark. It is poisonous snake.'

Today was an auspicious day. We were going to cross the Siang to the left bank. Jaro had some inside information on our proposed route, from the head *gam* of the village. It would be steep, slippery and in some places there would be no tracks at all. If an Adi warns one about terrain, it's going to be tough.

Our porters that day were six little boys and three girls. One of the smallest boys hefted my rucksack, some thirty kilos, on to his back. It was bigger than him. Topguy and the porters set off early while I delayed our departure by bandaging up my feet and attending to my injured leg. I had started a course of strong antibiotics the night before after noticing livid red streaks spreading up my thighs to my groin. I could feel the beginnings of swollen glands. However, the sheer beauty of that first half an hour took away the pain, as we walked along a pathway to heaven, across a carpet of clouds separating the earth from the sky.

We soon began to descend. It became a nightmare – a twisting, steep serpent of a track covered in treacherously slippery lichen-covered stones, dropping down 600 metres. It was like walking on ice. I must have fallen down about ten times in the first half-hour. Each time I picked myself up, Bhaiti licked my face in encouragement. Around midday, we reached the bottom of the chasm where another long cane bridge stretched over the Siang, here a raging white torrent hemmed in by thick vegetation. No chance of a log search here, I thought disconsolately. I hadn't seen my river for three days. Now I couldn't get near it.

I realised, as I negotiated the high, swinging structure successfully for a change, that the Siang seemed to have changed course. We were now walking up it. Jaro explained that the river swept around a long, looping bend here. Our descent that morning had been a detour to reach the bridge, the only possible crossing place between this point and ten miles farther down. The fury of the last monsoons had wiped all the other bridges away. We were now heading north again.

We started to climb. It was just the three of us: Jaro, Bhaiti and me. Classic and Shortcut had yomped on ahead. We were now struggling up a steep thousand-metre hill. In some places we traversed tiny, crumbling tracks by literally hugging the rock walls, inching our way across. It was a question of balance and luck. One slip would send you tumbling down a 300-metre drop.

We cut our way through jungle so thick that the sun could barely penetrate, only occasionally spotlighting the path in little golden pools. I had to let Bhaiti off his lead. Even Jaro found it impossible to walk with him. You needed all your balance, wits, and all your limbs. Bhaiti was a few yards ahead of me. Suddenly he turned round and started barking furiously, his hackles up, rushing forward and then retreating. I wondered what had bugged him as I took another step forward into one of those little golden pools.

'Do not move, Mark,' Jaro's voice suddenly whispered in my ear. 'Do not move at all.'

I noticed that the 'Mmmmm' had disappeared. There was a calm urgency in his voice. I felt something cold and sinuous wrapping around the back of my bare leg. Hyperventilating, I looked down. My right Noddy boot was pinning down a small, green reptile which was whipping its tail around my bare leg. But where, I thought in horror, was its head? Fortunately, I had stepped right on the back of its neck. An evil little head with two black horns protruding from either side was hissing and spitting in rage, trying to turn to strike my boot. I was standing on a horned viper.

I couldn't move. Bhaiti was going mad, jumping up and down and barking continously, almost hysterical. Jaro quickly tied Bhaiti up and then with amazing speed cut and fashioned a forked stick. The enraged reptile had now managed to turn and was repeatedly striking the thick leather upper of my boot, leaving a slime of transparent liquid. I was terrified.

'Mark,' Jaro said. 'When I pin snake – jump. Jump quickly.' Carefully, he lowered his stick and firmly pinned the enraged viper to the ground. 'Jump, Mark – now.'

I jumped. I've never jumped so quickly or so far in all my life. I must have broken some record. This time, Jaro did kill the snake, lopping off its head with his machete and throwing it into the bushes.

I hugged Bhaiti. He had saved my life. So had Jaro. I put my arm around his shoulders.

'Mmmm,' he said, now back to his quiet, calm self again, 'bad snake. This time is dangerous to walk in jungle. When sun shines, snakes come out for heat. Mmmm, better I walk first, Mark,' he added with a wry grin, 'or Bhaiti.'

About three hard hours later we reached a sunny clearing leading up to another steep but open path. We heard the sound of laughter through the trees above us. It was the little gang of young porters on their way home. They ran full tilt down the hill in bare feet to meet us. Jaro paid them, and told me the young boy who had carried my rucksack reminded me of his son.

Then he shook his head sadly. 'Mmmm. My son would never be able to do this. Not Adi any more. Too soft. But,' he added, 'my fault. I bring him up in town.'

At the top of the hill was the village of Paling. From Paling, you could see the world – all 360 degrees of it.

NINE

I had read about Paling in the book Yatish had given me. Kinthup had passed through it in 1882. I was still following in my hero's footsteps. But it had changed considerably from his description. 'About twenty houses . . . Hogs and cows abounded.' Now it was a large village – the largest I had visited so far – two hundred houses or so fringed the large open area that served as a football pitch and a helipad. But Kinthup was right about hogs and cows. Cows, anyway. They were everywhere, and remarkably inquisitive as I fought for space to put up my tent on the halfway line.

Paling was also a District Headquarters – and with the District Headquarters came the District Officer. Somewhere on any journey one comes across one of these gentlemen, a gentleman with an overblown sense of importance who enjoys demonstrating his power at whatever cost to other people. I knew there was one of his kind here when a group of young men wandered over and informed me that the District Officer was waiting to see me.

Reluctantly, leaving Bhaiti with Jaro, I hobbled over to his headquarters, a pretty bungalow, from which a tattered Indian flag hung sadly from a pole. He was sitting on a little wooden veranda. I wished I could have had the courage of Mahatma Gandhi who, one day a week, made a vow of silence and spoke to nobody.

The District Officer was squeezed into a small cane chair, his immense belly bursting out of a mustard-coloured wool cardigan. He beckoned to me with a disdainful crook of his finger to join him. He spoke perfect English. He seemed angry when he found out that I wasn't from Manchester. He then ridiculed me in front of his fawning court of cronies by dismissing my substantial injuries as nothing, and humiliated me even further when I told him that I had found the walking hard and the distances great. Adis were men, not snails, he told me, and he could walk from Paling to Yinkiong, a distance of fifty miles, in one day. I would normally not have doubted this, having experienced first-hand their speed and stamina, but considering the extent of his girth, I thought it a tall tale.

I finally got my own back when he grabbed my binoculars. He peered through them, handed them back to me dismissively, and informed me they did not work. I pointed out that it might be helpful to remove the lens cap. However, he did serve good tea made from ginger, and after a couple of cups and a couple more insults, he magnanimously announced that I could leave.

I returned in a sulk to my tent. It had started to rain, obscuring the amazing view. But I cheered up when I saw the supper that Topguy had prepared. It was just the kind of food one needed on a dreary, drizzly evening such as this. Good, substantial food – a hot, delicious meaty stew. Bhaiti and I tucked in. Apart from the many sharp small bones, it was delicious. We returned for second helpings. I noticed Topguy was hovering over anxiously over me, like a chef having prepared a meal for a food critic in a restaurant.

'Good, sir?' he enquired anxiously.

'Delicious, Topguy. Where did you get the chicken?'

He looked confused. 'No chicken, sir. Stew made from gift that young boy gave us back in Ningging. Small birds, squirrels and rats.'

My stomach churned. I felt the contents of any English country garden shift up and down in my digestive juices. An unpleasant, acidic wind was building in my stomach.

At that moment, Jaro came into the tent carrying a large plastic bottle.

'Mmmm,' he said, 'A pong.'

I reprimanded Bhaiti immediately. Blame it on the dog.

Apong, it turned out, was the local Adi brew – a milky-coloured beverage made from millet.

I found it delicious. It tasted sweet and fizzy, and after many cups it settled my digestion and put the world to peace. However, it evoked strange dreams. That night I dreamt that I had assassinated the British Ambassador to some European country by disguising myself as a tree and impaling him with a spear. I wondered what Freud would have thought of that, as I groggily made my way outside for the seventh time, cursing the diuretic qualities of the *apong*. I walked smack into a man. I thought he was a policeman who had come to arrest me.

'Sir?' he said questioningly.

No, I thought, it can't be. I must be drunker than I realised. But it was a voice I was sure I recognised.

'Neeraj?' I asked confused. What would Neeraj be doing here?

'Yes sir,' he answered happily. 'I am here.'

'Why?' I asked, 'and don't call me sir.'

'Sorry sir,' he said, following me into my tent to be knocked over by a delighted Bhaiti, who leapt into his arms whimpering and whining with pleasure.

Neeraj looked exhausted. I handed him a glass of apong. He downed it in one. Then he explained that Tiger Mountain had sent him straight from another long trek to replace the injured Yatish.

He had driven as far as he could from Pasighat and then walked for three days north, up the Siang, accompanied by a local Adi guide.

'You are injured, sir,' Neeraj remarked worriedly, looking at my swollen ankle.

'Neeraj,' I said, '*please* do not call me sir.'

Early the next morning, we set off into the mist after a substantial and luxurious breakfast provided by Neeraj – cornflakes, powdered milk, toast and jam. We had no porters. Topguy, Shortcut, Classic, Neeraj and Jaro managed somehow to distribute the load between them. I was forbidden, apart from my day pack, to carry anything. I felt pathetic.

The shortage of porters was my fault. I had been enjoying my breakfast when the District Officer appeared and demanded I take a picture of him. I refused. I told him I had run out of film. My irritation had only increased when I was packing up and noticed my towels were missing. I searched for them everywhere. I found them, or what was left of them, hanging from the mouths of those inquisitive cows. At least, I consoled myself, there were precedents for such bovine intrusions. Verrier Elwin once lost a prize copy of *Carry on, Jeeves* to a cow in a tribal village. The cow passed over other books by John Galsworthy, Jane Austen and T. S. Eliot, so it was, as P. G. Wodehouse wrote, 'surely rather a striking tribute'.

I had already informed Neeraj about my search for Kinthup's logs and he thought it was a great lark. Enthusiastically he told me of a perfect place for a search – a place he had passed on his way up – right on the banks of the Siang, where the river curled lazily round a bend. Neeraj was already proving himself to be a real asset to our little team. His enthusiasm, energy and sense of fun were infectious. I remembered our first meeting in Guwahati. Bhaiti had been right. Always trust an animal's instincts. They are rarely wrong.

We successfully crossed another little cane bridge over a deep chasm. The Anbo, another feeder of the Siang, rushed far below. Eventually, I caught sight of the Siang. A sense of peace descended upon me as I heard her pounding through another gorge, now on my right side. We descended lower on to a sandy path. I noticed the old marks of the river's waterline ringing the massive girths of the trees, a reminder of its awesome size during the monsoon. It was now flowing twelve metres below me. Following the river as it broadened and flowed quietly around a long bend to the left, we reached a small plateau of white sand, fringed by boulders and thick jungle, jutting out like a wedge of cheese into the current.

This was our campsite – a campsite so beautiful and so perfect that I thought some god had created it especially for me, or maybe a hundred or so years before, especially for Kinthup. I decided that we would stay here for a couple of days. We all needed the rest.

Those days on the sand were to be the happiest time of my journey down that part of the river. It was here that I finally really got to know her. For once, she couldn't escape. I watched all her moods. As she woke she gradually threw off her blankets of mist – yawning, stretching, at first almost silent, cold and blue. Then, as the sun warmed her, she became playful, a golden nymph – dancing, singing and frolicking to catch the sunbeams. As night fell and the moon rose, she prepared herself like a princess might for a magical ball, slipping into a gown of sheer black silk, fringed by a rippling necklace of brilliant cut diamonds. As dawn beckoned, she yawned again – satisfied, fulfilled, and slipped back under her lacy blankets.

It was during those happy days that I often felt her cold yet sensual kiss as I lay in her arms, washed by one of her handmaidens – the little waterfall that fell from the rocks above me.

There was one member of our gang who did not appreciate the river's icy kiss. One small, smelly dog. Bhaiti knew the terrible torture that lay ahead of him the moment Neeraj and I crawled into the tent, where he was dozing in the shade, armed with towels, soap and shampoo. He shot out the back and would have been in Pasighat if it hadn't been for Neeraj's impressive rugger tackle, cutting him off before he reached the safety of the tree line.

Bathing Bhaiti was so contrary, so different from the experiences I remembered with Tara and other elephants. It was always the most satisfying and peaceful time of the day when, in the early evenings, warmed by the last rays of the sun, I straddled their immense backs and scrubbed the acres of skin while they lay quietly in the water. Occasionally they sprayed me playfully with jets of water blown from their trunks. It was at this quiet time that one established the strongest bond with those wonderful animals. A bond of trust, mutual respect and understanding.

Bhaiti showed none of these feelings as we held him under the little waterfall and scrubbed his body with soap and shampoo. He howled and shivered constantly, occasionally giving me a wet, mournful look which made me feel guilty. He looked tiny as his usually fluffy hair, now wet and matted, sculpted his bone structure. I began to understand why some dogs hate baths. It's almost as if they are being forcibly undressed and then having to endure the embarrassment of standing naked.

We towelled him dry. He looked splendid. I noticed his coat had turned darker as if his hair had been run through with a sooty comb. Neeraj and I sat back and admired our handiwork, which was quickly destroyed. Bhaiti rolled over and over whimpering piteously in the warm sand. He soon resembled a dandelion – the kind you blow.

In the late afternoons, to avoid the heat of the sun, we commenced Operation Kinthup Log Search, organised by Corporals Shortcut and Classic. They had managed to drill some military discipline into this ragtag army. We combed the entire area, section by section, in neat lines, like soldiers on parade. Eventually, I accepted that it was really just a schoolboy's fantasy. We never found anything resembling one of Kinthup's logs, although I never gave up hope.

However, during those searches, Jaro introduced me to an Adi pastime: beetling. It is more than a pastime really – it is an obsession. Beetles are the Adis' greatest gourmet delicacy. But they are no ordinary beetles, as Bhaiti soon discovered when Jaro revealed their hiding places.

Bhaiti sat waiting, his ears pricked, quivering with excitement as Jaro rolled back a large boulder. Clusters of brown, shiny beetles shaped like triangles exploded in all directions, scurrying swiftly to safety. Bhaiti pounced, and trapped one between his paws. He was about to execute it when he hesitated. He looked puzzled, suspicious. The beetle had climbed up his nose. He panicked and shook his head frantically from side to side, dislodging it.

Jaro laughed, picked one up and held it under my nose. I reeled back. It smelt sharply of almonds, like cyanide. The Adis' greatest delicacy was deadly poisonous. I watched in fascination as Jaro gently squeezed the insect. A little jet of clear fluid arced through the air and then, turning the insect over, he popped it into his mouth, an expression of pure bliss spreading across his face.

'Mmmm,' he said. 'Good beetle. Hot, like chilli.'

The Adi delicacy, I found out, could not only make you very ill, it could also kill you. Admittedly, the odds were pretty high, about a thousand to one. It was a bit like playing Russian roulette. Ozing's wife had lost the gamble just a few months before. She had been hospitalised for three months, in a coma. The potency of the poison, Jaro explained to me, all depended on the season. I watched in horror as he popped another beetle into his mouth, this time without removing the poison. With bated breath, I waited for him to die. Very much alive, he picked one up, squeezed out the poison and handed it to me.

'Mmmm. Try. It's good. You will enjoy.'

It *would* be over my dead body, I thought. Cautiously I took the beetle and placed it between my teeth. It was still alive. One of its little scaly legs tickled my tongue. Evoking all the gods, I bit into its body. It tasted exactly as it smelt – like almonds – and evoking all those gods again, I quickly swallowed it. My insides started to boil. It was like eating a raw green chilli, one of those really deadly ones. I began to cough violently, tears pouring down my face. Jaro chuckled and offered me another one. Pouring with sweat, I spent the rest of the day sitting in my tent waiting to die.

It was our last evening at the campsite. We gathered around an immense bonfire of logs that weren't Kinthup's, collected by Classic and Shortcut. Sitting on a carpet of diamonds, as the moon reflected off the specks of mica in the sand, we dined on smoked squirrels courtesy of a couple of passing hunters, beetles fried in garlic (I passed on that dish), dhal, rice, and crispy spicy pop-padoms. We drank *apong* and rum – lots of it.

Spellbound, with the river murmuring softly behind us, we listened to Jaro's tales of the legends, myths and beliefs of the Adis, told to him by his parents. He related to us the creation of Doni Polo, the sun and moon deity, the supreme being of the Adis. A long time ago there were two suns. They were brothers. Each of them shone for twelve hours so there was constant daylight. The heat annoyed a frog, who shot one of the suns with an arrow and killed it. When the sun died, it got cold and now it shines as the moon at night. The splinters made by the arrows became the stars. In revenge, the two suns have shot their arrows at the earth ever since, sunbeams and moonbeams. To escape injury, the frog now hides in the water.

Jaro told us of how the firefly was born. There was a battle between two gods – one in the form of a human being, the other a mithun. The human god struck the horns of the mithun god with his *dao*. Sparks flew off and turned into fireflies. He told us of the magic tree that created animal life when its branches were chopped off by a god, turning them into deer, porcupines, bison, squirrels, and all the other species. He told us how water was created by a thirsty god who followed the droppings of a duck until they led him to a huge spring. From it, he gave water to the whole world. He told us the legend of how the elephant came to look like an elephant by annoying his mother. First he angered her so much that she struck him with an axe. The axe stuck and grew and grew and grew to become his trunk. Next, when they were winnowing rice, she became so angry at his clumsiness that she whacked him over the head with two winnowing fans that became his ears. Then she became even angrier because he was so greedy and threw a pair of tongs at him with which she was preparing the food. These became his tusks. Now thoroughly fed up, the elephant left home to live by himself. He walked so far that his feet became fat and podgy, like rice pounders.

Finally, he told us of the legend of the birth of the tiger. Two gods gave birth to a terrible striped beast with no teeth. Horrified, they banished him to the forest forever. There he roamed getting thinner and thinner. A jungle spirit took pity on him and gave him two sets of long, sharp, curved teeth. The spirit told the bewildered creature that he would now be able to eat, and the tiger became king of all the animals.

Later, I asked Jaro if he had ever shot a tiger. He shook his head ruefully. He had had one chance but the tiger was too quick. 'Mmmm,' he mused nostalgically. 'A missed chance never returns. But perhaps it better though. Not so many tigers now.'

I understood Jaro's desire to shoot that tiger. The Adis are the purest of hunters. It is about mutual respect and honour – one against one. Whoever wins gains the power and braveness of the other.

As night drew in, I hobbled down to the riverbank and dangled my injured ankle in its icy water to try and anaesthetise the pain. I was now wearing a different ankle weight. It was heavier, bulkier.

It was also a different colour. Yellow, filled with pus. There was no way, I realised, I would be able to sleep tonight without a little medicinal aid – a spot of opium.

Back in my tent, I filled the bamboo pipe with burning embers from a small terracotta dish sprinkled with incense that Topguy put in the entrance of my tent each night. It served a dual purpose. It perfumed the tent and got rid of mosquitoes. I added a little opium, puffed furiously to get the pipe going and then took a couple of long, deep hits. I settled back into my sleeping bag, exhaling the sweet smoke and closed my eyes.

I must have slept for a while, for I clearly remember waking up at some stage to float out of my tent into the moonlight to take a pee. I climbed back into my sleeping bag. So bright was the moon that it bathed the interior of the tent in a soft, pale light. Bhaiti was stretched out with his head resting on his paws, squeaking and fidgeting occasionally, deep in his secret world of doggy dreams. I stared at him for a long while, realising how lucky I was that, once again, this strange and complex country had worked its magic and blessed me with the companionship of another wonderful friend.

With these happy thoughts tumbling through my mind, I fell asleep. Or did I? If what happened to me that night was a dream, it was a dream unlike any other. It was so clear, so intense that I was able to replay it like a tape recorder and jot it down the next morning, word for word, detail for detail in my diary. It was spooky.

Nothing seemed to have changed. Everything was in its usual place – Bhaiti's shiny metal bowl filled with fresh water for the night – my torch, cigarettes, lighter and the tin I used as an ashtray, all beside my sleeping bag. If anything, the interior of our tent seemed brighter but also slightly diffused, like a film just out of focus.

Bhaiti had woken up. He was sitting by my side, staring at me intently. His stare was so hypnotic that I found myself being drawn into the vortex of those brown, liquid pools, tumbling, spinning, turning . . .

'Do you feel like talking?' he said. 'I can't sleep.'

I looked at him. 'Sure,' I replied.

He stared at me intently. 'Can I ask you a question?'

'Anything, Bhaiti.'

'Do you think I love you?'

'Well, yes,' I said. 'I hope so, anyway.'

'I'm really, really fond of you,' he replied, 'and I know I will grow to love you. Like Tara.'

I was astonished. As far as I knew, Tara and Bhaiti had never met.

'How on earth do you know about Tara?'

He smiled, revealing his sharp white teeth, and wrinkled his nose. 'Instinct. The old dog network. You see,' he continued, 'human beings are under the misconception that the moment they get a dog, that dog automatically loves them. But it's not necessarily so immediate and sometimes it never happens at all. Dogs too can be fickle. Many just hang in there, using their canine cunning to get fed, pampered and have a warm bed to sleep in.' He paused and scratched his head thoughtfully. 'It's really more about trust. Trust is everything. From trust everything grows. So what I can't understand is why, although I trust *you* totally, you don't trust *me*.'

I was bewildered. 'I do,' I said. 'Completely.'

'No, you don't,' he argued, 'because if you did, you'd let me off my lead.'

'Well, Bhaiti,' I argued, 'I'm terrified that you are going to run off, and something will happen to you. I mean you might get eaten.'

He sighed. 'Believe me, Mark, the streets of Guwahati were a good training ground. I've *had* to learn how to fend for myself.'

'I'm not convinced, Bhaiti,' I replied.

He sighed again – a deep sigh – and explained slowly and care-fully, as if he were talking to a young child. 'Are you worried I'll just run off? Do you honestly think I want to wander around by myself in the forest when I get fed regularly, and fawned over endlessly?'

He noticed I looked hurt – deeply hurt.

'I'm sorry,' he said, 'I didn't mean that. I'm not fickle. You're dif-ferent. It's just that I love chasing, hunting things. I can't help it – it must be in my blood.'

I explained to him about his genes – his breed – the Tripuri hunting hounds from the Lushai Hills of Assam.

He swelled with pride, his hackles rising. 'It's strange, but ever since I was young I've always had that feeling, deep inside, that I was a little different.' He looked sad for a moment. 'I wish I'd known my mother and father.'

'You never knew them?'

'No. I don't know what happened to them. Probably killed. But,' he added wistfully, 'I like to think they are living happily, like me.'

'Did you have any brothers or sisters?' I asked.

'Yes. Two brothers, two sisters. But I lost track of them. We all went our different ways. There are so many like us on the streets.'

'Perhaps you ought to stop breeding so much,' I suggested. 'Every corner of every city in India I have ever been to, you lot are always at it.'

'Well,' he replied indignantly, 'our *so-called* masters hardly set us an example.'

Touché. India's population had just teetered over the billion mark.

'What was it like, Bhaiti, when you were on the streets?'

He sighed again. 'Tough – very tough. It was a question of sur-vival, cunning and keeping your wits about you. We scavenged at night, in packs. It was safer then.' He shuddered. 'I'm not going to tell you what we ate to survive.'

I think I knew, remembering Mr Soman's description of the pi-dog, that they eat anything, from decomposed bodies to vegetation.

'But the biggest danger,' he continued, 'was human beings. You know how I got this scar? From a man! He hit me with a piece of metal. I was doing nothing – just dozing in the sun. And you know why I don't like water?' he added with a wry grin. 'A woman threw a bucket of boiling water over me once.'

Jesus, I thought. That explains everything.

We sat for a moment or two in companionable silence. I lit up a cigarette. Bhaiti wrinkled his nose. 'Do you have to smoke those filthy things?'

'Well, we all have our little weaknesses,' I replied. 'I don't eat insects. Anyway, you were lucky that Reeta found you.'

'Nothing to do with luck,' he replied, 'just a little of that canine cunning. I used to hang around that house. I was in a terrible state then. I had lost all my hair. I knew she was a good woman who loved dogs. It was just a question of time.'

'But what about when you met me?'

'Well, to be honest, Mark,' he replied, 'much as I was grateful to Reeta, I would have done anything to get out of there. It was nothing to do with her. She killed me with kindness. It was that other woman – sorry, I mean bitch, Rani. She drove me mad. She was very neurotic. She was always trying to, you know . . . '

'Yeah, I know,' I replied. 'She wasn't your type.'

'Exactly.'

'So, as I was saying, all that affection you showed me when we first met was just . . . '

'No, no, no,' Bhaiti interrupted. 'Remember, I told you. I trusted you. Right from the start. It's the instinct that we animals have – just like Tara had for you.'

'Bhaiti,' I said. 'I have to tell *you* something as well. There was another dog before you. I didn't know him for very long – he escaped.'

'You mean Pie,' he said.

'Yes,' I answered, now not at all astonished, considering the power of the old dog network.

'What was meant to be was meant to be,' he replied, mirroring Aditya's Hindu philosophy. 'There are no coincidences. Anyway, he's fine. He's a survivor. Trust me.'

I knew the question was coming. I had dreaded it.

'Mark,' Bhaiti asked, 'where are we going?'

'Well, we're following this river, Bhaiti, through Assam. Then, through Bangladesh until we reach the sea.'

'And then?' he asked, cocking his head to one side. 'What happens then? What happens to me?'

I paused. I didn't have the answer. Not yet anyway. 'Well, Bhaiti, I'm not taking you back to England.'

'That's a relief,' he said. 'I hear it's cold, and rains all the time and the food is filthy.'

'But trust me,' I said, with a smile.

'I do trust you,' he replied.

He climbed into my sleeping bag and yawned. 'I'm really happy we've had this little chat. It's sorted out a lot of things in my head.'

'Me too, Bhaiti. You've no idea how much you've taught me. And thanks, little brother,' I said, hugging him tightly, 'for saving my life from that snake.'

He licked me gently. 'It was the least I could do,' he replied. 'You saved mine.'

The next morning, as we were packing up to hit the road, Bhaiti disappeared. Neeraj was in a terrible flap, and confused that I didn't seem at all concerned.

'Don't worry, he'll come back,' I reassured him.

'But *bad* thing could happen to Bhaiti,' he replied worriedly. 'Very, very *bad* thing.'

'Trust me, Neeraj. Bhaiti knows how to look after himself.'

About half an hour later, a tired but happy-looking Bhaiti

ambled into the camp. I noticed a pale-coloured bitch slinking away across the rocks. I looked at Bhaiti. Bhaiti looked at me and then winked.

TEN

Early that day, I met my second mithun. Jaro had pointed out a pile of ancient black stones, decorated with a few fern leaves. He stopped and mumbled something inaudibly, as if he were talking to the stones, almost worshipping them.

'Mmmm,' he said. 'This is mithun.'

Bewildered, I looked around, searching eagerly for a glimpse of that most prized of Adi possessions. There was nothing – just the sound of Bhaiti scratching his head, the murmur of the river, and the keening of a hawk circling far above me.

'Where?' I asked Jaro, scanning the bushes again. Perhaps I had missed something. Jaro had hunter's eyes.

'Mmmm. Here,' he said, pointing at the pile of stones. 'This is mithun.'

'Come on, Jaro. Stop playing games.'

He smiled. 'Mmm, maybe you want to make bet with Jaro?'

'Done,' I replied. 'One bottle of *apong*.' We shook hands.

Reverently lifting off the little frond of ferns, he studied the stones for a moment, and then, picking them up, he spread them on the ground one by one. I squatted down with Bhaiti and watched. He studied them again for a moment, and then started piecing them together like a jigsaw puzzle. A few minutes later, he beckoned to me. A large black stone mithun lay in front of me, perfect in every detail, even the long, curved horns.

He chuckled. 'Mmmm. One bottle of *apong*.'

He told me of the legend of this ancient stone monument. Many moons ago, a villager from the nearby village of Lichor had owned the largest and fattest mithun in the district. He was envied by everyone. One night a jealous neighbour set out to try to capture his great mithun. He heard it bellowing and followed the sound. In a clearing, he found the fabulous beast. He tried to lead it away but it would not move. It had turned into stone. In fury, he smashed it into a thousand pieces. He returned home. The next morning, he was found dead. Ever since then it has become a special place of worship for the Adis. Each time they pass it, they piece it together. Outsiders, Jaro told me, cannot even begin to do it – only Adis.

To continue honouring the deal I had made with Bhaiti, I decided to let him off the lead. He slipped into the bushes beside the wide, sandy path. He had a wonderful day, and allowed me a fleeting glimpse of that elusive creature – a real live mithun as, howling with glee, he pursued it down a steep jungle-clad escarpment to the river far below. He kept his word. He always returned. He trusted me. I trusted him.

My ankle was so swollen by now that I could no longer wear boots, or even trainers. I was walking in *chappals* – rubber sandals. I wondered how I was going to reach Pugging, the next village twelve miles farther on, let alone Pasighat. I was walking more and more slowly. As usual, Topguy, the porters and the two Corporals had forged on ahead. Even Jaro pushed on, although he always waited for me. He was suffering from toothache and kept on slipping into the jungle in search of a particular plant.

Bhaiti and I reached a long, high makeshift cane bridge,

constructed recently to replace another large iron bridge that had been washed away by the monsoons. It started to swing alarmingly, even more so than usual. I looked ahead. In the distance, I could make out a figure approaching me. This was a new experience. On all the cane bridges I had crossed, I had never encountered somebody crossing the other way. I met my fellow traveller in the middle – a small fat man, smartly dressed in a blue shirt and pin-striped trousers, polished brown shoes and a pork-pie hat. He carried a small, brand new Samsonite suitcase, protected by a canvas cover in a camouflage pattern, which Bhaiti took a great interest in, sniffing it keenly. For one awful moment I thought he was going to cock his leg.

He raised his pork-pie hat in greeting, which made the bridge swing even more, and asked me if I was from Manchester. What, I wondered, was it about Manchester – first the District Officer in Paling, and now him? At least he wasn't belligerent like the District Officer. But he was certainly talkative. It wasn't the best place to hold a long conversation, but he was not to be put off.

I found out, as we swung together over the twelve-metre drop, that he worked for the Public Works Department of the Siang district, and had been sent up here to oversee the clearing of the roads. I also found out why he thought I was from Manchester. He had relations in Manchester, and although he had never visited them, he was convinced England *was* Manchester, that there was nothing else. I thought about putting him right about this geographical error, and then thought better of it. I would be here all day.

I nearly was there all day as it turned out – splattered on the rocks. The Siang District Officer's Public Works boss was clearly a newcomer to these wild parts. He could not understand that if we both tried to cross the bridge on the same side, it would tip over. After several attempts, as the bridge swung crazily from side to side, I grabbed him in desperation. Like ballroom dancers, we waltzed to safety.

Just the other side of the bridge, a few miles from Pugging, I heard a terrible noise – a noise that had become alien to me. It was the sound of a vehicle in the shape of an ancient battered yellow truck, gasping and wheezing, polluting the pure air with clouds of black smoke. In the passenger seat was Neeraj. In the open back were Topguy and the Corporals. Neeraj, god bless him, was worried about my leg and had somehow commandeered the Public Works Department's only vehicle. Knowing Bhaiti's hatred of motors of any kind, I handed him over to Jaro. At least there he would benefit from fresh air. I squeezed in the front.

It was strange getting into a vehicle again. But not as strange as meeting the driver. He was, without doubt, the gloomiest and thinnest man I have ever met. His name was, inappropriately, Antic. I have never known such a bond between man and machine – he was wedded to it. When I shook his hands, they were as smooth as the old bakelite steering wheel, from the hundreds of thousands of revolutions he had turned it through, around the twisting tracks. His left hand was like an atrophied claw, fitting neatly over the knob of the temperamental gearstick; his body was so angular that it seemed to mould into the sharp tin edges of the frame supporting the hard driving seat. His head, almost not visible, was embedded in the old plastic headrest. He looked like he was wearing earmuffs. He gave me the impression that he had lived forever inside this cab, that he had grown up in it, that he was never going to leave it. This machine was his home, and would probably be his tomb. I found out that he had been working this part of the road for over sixty years, carrying and removing rubble each year as, like clockwork, the monsoons wreaked their destruction.

Farther on, we met another long-term resident of this remote area – an ancient sadhu, his long, grey, matted hair entwining with the holy beads he wore round his neck. His home for the last seventy years – and, like Antic's, doubtless his tomb too – was a little temple with a corrugated roof, surrounded by papaya trees. He was a disciple, like me, of the great Lord of Protection, the 'remover of obstacles' – the half-elephant, half-man deity Ganesh. He blessed us all, even Bhaiti, and most importantly he blessed the tin machine. But he refused to bless the little holy thread that the *panda* had tied round my right wrist at the temple of Khamakya in Guwahati. He noticed I had been carrying Bhaiti's lead. Both ends were loops of leather – hide – a taboo for all devout Hindus.

A few miles down, the road was blocked by a crowd of heavily armed villagers, hunters from Pugging. They would dine well that night – a huge wild boar and a delicate russet-coloured deer hung from a pole they carried. We gave them a lift. They all piled into the back and as we entered Pugging they started shouting and hollering, waving their guns and bows to inform the village of their successful hunt. Above me I noticed a cobweb of wires running between telegraph poles, in odd contrast to the cobweb of bamboo tubes that spread through the village supplying each house with water – an ingenuous reminder of a more traditional way of life.

We camped on the outskirts of the village that night, in front of the Inspection Bungalow on a flat piece of ground that enabled us to pitch tents. No one got much sleep. The village celebrated into the early hours.

The next morning, the head *gam*, a sprightly old man wearing a battered khaki jungle hat came to have a cup of tea. He squatted down and took out a pipe from a leather bag studded with old coins, the same kind of pipe as my British-loving, leg-pissing ex-head *gam* from Pango. It was perhaps a little early, I thought, to indulge – except, of course, for medicinal purposes. I was disappointed when he filled the pipe with tobacco.

During the Chinese invasion of 1962, the head *gam* had been seconded as a scout by the Indian Army to show them the secret trails through the jungles, and he had supplied them with chickens and pigs from the village. He was still angry with them, he said. For all his work he had received just one bottle of rum. I studied the exquisite turquoise and silver pendant which hung round his neck. It looked Tibetan. As a small boy he had accompanied many trading expeditions over the cold, high passes into Tibet. He even remembered Lhasa, which he described as 'a stone mountain with holes and long poles'. In an area called Pemako in Tibet, they had bartered with the local villagers. One cup of rice for one cup of salt, and locally woven cloth in exchange for brass bowls.

This little titbit of history reminded me again of my hero, Kinthup. He too had visited Pugging in about 1884, where he found 'the inhabitants prepared cloth which they sold in the market of Pemako'.

When the head *gam* stood up to leave, he blessed me for a safe journey and told me that as long as he lived he would protect his world, his forests. I wished he could have done something much simpler: cured my leg. It was agony.

My reputation as a hypochondriac has been enhanced over the years due to the immense medicine chests that accompany me on my journeys. Unfortunately, short of amputation, there was no remedy this time and nothing in the chests even to alleviate the pain. Not even Bhaiti could help me here. I could, of course, fall back on the opium. But I felt I was overdoing the old pipe some- what. Sadly, I realised my walking days were over. More than anything, I needed to rest my leg. Another kind of transport was now required – four wheels instead of two legs.

Salvation came in the form of a temperamental Indian jeep sup- plied by Neeraj, who had left early that morning on the back of a motorbike to Yinkiong, the Regional Headquarters of the Upper Siang, thirty kilometres away. It would only start by pushing it. It then belched into life, polluting both inside and outside in a fog of black smoke. Neeraj apologised profusely about the quality of the machine but it was the only one available. Every other vehicle had

been commandeered for the arrival in Yinkiong of the Chief
Minister in a few days time.

Somehow six men, a mass of equipment and one reluctant dog
squeezed into the jeep. Puffing and hissing like a steam engine, the
wheezing old banger was coaxed up and down and around the
snaking hairpin bends. I wondered what Kinthup would have
thought of us, as we barrelled towards Yinkiong, following in his
footsteps. I felt ashamed as I imagined him loping along effortlessly
by himself, and miserable too for Bhaiti, who once more was
buried under my shirt.

Yinkiong felt like a proper town after all the little villages we
had passed through. A thorough spring-clean was in full swing, in
preparation for the Chief Minister's visit. People were sweeping the
streets. Agile young men hung precariously in the trees lining the
road, removing the countless pink and blue pastic bags, an un-
welcome decoration in most Indian towns nowadays. Proud
homeowners were busily clipping privet hedges and retouching the
white fences bordering their gardens, ablaze with scarlet from the
overhanging hibiscus bushes. Security was tight as well. Even with
two soldiers as passengers, we were regularly stopped at road-
blocks and my permit thoroughly checked.

We passed garages, auto repair outfits, *dhabas*, and rows and
rows of shops displaying the latest Mumbai fashions. I felt disorientated. We stopped at a chemist to restock our medical supplies
and then made contact, for the first time in three weeks, with the
outside world from a telephone booth. Much to his chagrin, and
breaking my word, I kept Bhaiti firmly on his lead while I made my
calls. Yinkiong's streets were patrolled by packs of dogs and their
flirtatious girlfriends, whom Bhaiti eyed longingly. I was all for a
good scrap, but we were heavily outnumbered.

First I rang home. I got the answering machine. I called Tiger
Mountain Headquarters in Delhi. Yatish had been hospitalised
with badly torn knee ligaments, they told me, but was slowly

making a good recovery. And a couple of friends were on their way to Pasighat, to do some fishing. One of them was Dinesh Kumar of the British High Commission, who had led me to the centre of Delhi's bureaucratic maze to pick up my unique permit for Aranachal Pradesh. The other was John Edwards, the Managing Director of Tiger Mountain. He, I knew, was a fanatical fisherman. Above his desk in Delhi hung a sign, 'As two-thirds of the world's surface is covered in water, surely God created man to spend more time fishing than working.'

Perhaps I would join them, I thought. I still had a few days in hand on my Arunachal permit, and a little R & R would do my leg the world of good. In any case, the next part of my journey down the river through Assam would be much less strenuous. I would be travelling by boat. Which reminded me to call Manju, my boat fixer in Guwahati.

It was an appalling line. From what I could make out Manju had now rented me the *Titanic*, a Government ferry that had excellent conveniences, a passenger capability of 150 and a conference room. Diplomatically I suggested something smaller. He grumbled something about not being a yacht broker. However, he did give me some good news – great news in fact. It turned out that Aditya was on a photographic assignment in Assam and would meet up with me at some point. I was over the moon. Not only would the old team be reunited, but Aditya always managed to add that little something to our journeys – a bit of Maratha magic.

We pitched camp that evening on a broad, white sandy beach a few miles south of Yinkiong. Here the river was not in quite such a benevolent mood as she rushed over a series of small rapids. Because of my leg it would be my last chance to be close to her in her present form, for in Pasighat she would change in name, mood and sex: from the Siang, a roaring, capricious mistress, into the Brahmaputra, a wide, majestic, calm deity, son of the great Lord Brahma and the only male river on the continent.

In the dying rays of the evening sun, I paid my last obeisance to her. She bade me farewell with a thousand cold, sensual kisses, rushing over me as I held on tight to the slippery boulders. Later I toasted her with a mug of rum. I was going to miss her. Like Verrier Elwin, I almost felt like laying my body beside her waters.

The next morning after an embarrassing moment when, in the shifting mist, I had been surprised, as Neeraj would describe it, 'attending to potty', by a group of female beetlers, I said goodbye to the Corporals. Classic and Shortcut were staying on here for a few days before moving on by truck with another regiment. I presented them with a case of rum. We all embraced – big bear-hug embraces. They told me that this journey had been one of the finest experiences of their lives. It had been an honour for them. They were wrong. It had been an honour for me. They saluted once and then, with the sun flashing off their bayonets, marched away across the sand.

A little lighter now, we set off for Pasighat. En route I finally bid farewell to my hero, Kinthup. He had stopped here before return-ing home. I apologised for not finding even one of his logs. I felt I had let him down. Later on, we crossed the river on a large metal bridge to the right bank, leaving the wilds behind and hitting more urban areas. We passed trucks, other vehicles and road signs telling us, rather affectionately, to 'treat the kerbs kindly'. At one of the many *dhabas* that lined the road, we stopped for tea. Inside was a refrigerator. It all seemed very odd – modern and civilised. I felt as if I were a long way from the river. But I wasn't. When we set off again she was always there beside me, glittering like a silver ribbon far below us in the moonlight, as Bhaiti and I, both overcome from the fumes, hung our heads out of the window.

We reached Pasighat late. A familiar figure was waiting for us expectantly at the Circuit House, rubbing his podgy hands together. It was Cookie.

'Welcome back, sir,' he said, and announced, 'full meal, soon coming.'

After dinner, John and Dinesh turned up, feverishly excited about their fishing expedition. Ozing, who was supposed to be organising the trip, soon joined the party too.

'G-g-god,' he said to me. 'W-w-what a pity. Y-y-you are alive. I thought I had only one b-b-bloody Englishman to look after.'

After a few drinks Bhaiti and I went to bed to let them bang on about forward shooting lines and the ones that got away.

The next morning John and Dinesh set off towards the Yamne, a major tributary of the Siang, with Jaro, Topguy, Neeraj and Ozing. I decided to stay on here for a while to rest my leg before joining them.

Bhaiti underwent a complete change of character during those few days we spent recovering in Pasighat. It was very bizarre. He was like a different dog. I asked him to share his problem with me, but it seemed I had lost my powers as a dog whisperer. Most of the time he lay in our room with his face turned to the wall. Cookie was most concerned as well. He surpassed himself in his culinary expertise each day, trying to tempt Bhaiti with new, innovative tit-bits. One night he prepared a feast of what he called 'special boiled dinner' – boiled chicken, boiled meat, boiled cabbages, boiled rice, boiled eggs, boiled milk and boiled water.

There were other temptations as well. Bhaiti had become a bit of a star and the groupies – dishy little numbers desperate to sample a bit of the infamous Tripuri hound – lined up, howling outside the Circuit House each day. But he wasn't interested. Like some prima donna rock star he walked occasionally out of our room, stood at the top of the stairs and barked, as if calling for room service. Cookie would faithfully rush up and down the stairs carrying trays with more titbits. It was almost as if Bhaiti blamed me for bringing him back from the wilds and into a town and was going out of his way to embarrass me – not a side of him I had seen before.

The Circuit House, like Yinkiong, was going through a bit of refurbishment due to the imminent visit of the Chief Minister. Everything was being retouched and painted white. Outside the front of the Circuit House there was an immaculate lawn, demarcated by a circle of round stones. An old man was carefully retouching these stones. On one of our few forays outside the building, as the old man had just finished painting them and was admiring his handiwork, Bhaiti, with what I thought was almost pleasure, cocked his leg on them. The old man was not furious. I apologised to him and reprimanded Bhaiti. For the first time in days he smiled at me and wagged his tail. He thought it was a great joke. On our return, the old man had just finished repairing the damage. To my horror, Bhaiti repeated his little trick. It took intervention from Cookie to cool things down.

On another occasion I was engaged in conversation by three Indian housewives. As we chatted, Bhaiti decided to relieve himself once more. It was extremely embarrassing, and I found it hard to concentrate while he squatted and strained beside me.

My leg had by now nearly healed. It was time to join the others for a spot of fishing. Before we left, I received a telephone call from Manju, telling me that he had now found another boat. It was just right, he told me – much smaller than the previous one. It would be arriving soon in Dibrugarh, a large town on the south bank of the Brahmaputra from where I would be starting the next part of my journey. But, he warned, certain stretches of the Brahmaputra were on 'red alert' because of insurgency. I was sure Bhaiti would look after me, provided he got his good humour back.

One of Ozing's jeeps had been sent to pick us up. We soon reached the broad reaches of the son of Brahma where it merged with the Siang. We crossed the river on an old landing craft, pushing way upstream to combat the huge and powerful current. The moment we were on the river, my river dog returned. He rushed around, barking orders at the crew. However, he paid dearly for his earlier insolence by sitting on the hot tarmac of the roof and covering his backside in a black, sticky mass of tar.

We disembarked and drove up a steep, twisting track. I asked the driver to stop. Here there was an historical site that I wanted to see – a broad, pebble-strewn beach across on the far side of the Brahmaputra. It was here in October 1911 that the British amassed a large force to quash once and for all the troublesome Abors.

The British hardly had a good word to say about the Abors. The wife of an officer attached to the Abor expedition of 1911 summed her feelings up in a series of puns: 'It is such a bore that my husband has to go off on that silly Abor expedition to fight those stupid Aborigines with their queer aborial habits'; and a political officer wrote dismissively, 'they are truculent and aggressive. Like all savages, the only law they know or recognise is that of force, and in the ability of awarding prompt and speedy punishments.'

The trouble had started back in the nineteenth century when various British expeditions set off from Sadiya and Pasighat up the Siang to establish whether the Tsangpo and the Brahmaputra were the same river. In 1858 the Abors raided a village near the military headquarters at Dibrugarh. They ambushed the soldiers sent out to punish them, chasing them back to Dibrugarh with considerable loss of life. Intoxicated by their victory, the Abors then sent a challenge down the plains, daring the British to give them a return match.

It was time to restore the honour of the Raj by, 'inflicting such chastisement as will teach these savages to respect its power'. A second military expedition, loaded with elephant-drawn howitzers, was dispatched and defeated with the loss of three of its officers. A third attempt ended in a political victory for the Abors when it was agreed that they would keep to their tribal lands in return for an annual payment, in cash or kind, of 3400 rupees.

Unfortunately, this wasn't the end of the trouble. In 1893, Jack

Needham, another British political officer, led a peaceful expedition through Abor country with disastrous consequences. His small force of some sixty sepoys and camp followers were murdered just north of Pasighat. But it was the killing of Needham's successor, Noel Williamson, and a doctor called Gregorson in 1911 that effectively sealed the fate of the Abors. The two men had set out to trace the Brahmaputra, carrying a gramophone, a magical lantern, no military escort and forty-seven porters bearing gifts and medicine.

The massacre was triggered by an absurdly trivial incident, and a catastrophic misunderstanding. In the village of Rotung, which I could see now across the river, some rations and a bottle of whisky were stolen from the party. Williamson warned the villagers that they would be punished on his return, and then crossed the river into the territory of the Abors. Here some of the porters fell ill and Williamson decided to split the party up, leaving the sick with Dr Gregorson while he and the rest headed on.

Back in Rotung, the villagers were considering what best to do about Williamson when his mail runner arrived carrying three letters for posting. Their white envelopes were edged in black, as a mark of mourning for the recently deceased King Edward VII, and sealed with red wax. The Abors, having no written language, placed great importance on signs and symbols, and interpreted the envelopes accordingly: the white envelope signified the white man, the black border his soldiers, and the red seal Government anger. The letters were, in effect, the death warrant of Williamson and of the entire party. As a result of seeing them the villagers decided to pre-empt their punishment by killing the mail runner and sending a war party, about a hundred strong, to find Dr Gregorson and his invalids and dispatch them all on the spot. The following day they caught up with Williamson, hacked him to death and speared all his porters as they tried to escape.

Six months went by until word came that the British were out

Gamma puffing on his chillum.

Bhaiti and Gamma – stoned – dreaming the river.

The perfect camp on the Brahmaputra.

Morning – Mark and Bhaiti.

The hunting dog at full stretch.

The *Koyel*, Jamuna River, Bangladesh.

Floating haystacks on the Dhaleshwari River approaching Dhaka.

Dholias at sunset on the
Padma River, Bangladesh.

The end of the journey, about to pay
obeisance to the River in the Bay of Bengal.

Entering India *with* E/Dog Small size.

Entering Bangladesh *without* E/Dog Small size.

The Gallery of River Rogues

MARK SHAND

Yatish Bahuguna.

MARK SHAND

Neeraj Pathania.

PADDY MARK

Ozing Dai.

MARK SHAND

Jaro Dai.

ADITYA PATANKAR

ADITYA PATANKAR

Topguy.

Ranesh Roy.

ADITYA PATANKAR

ADITYA PATANKAR

Manju Barua.

Shaams.

JARO DAI

MARK SHAND

Mark Shand.

Aditya Patankar, the Maratha.

MARK SHAND

Bhaiti.

for revenge: an army was on its way. There was huge excitement among the Abors: for the first time all the main villages got together to plan a united defence. Women and children were sent to the mountains, while the men prepared for the jungle warfare of which they were masters. They demolished cane bridges, built stockades and prepared booby traps of hidden pits lined with poisoned stakes and ingenious spring traps that sprayed the track with poisoned arrows.

The Abor expeditionary force sent to fight them was enormous. This time, the British meant business. It consisted of 725 Gurkhas, military battalions from Assam and elsewhere in India, and 3500 spear-carrying Naga tribesmen. The Nagas were magnificent and sworn enemies of the Adis. They marched in columns six abreast and their peculiar two-note chant – 'he-hah, he-hoh' – echoed through the jungle terrifying all who heard it. The Nagas were greatly looking forward to taking a few heads from the Abors so there was a marked drop in morale when the commander of the expeditionary force announced that head-hunting would not be allowed.

Letters home from the British troops on this long, drawn-out campaign give a much livelier and more honest account than the official published versions. 'Don't be worried if you read in the papers that the Abors used poisoned arrows,' a young captain in command of the Second Gurkhas wrote. 'The poison (aconite) is not usually strong and rarely has ill-effects if the wound is treated properly at once. We all carry squirts and an antidote. So there's nothing to worry about . . . You should not be concerned at the exaggerated stories you see in the *Daily Mail*.' Good advice, I thought.

The Abor war eventually came to a conclusion on a cliff above Rotung in the autumn of 1912, when the hostile chiefs came in waving newspapers as flags of truce. By Christmas, it was all over.

An astonishing change came over the tribe in the early 1940s and '50s. They were transformed into a friendly, co-operative and progressive community. Perhaps this had something to do with the work of my old friend, Verrier Elwin. They changed their name from Abor, which means 'unruly or disobedient', to Adi, which means 'hill men'. Considering the insults heaped on them over the centuries, and their final pacification by the British, they certainly did not bear any grudges. In the Second World War they provided a labour corps of two thousand men to help the Allies fight the Japanese.

We spent a pleasant few days in the Yamne Valley, although the weather was dank and drizzly and there was no food. Ozing had forgotten to bring any. We survived on one small mahseer – India's infamous fighting fish – caught by John, beetles, a few potatoes and local spinach. We were also besieged by a dreaded insect, aptly named 'dam-doom' or 'dim-dam'. Unlike the mosquito you don't hear the dim-dam coming: there's no whine to warn you. And its bite is only felt sometime later, when a little blood-filled blister appears and drives you mad with itching.

But Bhaiti had a great time. Unaffected by the dim-dams, he spent his days flushing out mithuns from the vast bamboo groves and pursuing them, howling with glee, through the jungle. At the fishing camp I met a very interesting man, a friend of John's, who joined us for a day on the river. His name was Tobu. His grandfather had been hanged by the British. His crime? Murdering Noel Williamson. Tobu now held an appropriate job in the Government. He was the Minister for Tourism.

We spent our last night in Arunachal Pradesh at Ozing Dai's camp – the very luxurious camp he had offered to show me when we left Pasighat. It is *the* place to stay in Pasighat. It has unbelievable charm. It is the Fawlty Towers of the north-east, with Ozing as Basil, his wife as Sybil, and a demented Nepali servant cum cook cum houseboy as Manuel. Accommodation is a row of rather flimsy tents that have a habit of collapsing. The service is – how shall I put it? – questionable.

But it is the water system that really defies imagination, considering that the camp is situated about a quarter of a mile from the largest river in India. At the bottom of the camp, Ozing had recently constructed an extremely grand bathroom complex consisting of six showers and six latrines, all furnished with a stunning array of chrome fittings. The water supply to this ablutionary marvel is siphoned in through a long hose that snakes through the camp from the kitchen. The number of times that I found myself naked, covered in soap, or squatting, flushless above one of the loos was beyond belief. The excuses were even more so.

'S-s-sorry, Mark,' a harassed Basil (or Ozing) would inform me. 'S-s-someone's watering the g-g-garden.' Or 'M-m-manuel is w-w-washing up.' Or, 'S-s-sorry, Mark, s-s-someone's parked the j-j-jeep on the hose.'

We celebrated our last night in Arunachal Pradesh with inordinate quantities of *apong*. Ozing presented me with a litre bottle of rum, and made a speech along the lines that he was honoured as an Adi to have two b-b-bloody Englishmen staying, and even more honoured as an Adi to be getting rid of two b-b-bloody Englishmen.

My new friend, and guide, the renowned Adi hunter Jaro presented me with the beautiful rattan backpack that he had carried on our journey and his own antique *dao*, with a belt made from the skin of a Himalayan black bear that he had shot. I presented him with my binoculars. He turned them over reverently in his hands.

'Mmmm,' he said. 'I will lend them back to you Mark when you return for your new job as Safety Officer to Cane Bridge Department.' Then he added, with a chuckle, 'With these Mark can check bridge, not break bridge.'

In the middle of the night, Fawlty Towers was hit by torrential rain. My accommodation leaked so much that my bag floated out of the tent. I pursued it as it sailed merrily down a small river. A figure, standing under an umbrella, watched with amusement.

'Y-y-you know what y-y-you can call your n-n-new book, Mark? *T-t-t-travels on my S-s-suitcase.*'

The next morning, we caught a little wooden ferry for the four-hour trip down the Brahmaputra to Dibrugarh. I sat quietly on the roof, the vast expanse of the river stretching out on either side, and looked back on the lush valleys and the snowy peaks as they slowly disappeared in the mist.

In 1957 Jawaharl Nehru wrote,

I am alarmed when I see – not only in this country but in other great countries, too – how anxious people are to shape others according to their own image or likeness, and to impose on them their particular way of living. We are welcome to our way of living, but why impose it on others? This applies equally to national and international fields. In fact, there would be more peace in the world if people were to desist from imposing their way of living on other people and countries. I'm not at all sure which is the better way of living, the tribal or our own. In some respect, I am certain theirs is better. Therefore, it is grossly presumptuous on our part to approach them with an air of superiority, to tell them how to behave or what to do and what not to do. There is no point in trying to make of them a second-rate copy of ourselves.

The Adis would never be a second-rate copy of anybody. They were far too proud.

ELEVEN

More than anything, it was the sense of space that blew my mind. Having been effectively hemmed in for the last three weeks by the steep valleys of the Siang, my vision was now limitless. I could see forever: sky and water, water and sky. By contrast, space was limited on board the little wooden ferry, the *Sisi*, named after a local river. A combined weight of cargo and people forced her dangerously near the waterline. We were in the hands of a very powerful and familiar God – Ganesh, the 'remover of obstacles' and the Lord of Protection – in the form of two little red plastic elephants, surrounded by a garland of fresh marigolds guarding us on the prow.

The *Sisi* had been almost empty when we set off, but she had quickly filled up after a few stops along the river's crumbling banks, where cheeky little girls offered oranges, papayas, lemons, vegetables and baskets of tiny, silver dried fish. We now carried a cargo of bundles of wood, sacks of rice, scrap iron, chickens, goats and large vats of fresh milk – in fact anything that was saleable in the big city of Dibrugarh.

Then there were the people. There were groups of Indian families, dazzlingly dressed in their finery like spring flowers in a meadow, on their way to meet their relatives. Their children politely called me 'uncle'. There were merchants, jealously guarding their goods; a young cricket team on an 'away' game; and a group of Adi wildlife rangers who were on their way to Guwahati to lobby for the reinstatement of the timber ban. And there were crowds of refugees from disaster, who had lost everything in the fury of the past monsoons, on their way to find work.

It was through these desperate people that I again was given an insight into the power and destructive force of this great male river. In the most devastating floods that Assam had ever suffered, five million people had been affected in twenty-one of its twenty-three districts. Thousands of people had died. Millions had been made homeless. Eighty per cent of all livestock had been destroyed, and even endangered wildlife had been affected. Five hundred wild animals, including rhinoceros, tigers and elephants had been swept away from the Wildlife Sanctuary of Kaziranga. I chatted with the milk merchants. Before the floods, they told me, they could guarantee about two or three thousand litres of milk on each run, which they sold for fifty paisa (about two pence) a litre. Now, they were lucky to collect two hundred litres.

We passed a *char*, one of those fickle, ever-shifting deposits of silt whose mineral content guarantees the richest of soil. In the monsoons they disappear beneath the fury of the river. A flotilla of little dug-out canoes filled with bamboo was bobbing in the shallows, while the villagers toiled in the sun to reconstruct their homes. As everywhere in rural India, I am always amazed at the tenacity, the spirit and, above all, the belief of the people. Whatever was thrown at them, they would fight back. It was their lot. They accepted it with dignity, without complaint.

A bell rang on the *Sisi*. It was lunchtime. The boat lurched alarmingly as a flood of people rushed to the little kitchen situated below deck, amidships. Silence suddenly engulfed our little craft as everybody concentrated on the most important ritual of everyday Indian life – eating. I went to find Bhaiti, whom I hadn't seen for a few hours. I found him looking miserable, wedged between some sacks of rice that were splattered in vomit. That boded well, I thought, for the rest of our journey. I was travelling with a dog who suffered from seasickness. However, it turned out not to be seasickness but greed. The deck was littered with empty sweet packets. The children had been feeding him. He looked at me guiltily as if to say sorry. I cleaned up the vomit and forced him to drink lots of water. He soon perked up. Late in the afternoon the wind changed, scenting the air with a familiar smell – a strangely sweet and evocative smell – of smoke, rotting vegetation, spice, sweat and shit. It was land.

Lines of battered open jeeps waited at the ghat, the landing area, to transport us across the river bed to Dibrugarh. Over the years, during the monsoons, the river has been eating away at the foundations of this busy town. Once the nerve centre for all trade and commerce in Assam, it has now been replaced by the capital, Guwahati.

Dibrugarh means 'fort on the banks of the river'. The British built it in the early nineteenth century to repel invasions from the Abors. Originally the town was situated on the banks of the River Dibru but after the great earthquake of 1950 the river merged with the Brahmaputra and eroded vast tracts of the town. The British, usually pretty sound in their construction of defence systems, had for once been beaten not by an army but by a river. They had underestimated its power. I later found out that residents of Dibrugarh reckon that in a few years the town will disappear altogether.

But, for the moment, it was here. An abrupt and noisy reminder that I had re-entered India again, as we inched our way through the kaleidoscope of colour, the ear-splitting bedlam of any large Indian town. I wasn't prepared for it, particularly for the pollution. My eyes streamed and stung even through the towel that I had wrapped round my face. Bhaiti just buried his head in my shirt, occasionally sighing in resignation – he had seen it all before. He made me feel guilty. It was as if I were taking him back to prison.

At our hotel, we bid farewell to John and Dinesh. They were continuing on to the airport to catch a flight to Delhi. I wearily climbed the stairs to our room on the top floor. I felt depressed, out of sorts. But not for long. I suddenly heard a deep, infectious chuckle, and then a voice. 'Welcome to my country, Mr Sands. I will be showing you many strange and wondrous tings.'

Standing at the top of the stairs, dressed like a football coach in a black shell suit, Nike trainers, his eyes covered by Rayban shades, was the Maratha – Aditya Patankar.

'And this is?' he asked, indicating the small russet bundle that was sitting despondently at my feet.

'This is Bhaiti, Aditya. Reeta gave him to me.'

'Little brother, eh?' he said. 'Good name. He's a beautiful dog. Funny, he doesn't look like a pi-dog, more like a pure breed.'

He noticed my surprise.

'Dog instincts,' he said mysteriously, tapping his nose.

I remembered I was not in the company of a mere mortal. I was in the company of India's ace dog catcher, ace dog trainer, ace dog loser and, most importantly, devout dog worshipper – a man with mystical canine powers.

'He *is* a pure breed,' I announced proudly. 'He's a Tripuri hound from the Lushai Hills of Assam.'

'The Lushai Hills, Mark, are *not* in Assam. They border the states of Mizoram and Tripura.'

'Well, they were once,' I argued. 'All those states were part of Assam. They got their independence in the 1970s.'

He looked at me suspiciously. 'You know nothing about dogs. Where did you learn this nonsense about Tripuris?'

'Dog instinct,' I replied, tapping my nose.

'Bollocks,' he said. 'You got it from that book. By Salmon or whatever the bloody hell his name was.'

'Soman, actually. Anyway,' I continued, 'Bhaiti and I understand each other. We've talked. We know everything there is to know about each other.'

'Well,' Aditya replied, 'I hope he listened to you – and you listened to him. Those endless midnight mumblings with Tara didn't do much good. She was always taking off and causing havoc.'

At that moment, Bhaiti did something odd – something I hadn't seen him do before. With his ears back, and a look almost of devotion in those extraordinary eyes, he slid slowly across the floor towards Aditya and gently licked his feet.

'You see?' Aditya announced. 'It takes one to know one. It's in our blood. The old Maratha ancestor dog worship.'

I stifled a giggle. It should, I thought, be the other way around – the Maratha should be on all fours in front of Bhaiti, licking *his* paws and barking like a dog in obeisance. I wondered, with relish, if Aditya was going to eat out of Bhaiti's shiny metal bowl.

We dined in style that evening – on finger chips and fish curry, Lamb's Navy rum and beer. Neeraj was quiet. He was a little in awe of the legendary Maratha, but Aditya, with his innate ability to put anybody at ease, soon had him regaling us with tales of Arunachal Pradesh. Topguy was his usual energetic, diligent self, dashing up and down the stairs and berating the harassed staff for more supplies.

We were joined by another guest that night, a young man called Rajan. He was Manju Barua's nephew and occasionally worked for him as a tourist guide. I had a suspicion he'd been sent by Manju to keep an eye on us, to keep us out of mischief. But Rajan was mischief personified. He was delighted to be in the company of a different breed of traveller. He was obsessed by two things –

women and music, the blues in particular, and he played in a local band.

By the end of the evening, it was arranged that Rajan would meet us at Majuli, the largest river island in the world, farther down river. He wanted to introduce us to the monks there. There was, he told us mischievously, something strange about them. It sounded intriguing, but as yet we had not found a boat. Rajan was terrified of his uncle and begged me to ring him in Guwahati to find out where it was. Communication between Dibrugarh and Guwahati was sporadic. There were regular, annoying power cuts. Eventually I got through.

'Hi, Manju,' I shouted. 'How's it going with the . . . '

'Hear me out, Mark, hear me out,' he yelled.

'I'm listening, Manju,' I replied, holding the telephone a foot from my ear.

'The boat is coming,' he yelled again. 'It left four days ago.'

'Four days!' I exclaimed incredulously, 'but . . . '

'Hear me out, Mark,' he yelled even louder. 'It's a small boat. It's coming upstream, against the current.'

'Are they rowing it?' I asked facetiously.

The line went dead.

The next morning, I was awoken by an urgent knocking on my door. I had a killer hangover, I felt like hell. Groggily, I looked at my watch. It was only 7 a.m. I stumbled out of bed and opened the door. The Maratha was standing there impatiently, smartly dressed in a dark blue shirt and knife-creased green khaki trousers, the turn-ups hanging at exactly the right level above a pair of carefully brushed suede desert boots. He was shaved and pomaded. He looked immaculate.

Unlike me, Aditya, even after the heaviest nights, had this extraordinary ability to look like he had gone to bed at 7 p.m. and drunk milk. It drove me mad. The only giveaway was the colour of his eyes. They were always just a little bloodshot. This morning, he blamed it on the quality of the 'polluted Brahmaputra water' in which he had washed his face.

'Hurry up, Mark,' he said impatiently. 'I'm bored. I want to do something. Go somewhere. I'll take Bhaiti for a stroll while you think of something.'

Dibrugarh and its surroundings offered so many fascinating things to do. For a start, we could take in a movie in the 1930s cinema hall in Talkie House Road, named when talkies replaced silent films. They were showing a double bill: *Twogether* and *Girls with Guns*. They were what is known in India as 'A' movies – adult movies. The larger the 'A' on the poster, the racier the movie.

We could venture farther afield and visit St Luke's Hospital where the actress Julie Christie was born; or if industry was of interest, the possibilities were endless. We could visit the great coal-fields of Marguerita, named by the immigrant Italian workers after their Queen. Or visit Chabua, where the first tea plantation was established in India in 1823. Or take a trip to Dighboi, where oil was first found in India, by elephant. In the 1880s a railway line was being constructed between Dibrugarh and Marguerita with the help of working elephants. One day on finishing their work, the mahouts noticed a sticky black substance on the elephants' feet. They reported it to the authorities. It was crude oil, of the very best quality. Today Assam is still India's biggest supplier of oil. The country owes so much to these majestic and loyal subjects.

Aditya appeared a few minutes later with Bhaiti. Aditya looked exhausted. Bhaiti was panting happily. He looked almost elated.

'Bloody hell,' he said. 'Bhaiti sure likes a scrap. We took on five at one time.'

I patted Bhaiti proudly. 'That's my boy.'

'Well, what have you come up with?'

'Do you remember when Charles Allen came down to visit you? When I was living in the country. When you were staying with us recovering from your operation?'

'Yes,' he said slowly.

'He told me about a really weird place that he'd heard about when he was a kid, growing up in Assam. Farther east, up the river. A penis park.'

'A what?' Aditya asked incredulously.

'A penis park,' I replied. 'I know it sounds odd but apparently there was a penis park. That's what the British called it anyway. What do you say? It should only take a few days or so.'

'Did Charles tell you *exactly* where this penis park was, Mark?' Aditya asked suspiciously.

'Well, sort of,' I replied. 'I've got maps. They are on rather a large scale, though. Charles marked the place with a pencil cross.'

Aditya sighed. 'Look Mark, you well know Charles can be a little vague. I think we should stick to something a bit more factual and closer. I met Rajan in the street when I was taking Bhaiti for a walk. He suggested we visit Sibsagar, the old capital of the Ahom kingdom. What we need is a bit of culture for a change. Rajan has given us the name of a cousin of his, a Dr Diptomonto Baruah. He's a twitcher, a bird watcher, and he runs a chemist there.'

It was perfect, I thought. Aditya was an avid twitcher. I was an avid hypochondriac.

Leaving Bhaiti in the safe hands of Neeraj and Topguy, who were going on a shopping expedition to revictual the boat, if and when it ever turned up, Aditya and I set off in a cab to Sibsagar to meet the twitcher chemist, Dr Diptomonto Baruah.

We found him in his establishment, the Das Pharmacy, which fronted the main street of Sibsagar. On the instructions of Rajan we had arrived at five minutes to noon. Dr D was a trifle eccentric. He only opened his surgery from nine till twelve each day. The rest of the time he twitched, ate fish curry and wrote poems with his wife.

Dr D was sitting quietly at his desk, dreamily looking at a

picture in a book of a pair of tits. He seemed to be in a trance. Above his desk hung a picture of India's most revered holy man, Sai Baba, garlanded by beads and a stethoscope.

'Dr Baruah?' Aditya said.

He looked up dreamily. 'I don't get to see these much nowadays. It's really sad. I handled a pair once. Beautiful things,' he said, closing a book on Indian birds.

We introduced ourselves and handed him the note which Rajan had given us. His whole demeanour changed.

He shook our hands. 'Splendid, splendid,' he chirped, his little beady eyes glittering behind his bifocals. Dr D was tiny. He was wearing an old pair of brown trousers and a red shirt. He resembled exactly, both in colour and mannerisms, a species of robin – the main focus of his bird obsession. He pecked and hopped rather than talked or walked. He was busy, industrious and nosy.

'We'll do a tour,' he announced eagerly, rubbing his little hands together. 'I'll just pop back for lunch.' He smiled, 'My wife makes a wonderful fish curry. I'll meet you back here in an hour.'

An hour later, we set off in our cab to visit the remains of the Ahom kingdom. In the thirteenth century the Ahoms, descendants of the Shan civilisations of Burma, crossed the Paktoi Hills and invaded Assam. They ruled Assam for a staggering six hundred years, allowing the Hindu culture to flourish in relative peace and repulsing all invasions, including seventeen attempts by the Moghul Empire, which lost over a hundred thousand horsemen and four hundred boats in their efforts.

The long continuance of Ahom rule in Assam was almost without parallel in history. Their vanquished enemies spoke in grudging awe of their bravery, patriotism and indomitable spirit. As well as the courage and organisation of their army, nature also played its part in helping them to resist invasion. Disease, pestilence, monsoons and the huge forests of Assam did a great deal to hold their enemies at bay. Establishing their capital at Sibsagar, the Ahoms named the region Assam, which means 'undulating land'. Their empire lasted until the Burmese invasion in 1817, a five-year campaign that killed one in every three inhabitants of the region. And in 1826, the British drove out the Burmese and Assam was ceded to the Empire.

We paid our obeisance to Bholay Shankar, the great Lord Shiva, beside a huge artificial tank – or reservoir – that is said to be the largest in India, at the great temple of Shivadol – thirty-three metres high, the tallest in the country. Then we moved on to the eighteenth-century Rhang Ghar, an oval two-storied honeycombed pavilion, its shape and structure clearly indicating influences of the Ahom's Shan ancestors farther east. Here, the Ahom king sat surrounded by his court, looking on to a natural amphitheatre, enjoying the spectacle of elephant and buffalo fights. Here too, in 1979, Dr D told us, a secret meeting led to the foundation of one of Assam's most powerful insurgency organisations – ULFA – the United Liberation Front of Assam. But gathering these extra titbits of information was difficult. At any given moment Dr D would flit off in hot pursuit of another rare feathered species.

At the once dignified, but now almost totally defaced complex of Kareng Ghar – the 'palace of the kings' – I left Aditya and Dr D to argue about the mating habits of the wire-tailed drongo. Kareng Ghar in its full splendour must have been a remarkable construction, with seven storeys above ground and three below. It was said to contain two tunnels – secret escape routes – one of ten and a half miles and one of two, linking it to two other, now ruined palaces. I found the opening of one of these tunnels, deep in the bowels of the palace. I could just have squeezed through but decided against it, not wanting to end up like two of my fellow countrymen. In the 1950s two British archaeologists set out to try and trace the tunnel. They never returned. Somewhere in those dark, dank snake-infested caves lay not only their remains, but the remains of perhaps thousands of others – enemies of the fearsome Ahoms.

A 1906 gazetteer describes some of their methods,

It is needless to mention instances of the savage violence of the times but the different forms of punishment in vogue called for some remark when life was spared. The ears, nose and hair were cut off, the eyes put out, or the knee pans torn from the legs – the last penalty generally proving fatal. Persons sentenced to death were hung, impaled, hewn in pieces, crushed between two wooden cylinders like sugar cane in a mill, sawn asunder, burnt alive, fried in oil, or shorn of their hands and feet and placed in holes until they were used as latrines. In the seventeenth century it was no uncommon thing to compel conspirators to eat their own flesh. There is one case in which the father was forced to eat the liver of his son – a meal that was usually his last in the world. Methods such as these could hardly fail to have a terrifying effect.

It was near the entrance of one of these catacombs that we discovered the last king of the Ahoms. We could smell him before we saw him – the stale smell of moonshine. He was very drunk, very dishevelled and very old. He told us that every day, after working hard in the fields, he came back here to guard the palace. He also always brought a little bottle of moonshine, which he said made him feel like a king.

Dr D was so excited that we had found the last king of the Ahoms that he asked me for a cigarette. He had given up smoking twenty years ago. Puffing furiously, he bobbed up and down, and then handed the old man a hundred rupees. Aditya and I added another two hundred. Dr D then adopted a totally different demeanour. He became solemn. However, there was a slightly mischievous twinkle in those little beady eyes.

'Sir,' he announced. 'I now crown you the last king of the

Ahoms. With these gifts you will buy a little moonshine every day. You will defend the palace with your life.'

The old man couldn't believe his luck. His hands shook as he took the money. He puffed himself up proudly. 'Until I die, sir. I give you my word, I will defend the great palace. For I am the last of the kings of the Ahoms.'

We dropped Dr Baruah back at his pharmacy. He bobbed up and down as I shook his hand.

'Thank you so much for a wonderful day,' I said. 'It was very nice meeting you.'

He held on to my hand. 'Yes,' he replied. 'It was *quite* nice meeting you. Your visit today has stimulated me – just a little.'

Late that night, we arrived back at the hotel. We found a despondent Neeraj and Topguy and an embarrassed-looking Rajan surrounded by an immense pile of pots and pans, sacks of rice, ropes, cases of mineral water, vegetables, a case of rum, and even a new pressure steamer, mysteriously called Miss Mary.

'The boat's arrived, boss,' Neeraj said. ('Sir' had now been replaced by 'boss'. I was getting there.)

'Well, that's great,' I said excitedly. 'What's it like?'

'Boat no good, boss,' Neeraj replied. 'Too small. No shelter. Useless.'

It seemed that Manju had taken me seriously when I suggested something smaller. He had chartered me a rowing boat.

Aditya immediately took command. 'OK,' he barked. 'First thing tomorrow morning we'll go to the ghat and check things out. If the boat's no good, as Neeraj says, we'll try to find another one. You stay here. One glimpse of that pasty English face of yours and the price will go through the roof. You can sort out the provisions.'

'Yes, sir,' I said, snapping to attention and saluting smartly.

The next morning, while Aditya and the crew left for the ghat, the boss relaxed. I settled back into a comfortable armchair with Bhaiti, propped my feet up on a sack of rice, and flipped the cap off a bottle of ice-cold beer. Then I turned to the pages of Mr Soman's book on the Indian dog to gain some useful tips from the chapter 'Management of Dogs on Board Ship'.

'It is important to take the trouble every morning and evening to let the dog out of its kennel for a walk on deck, and to see that the animal's habitation is not too close to the boilers, or unduly exposed to the sun's rays. If he be a water dog, bath twice a week (in fresh water if possible, but if not procurable, then in sea water). It is absolutely indispensable to keep the skin in order.'

Bhaiti shifted in my lap and stared at me suspiciously. I read on.

'If, as frequently occurs, there are signs of constipation after the first few days of confinement on board, give a mild aperient, to be repeated as occasion requires. Many animals which are usually good-tempered become snappish and surly on board, so it must not be forgotten before starting, to supply not only the dog chain but also a muzzle for use whilst out exercising, or the dog's daily walks on deck may be objected to and prohibited. Plenty of clean, loose straw should be put in the kennel to lessen the annoyance caused by the motion of the vessel.'

At lunchtime the crew returned, looking dejected.

'Neeraj was right,' Aditya said, looking fed up, 'Manju's boat is far too small. It'll be extremely cramped. It's already got a crew of five.'

'Well, what *are* we going to do?' I whined, anxiously.

He roared with laughter. 'For a start, get your arse off that chair and pack up! We're setting sail on the midday tide. I've found you a boat – *the* boat – the only boat suitable for you. You know why?'

'Why?' I asked.

'It's called the *Kailash*! You see, there are no coincidences.'

There was nothing aloof, mysterious or forbidding about the good ship *Kailash*, unlike that perfect white crystal cone on the roof of the world. In contrast, she was cosy, inviting and friendly. She almost seemed to be smiling as she bobbed gently in the water at the ghat, a battered old wooden tub with chipped and peeling paintwork the colour of the sky – indigo blue. Her crew – known as *majhi*, or boatmen, the generic name for people who ply the great rivers of India – were just as battered as their boat. There were four of them, all Biharis, all burnt black by the sun.

Gamma, the captain or pilot, was an ancient old riverdog who sported a splendid handlebar moustache. Bachha Das, or Pandit as he was known, was Gamma's second-in-command and in charge of anchoring. Laxman, a dignified man with sad eyes, was the engineer, and young Vijay – only twelve years old, his youth belying his experience – was the baler, the cook and the vital link between the other three senior crew members.

The *Kailash* was well appointed, seventeen metres long, and built on two tiers. The lower deck, at the back, housed the engine – a truck engine with five forward gears and no reverse. An open gap led to the galley, which also doubled as the crew's billet. The top tier, above the engine, was flat, affording a splendid space for sunbathing and birdwatching. Above the galley was the bridge, a little wooden structure where Gamma piloted the boat with a tractor's steering wheel connected by oily chains that ran along and inside to the engine and the rudder. The 'convenience' as Manju would have described it, was light and airy – a little raised platform situated discreetly at the back, an inch or so from the waterline.

The prow was short, stubby and proud. On top of the bridge,

surrounding the little rusty spotlight, was Gamma's garden, planted in old tin boxes – pretty arrays of flowers, shrubs and basil, a herb sacred to Hindus. Also, I noticed with pleasure, a good healthy crop of ganja. Behind Gamma's little wooden bridge was another small area of flat, open decking – the senior members' billet for Aditya and myself. Neeraj and Topguy would share the crew quarters down below.

From the bank, Aditya and I watched the hive of activity as the crew and the boys scurried over the boat. Topguy fussed about in the galley, while Neeraj, after cutting down a couple of bamboo poles, constructed a sun shelter from the flysheets of our tents behind the wooden bridge. Bhaiti did his bit as well, checking every nook and cranny for stowaways, resulting in a mass genocide of insectocution. Even the *Kailash*'s resident rodent didn't last long. He was quickly dispatched with a snap of those wicked jaws.

Provisions were quickly loaded and fuel rolled on board in big drums. There was now one last thing to do. Our puja. We all gathered round the front of Gamma's bridge, which was decorated with silver tinsel. As the sun flashed off the tinsel, it reminded me of Christmas, when I was due back in England. It was now the first of December. The great river was going to have to carry me swiftly home.

Neeraj tied a garish plaster effigy of a plump-bellied Ganesh to the railing below the bridge, so the deity looked out over the prow of the boat. In a cloud of scented smoke, we cracked a coconut and, steepling our hands together, mumbled our mantras and asked for guidance and safety for our journey from that great Lord of Protection.

Everything was now shipshape. Aditya was certainly dressed for the occasion. He had changed into white cotton trousers, boat shoes and a jaunty peaked cap. He looked like a retired admiral during Cowes week. I almost felt I should pipe him aboard. At exactly 12.01 p.m. Laxman started the engine. It roared into life, spewing a great plume of black smoke from the little car exhaust positioned on the top deck, darkening the blue sky like an approaching storm.

He then rang a bell – the signal to let Gamma know he was about to engage first gear. There was a slight pause. Communications between the engine room and the bridge involved a third member of the crew, Vijay, whose job it was to alert Gamma that the bell had rung. Gamma was almost stone deaf. Having received the signal, Gamma rang his bell twice – his signal to Laxman that he was ready. Laxman again rang his bell once, and Vijay relayed to Gamma that Laxman was ready. Gamma turned the wheel and the *Kailash* chugged proudly out in a broad, sweeping circle, heading south down the vast reaches of the Brahmaputra, amidst cheers from all of us and bewildered onlookers on the bank.

We soon settled down to a happy rhythm, each of us finding our own space. Bhaiti found his immediately. Apart from shore leave and the odd patrol for a spot of insectocution, he never left it. He curled up happily under the little wooden bench that served as a seat for our pilot, Gamma. It almost seemed that he had read my manual of 'Management of Dogs on Board Ship'. He was well away from the heat of the boilers and sheltered from the rays of the sun. Instead of plenty of clean, loose straw for his kennel, he slept on a pile of soft rope. He was a born river dog.

Aditya and I settled into the first-class accommodation – the little wooden deck behind the bridge, protected from the sun by the flysheets. I noticed he had changed again into a pair of multi-coloured surfer's shorts.

'What do you think?' he said. 'Pretty snappy, eh? They're the top of a new range, designed by one of Hawaii's greatest surfers, Duke Kahamamoku.'

'Where do you get *all* these clothes?' I asked. 'You look like a male model.'

'Presents,' he replied enigmatically. He pulled another garment out of his bag, a bulkier garment with a lot of straps.

'What's that?' I asked.

'My life vest.'

'A life vest?' I asked, astounded. 'We are not exactly embarking on a round-the-world yacht race.'

'Listen,' he said, trying to struggle into the life vest, pulling and tugging on a multitude of straps. 'I'm not taking my chances with you on board. I know all about your sailing skills. You've sunk not one, but two boats on previous expeditions. You're a Jonah. Look, it's even got a whistle,' he added happily. He blew it hard.

Laxman, mistaking the whistle for the bell, a signal from Gamma to cut the engines, slammed the gear into neutral and switched off the engine. The *Kailash* came to a juddering halt.

'There's only one Jonah on this boat,' I remarked acidly.

I climbed down on to the lower deck to check out the kitchen facilities. It was immaculate and a delicious smell was already emanating from it. Out of nothing, Topguy had created a galley that any yachtsman would be proud of. Gleaming pots and pans hung from little nails. A selection of sharpened swords lay neatly on a chopping board, fashioned from a bit of driftwood. A little Primus stove burnt merrily, heating up a large aluminium pot. But it was Miss Mary, the steamer, that was Topguy's pride and joy.

'Good,' he smiled, as he took off the lid and carefully checked the contents.

'First-class, Topguy,' I said.

'Lunch ready five minutes.'

I went to find Neeraj. He was sitting next to Gamma on the bridge, intently watching the old man, clearly contemplating a new career. Gamma, his eyes never leaving what seemed to me just a vast, plain, brown sheet of water, turned the wheel tirelessly, endlessly shifting the prow of the *Kailash* in a series of twists and turns. It seemed that he was following a map. He was reading or, as he put it, 'dreaming' the river. Beneath that deceptively calm water was a labyrinth of eddies, shoals, sandbanks, cross-currents and whirlpools. In his dream, he told us, he saw a clear path. One step off that path meant instant disaster. It was tradition, an ancient, old and skilled tradition, handed down generation after generation by these master pilots.

The usual instruments – compasses, landmarks or celestial sighting – were of little use for navigating this river, where everything changed all the time and yesterday's channel could be non-existent today. Instead the steamers' captains had to learn the *majhi*'s art of reading the water – detecting the way by the shifting patterns of the current, by the movement of debris on the surface, or even by the subtleties of light and shade in the muddy colours of the river.

Topguy's culinary skills had reached new levels with the aid of his new baby, Miss Mary the pressure steamer. We were all spoilt. Lunch arrived on brand new tin plates: mountains of fluffy white basmati rice, a bewildering variety of fresh, perfectly cooked crisp vegetables from the markets of Dibrugarh, and a new kind of spicy dhal, less oily but hotter, its piquancy giving that perfect little extra zing.

'He's a marvel, Topguy,' Aditya remarked. 'A rare breed. He's what we call in Hindi a karma yogi. For them, work is worship. They never expect rewards.'

After lunch, Aditya and I unfolded our sleeping bags. We dozed, lulled by the gentle rolling of the boat and the dull echo of the engine, protected by the awning from the sun that was now slamming off the metallic surface of the river in a haze of heat. In the late afternoon, the sun dropped, turning the river into a gigantic canvas. It was as if some god had reached down and with a few lazy strokes of a brush had painted a picture. One didn't need to look up for it was all here stretching into infinity, the clouds, the hills, the colours, the whole universe reflected in perfect detail on the river's mirror-like surface. Lone fishermen waved to us languidly, as they slid past silently in their slim, elegant canoes. We passed a bamboo raft completely obscured by piles of banana and bamboo fronds. A group of people sat on top like a little family of birds on a floating nest.

For a twitcher like Aditya, it was a paradise. All kinds of water birds – shovelers, egrets, cormorants, cranes – lined the little sand-banks like small armies. Occasionally, one caught a glimpse of bright copper, identifying the plumage of groups of ruddy shel-drake. Above us the music of the wind passing through a thousand flutes announced the arrival of flocks of whistling teal as they cir-cled, and then dived, landing in a flurry of wings.

At about 4 p.m. three long rings of the bell in the engine room informed Laxman to slow down. The *Kailash* shuddered as he dropped down into the lowest gear and then, switching off the engine, we glided slower and slower until the side of the boat nudged against a sandbank. This was our camp for the night. I was disappointed. I had been looking forward to the experience of steaming down the river under the light of a full moon. But these are dangerous waters at night, even for the most experienced of *majhi*.

We found we had our own private desert island. Aditya and I walked across cool, clean, crunchy sand. There was pin-drop silence, only slightly disturbed by a soft thud as a wedge of crum-bling sand fell from the high banks, or a distant yelping of glee as Bhaiti pursued some new form of prey. When we returned, a fire was burning brightly. The crew and the boys were huddled around it in blankets. The temperature had dropped.

Topguy produced a pudding – a pudding that I would never forget – Topguy's special lemon pie. Gamma filled up his old black-ened *chillum* and after a few hits and a few tots of rum, we settled to listen to the old man's tales. He told us of the history of our little vessel.

Fifteen years ago, a young man from Uttar Pradesh with a large family to feed could not make ends meet. Leaving his family, he migrated to Dibrugarh to make his fortune. He came from a family of devout Shivites who named their first-born son after the great Lord Shiva's snowy and lofty abode on the Tibetan plateau. They called him Kailash – Kailash Rai.

Kailash Rai was a bright young man. In a few years he had built up a profitable little business. He became an agent, a middleman for all sorts of ventures, disposing of garbage, hauling wood, and dealing in scrap iron. As the years went by, he opened a timber yard, a trucking company, a mill, and built a fleet of boats. He became an important man. Everybody knew Kailash Rai in Dibrugarh. He became rich, which was to become his downfall.

In 1991 he was abducted by terrorists of ULFA, the United Liberation Front of Assam. He was never seen again. His business was broken up and sold – the mills, the timber yards, the trucks and the fleet of boats. Just before he was abducted, he had designed a special boat for himself. It was to be the flagship of his little navy. It remained unnamed. The present owner, a friend, bought the boat and named it in his honour – the *Kailash*.

Gamma had been a *majhi* all his life, like his father and his father before him and so on. He remembered as a kid working the lookout shift on the great steamers that plied up and down the river, taking just six days to reach Calcutta from Dibrugarh. These early boats were known as the 'giants', the largest mail steamers ever built. Each was licensed to carry over thirteen hundred passengers. He remembered the sounds, the laughter and the music that echoed across the great river as the 'tea sahibs', as he called them, celebrated late into the nights, dancing and drinking. He remembered the pungent smell of their cheroots and the sweet musty smell of freshly packed tea. These boats, he said, in awe, were like river palaces.

Later, Gamma had also worked during the Second World War

on the steamers that carried the military supplies and fuel up the river to Guwahati and Dibrugarh. He called them river trains. Sometimes, the volume of traffic on the river was as busy as the road traffic today in Guwahati. It was an odd contrast to the empty river that now flowed before us. In the war, the Brahmaputra had been a vital conduit for the transport of materiel – nearly two million tons of it in 1944. And it could be hazardous – aviation fuel was carried in bulk in seventeen specially converted flats – barges – towed by eight specially adapted steamers.

Gamma told us of the fury of the monsoons. His gnarled and knotted hands shook as he refilled his *chillum*, as if reliving a nightmare. Twenty years ago, he had been crossing the river by canoe when it was in full spate. He was ferrying food to another family in a village on a *char* flooded and cut off, north of Dibrugarh. He heard what he called a big splash of water behind him. It was a huge bore wave that threw him and the canoe into the air. He found himself being swept down the river. He thought he would die. He prayed to the gods to save him. He felt something slam into his back. It was a long, cut log. Then another hit him hard, almost drowning him. He was surrounded by logs, hundreds of them, from an overturned timber boat. He quickly grabbed a log and hauled himself out of the water. He clung to that log for twenty-two hours. The river took him forty miles. He eventually managed to hit land just south of Guwahati.

The river, he told us, was a god and must be respected. There is nothing else but the river for the *majhi*. It has ruled their very destinies through history. With the advent of steam his ancestors had been impoverished, their country boats made redundant. Then the river had given them life again. They were employed as pilots on the steamers. Then the river had taken it away again, with the coming of modern land transport – railways, roads, and bridges. But the river had always kept its word towards the *majhi*. It had repaid their loyalty. Now, the river's once deep waters were a fickle

sea of shoals and sandbanks. Only the *majhi* knew how to find its
secret ways.

For a long while, Gamma didn't speak again. He sat quietly
with his eyes closed, as if in deep meditation, the flickering flames
of the fire occasionally illuminating his calm, weather-beaten face.
Then, quite suddenly, he began to sing. He sang the songs of the
river, the songs of loved ones left behind, and the songs of the
majhi, his creaky, ganja-soaked voice amplified by the hollow
silence of the sand. Then it echoed softly away into the mists that
hung like strands of cobwebs over the river.

I lay awake for hours that night, the full moon bathing Bhaiti
and me in a fretwork of pale light filtered by my mosquito net.
Suddenly, far, far above me, I heard the sound of wings. I looked
up. Thousands of bar-headed geese were crossing the moonbeams
in skeins, like squadrons of bombers, as they migrated south, fleeing the icy prison of the Tibetan plateau to the warmer climes of
the Indian plains. Life, I thought, couldn't get much better than
this.

TWELVE

We set off early the next morning through the rolling mists towards Majuli, the largest river island in the world. Bhaiti and I joined Gamma on the bridge. He really must have 'dreamed' that safe passage as he wrestled with the old tractor wheel, steering the *Kailash*, twisting and turning like a dodgem car. He couldn't see the river at all. The mist hung like a wet blanket, right over the little prow. I wondered if the hallucinatory effect of the ganja was blurring our view further. It was only 5 a.m., and the little cabin was as foggy as the river from the sweet-scented smoke that Gamma blew out in clouds, after sucking on his old *chillum*. Smiling, he passed the *chillum* to me. A little early, I thought. But why not? According to the Assam Ganja and Bhang Prohibition Act of 1958 I wasn't breaking any laws. It prohibits possession and consumption of ganja and bhang, and its smoking apparatus, except for 'social, religious, medical and scientific purposes'.

If it came to court, I was certainly clear on three counts, maybe all four. This was a social occasion, a religious one, as both Gamma and I were devotees of the great ganja-smoking Lord Shiva, and without a doubt medicinal – I had enough old injuries to sway any jury. Scientific? An in-depth study of the course of one of Asia's most important rivers? That would be a tough one for the prosecution. I sat on the bench next to Gamma, took the *chillum* and inhaled deeply. Something cold touched my leg. I looked down. Bhaiti was staring at me questioningly from his kennel beneath the bench, with a look that said, 'Hey, what about me?' Bhaiti certainly didn't need any more. He was stoned all day from the fumes that filled the little cabin. No wonder he never left it.

I stared intently at the wall of mist in front of me, hoping that at any moment it would open like the parting of the Red Sea. Nothing happened. If anything, it got thicker and more colourful. It had now turned into a rainbow, filling the little cabin in dazzling, glittering strands, encasing my body, tickling me. I giggled. Gamma smiled back at me. Still giggling, I floated out to the luxury berth where Aditya was dabbing cologne on his freshly shaved face.

'Good morning, Aditya,' I said happily. 'What a *beautiful* day!'

He looked at me oddly. 'I can't see it as yet. What have you been up to? Your eyes are spinning like saucers.'

I giggled again. 'Trying to "dream" the river with Gamma.'

'Well, you can wipe the smile off your face,' he replied. 'You've got work to do.'

'Work. What work?'

'As commodore of the *Kailash*,' Aditya announced, 'I've decided to change the rules of traditional nautical hierarchy. From now on, the *Kailash* will be an equal opportunities boat. Everybody will contribute. You're on the washing-up detail. Effective immediately.'

'And what are you going to do?' I asked.

'I will be lookout,' he replied. He settled himself comfortably against the cushion of his rolled-up sleeping bag, took out his binoculars and started to survey the horizon. 'These are dangerous waters,' he said.

I climbed down and entered the galley. I saluted Topguy and Neeraj.

'Reporting for duty,' I announced.

Topguy looked appalled. Neeraj smiled – a silly smile. His eyes were spinning too. I knew where he had been that morning.

'No, Topguy, I must,' I said, as he tried to stop me collecting the pile of dirty plates and pots.

'OK,' he said reluctantly, 'but be careful.'

I saluted again. Washing up, not usually my favourite domestic chore, was rather fun under the influence of Assam's finest weed, I thought, as I slung a bucket attached to a long rope over the side of the boat to collect water. Each tin plate took on a character of its own. I spent a long time polishing them until they shone like mirrors. I hurled the bucket over the side again to get some more water, letting the rope play out like a fishing line. I was so stoned that I forgot to let go. The next thing I knew, I was floating in the bubbling wake of the *Kailash*, as she disappeared into the mist. The water was nice and warm, I thought contentedly.

'Man overboard!' a great roar echoed across the river, followed by a familiar bark.

I heard the crunch of gears as Laxman slammed the boat into neutral. A few minutes later, the welcoming prow of the *Kailash* loomed out of the mist towards me. A figure with a pair of binoculars around his neck towered above me as I floundered in the water.

'I told you,' Aditya called. 'These are dangerous waters. Lucky I was on full alert.'

Laughing their heads off, Vijay and Laxman pulled me on board. I was now pretty clear-headed. My early morning dip had swept away the hallucinatory cobwebs in my mind. Topguy kindly gave me a hot cup of coffee. He was the only member of the crew who showed any compassion. Neeraj was lying in the galley, his legs waving in the air like an upturned beetle, howling with laughter. Not even Bhaiti paid me any attention. Seeing that I was soaking wet, he retired hastily to the cosy confines of his drug den. There was no way *anybody* could get Bhaiti voluntarily into *any* water.

After drying off and changing my clothes, I joined the commodore on the poop deck. 'Now,' he announced, 'as commodore, I'm introducing another new rule on board the *Kailash*. There will be no narcotics or alcohol, nor any mind-altering substances, consumed before the sun dips below the yardarm. Except, of course, for Gamma.'

'Yes, sir,' I saluted.

By now the mists had disappeared. It was a glorious day. Gamma threaded the *Kailash* up a narrow channel, close to the steep south bank. River life passed us by in a kaleidoscope of colour. I could clearly see the flood mark of the river from the monsoons. It was at least ten metres up.

In the shallows, lean, sun-blackened men washed their buffaloes, while the women bathed, turning away giggling, coquettishly protecting their modesty as we swept by. The commodore, I noticed, was 'twitching' a lot that morning, as he scanned the banks through his binoculars. Lines of beautiful fishing boats, shaped like sampans with high, pointed prows and intricately woven rattan domed awnings, bobbed gently in the *Kailash*'s wake.

On the banks, the sun flashed off great stacks of beautiful little clay pots – all shapes and sizes – waiting to be loaded into the boats, to be sold in the local markets. Expertly and patiently, again and again, a lone fisherman flicked out his heavy net like a matador's cape and then slowly drew it in. A few tiny silver fish struggled in the thin mesh like sparklers. On top of the banks, villagers waved to us from their little temporary bamboo houses, surrounded by tall palm, coconut and toddy trees. Stands of jute and sugar cane waited for collection. Here and there, I caught flashes of emerald – little rice plantations.

It was impossible to tell how wide the river was. We looked across the expanse of water, gleaming like a mirage in the sunshine. It could have been three or four or even twenty miles wide. It was endless – here nothing was stable or well defined. You could not even be sure about the main banks: they could move miles in a single season, the power of the monsoons had overwhelmed such huge areas that the paddy fields of a few weeks earlier could now be anywhere in the middle of the river. It was just an infinite vista of water beneath the canopy of the hot blue sky.

Only the *majhi* could tell where we were. Gamma steered the *Kailash* towards what I thought was the right bank. In fact, it was just a huge sandbar, the Nimati Chapari, the 'silent sandbank', so-called because it was large enough for human voices to get lost in. But it was far from silent. The Maratha swung his binoculars to study the different species of bird bathing in its shallows. Excitedly, he identified them for me – pond herons, river tern, black-headed storks, open-billed storks, adjutant storks, lesser adjutant storks, ibis, and even a flotilla of low-flying grey pelicans with their strange, shopping-bag-shaped beaks, skimmed over the surface. No wonder, I thought, the fishermen struggled here. There was stiff competition.

Dark clouds suddenly appeared in the clear blue sky. At first, I thought they were swarms of locusts but Aditya identified them as wire-tailed swallows on their migration south, fleeing the cold Siberian wastes for the warmth of the Indo-Gangetic Delta. Some never made it. I watched as two exhausted stragglers dropped like stones into the river. They struggled for a moment, desperately trying to beat their wings, but the current rolled over them, taking them to a watery grave.

At midday, we arrived at Majuli. According to myth Majuli was formed by one of the breasts of the beautiful Sati, who took her

own life after being outcast by her family for marrying the great
God Shiva. A familiar figure was standing there, waiting with
a small bus. It was Rajan, Manju's nephew whom we'd met in
Dibrugarh a few days ago. Apart from women and the blues,
Rajan was an expert on the strange monks of Majuli. He was
going to be our guide to Kamalabari, the largest of the thirty-three
satras or monasteries that were founded here in the seventeenth
century.

Majuli Island always suffers badly during the monsoons, but this
year, because of their ferocity, two-thirds of the island had disappeared under water. It took us nearly four and a half hours to
cover the eight miles to the monastery, most of them spent pushing
the bus out of the sandy track that just a couple of months ago had
been a tarmac road. We would have been better off with the old
Majuli mode of transport – a high-wheeled cart drawn by an elephant.

A group of boys were sitting, laughing and chattering on a wall
outside the monastery gates. They were dressed in simple, clean
white dhotis, their freshly washed hair swept back and tied in
buns.

'These are the novices, the disciples,' Rajan explained. 'Notice
anything about them?'

For a start they were all extraordinarily beautiful – a sloe-eyed,
slim-hipped, high-cheekboned, pouting-lipped, sensual kind of
beauty. But there was something else. Strangely, they all looked
exactly the same.

'Odd, isn't it?' Rajan said, as if reading my thoughts. 'It's almost
as if they were interbred. There are about a hundred and twenty
devotees here at Kamalabari.'

I went up to the boys to shake their hands.

'No, no, no, Mark,' Rajan whispered urgently. 'You can't do
that. They can't be touched after they have bathed. And never
inside the monastery.'

An older but almost exact replica of the young boys led us into the compound of the monastery. It was cool, clean and tranquil, nestling in a grove of giant peepul trees. Doves cooed while squadrons of fruitbats glided silently in the air above us, on their way home to roost. A great sense of peace enveloped me. The monastery had an almost saintly air about it.

The older monks each had their own rooms overlooking the pretty courtyard. They too seemed oddly similar, their fine-boned faces curiously young and alive, their brown bodies still muscled and well defined. They smiled at us when we passed – an enigmatic, empty kind of smile, almost hypnotic. I found myself dragging my feet, my whole body overcome by a calm that bordered on indolence, pulling at me like a spiritual magnet. It was so strong that I found myself not wanting to leave. Everything was so perfect – too perfect.

In any other temple or monastery I have ever visited in India, the *pandas* or priests descend on you in flocks, fleecing you at every opportunity. At Kamalabari there was absolutely no venality. Even when we left, I had to force my donation on them. They needed nothing and they wanted nothing. But the moment the big wooden door of the monastery closed behind us, it was like coming out of a dream, back into reality. It felt like a film I had seen, *The Stepford Wives*, about a town where everything was perfect and the women were all the same.

Immediately we peppered Rajan with questions. 'Are they . . . you know . . . ?' Aditya and I asked almost simultaneously.

'What?' Rajan smiled innocently.

'Well, you know what I mean, Rajan,' I probed delicately. 'They're all men and boys. They all live together. They're all incredibly beautiful. You know, are they, er—'

'Cut the crap, Mark,' Aditya interrupted. 'Are they gay, Rajan?'

He smiled enigmatically. 'I wouldn't know.'

'Well, I'll tell you something, Rajan,' Aditya announced. 'You've got a gold mine here. You could run the first gay tour to India. You'd make a fortune.'

Rajan laughed. 'Funny you should mention that. I once acted as guide for an American photographer. It was a nightmare. He wouldn't bloody leave. We spent ten days here, *outside* the compound.'

'Why?' we asked.

'I don't know. Perhaps,' he said mischievously, 'it was the only place he could touch them.'

The wet rasp of Bhaiti's tongue awoke me from my dreams the next morning. He stared at me, those deep eyes filled with affection and trust. Suddenly my stomach churned, there was something in that look that brought me to a realisation with a thud. It hit me how fast we had been moving. We had already covered a quarter of the river in Assam. Cocooned by the cosy, battered old frame of the *Kailash*, we had become one big happy family. Days had melted into one another, but it couldn't last. In just over a week, it came to me with dread, Bhaiti and I would be crossing over the Bangladeshi border and there was no way that my little Hindu brother was going to find a home in a Muslim land. Bhaiti, my Tripuri hound from the Lushai Hills of Assam, belonged here. What was going to happen to him? He trusted me – I'd told him to.

We were making our way that morning to Wild Grass, to visit Ranesh, Reeta's brother, whom I had last seen in Guwahati. The river was so wide here that I could not see the banks. It was really part ocean, part lake – only geographically a river. It was so riddled with a bewildering labyrinth of sandbanks that even Gamma got confused trying to find the little tributary that led to the Kaziranga ghat. However, the Maratha, I was relieved to see, had everything under control. He was studying a map intently. It was, I noticed, an Indian road map.

'Well,' I said, 'where are we?'

'What?' he replied vaguely, looking up, his glasses perched on the end of his nose. 'I have no idea. But I had no idea either that TTK Limited, the printers of this map, had a publishing division.'

'What on earth has that got to do with anything?' I said in exasperation.

'Nothing, really,' he said. 'Just that TTK are the largest manufacturers of condoms in India.'

We circled a few times until Rajan, to whom we had given a lift, recognised the narrow tributary. Even at a distance, I could identify the figure waving at us from the top of the ghat. It was Ranesh. As we moored the boat, I knew where *his* heart lay.

'Where's the most important passenger?' he shouted, searching the decks for Bhaiti, even before greeting his old school chum Aditya, whom he hadn't seen for nearly thirty years.

Hearing Ranesh's voice, Bhaiti ambled out of his kennel, wagging his tail. He barked happily.

'Ah, he's a real river dog now,' Ranesh said. 'Sumo can't wait to meet him.'

Sumo, I discovered when we reached Wild Grass, was the love of Ranesh's life – a pretty little tan and white bitch. She threw herself immediately at Bhaiti, licking, sniffing and yelping in pleasure. Bhaiti grabbed her softly by the neck and dragged her towards me, as if seeking my approval. I looked at Bhaiti. He looked at me questioningly, then back at Sumo. For the second time that day, my stomach lurched. Suddenly, when I had least expected it, everything had fallen into place again. I could see it in Bhaiti's eyes as well. It was karma – trust had been repaid. This was his home – in Assam, at Wild Grass with Sumo.

Bhaiti was now gently leading a willing Sumo out of the house to find a bit of privacy. I understood. He was like a sailor, finally back on land after a long stretch at sea.

At that moment, Rajan appeared. 'God,' he said enviously. 'In my next life, I'm coming back as a dog.'

It was as if a great weight had been lifted from my shoulders. The Tripuri hound from the Lushai Hills of Assam had moved just a little farther north to the Karbi Anglong Hills of Assam. At Wild Grass, only a few miles away from Kaziranga and the Brahmaputra, the river that had guided him to his destiny, Bhaiti could hunt to his heart's content. In the evenings, he could return to his new home, to be spoilt rotten by Ranesh and his new girlfriend. Who said it was a dog's life?

There were, however, a lot of problems still to address. I needed to find another boat to take us down the river through Bangladesh. Although my permit clearly allowed me to enter Bangladesh by the Brahmaputra, the *Kailash* was an Indian boat. It would not be allowed to sail in Bangladeshi waters. Relations were a little strained, to put it mildly, between the two countries.

Ranesh handed me an enormous sheaf of faxes from my exasperated yacht broker in Guwahati. Manju, who by now was deeply embroiled in the task of finding me a boat, had become a sort of international middleman as he tried to negotiate boats across two countries. He clearly wasn't enjoying his new role.

I realised that I needed to sort this out as soon as possible. I decided to drive down to Guwahati the next day to go through it with Manju, and then come back to Wild Grass to rejoin the *Kailash*. Aditya would come with me. He had to get back to Delhi for another assignment and I could drop him at the airport.

In the meantime, the *Kailash* would stay here until my return. Neeraj had a fever, Gamma needed to stock up on ganja, and most importantly Bhaiti could get to know his girlfriend and his new home before leaving for Bangladesh.

Wild Grass was a beautiful place, set in five acres of bamboo groves and many different species of flowering tree. Accommodation was old-fashioned and comfortable: a cluster of traditional Assamese houses with light and airy rooms and creaking wooden floorboards.

We dined that night at Ranesh's home at Wild Grass. There, I met a fascinating old woman. She swept into the room in a stunning blue chiffon sari with a matching blue 'tikka' between her eyes. Her white hair was elegantly coiffed and her wrists, arms and neck were ablaze with silver tribal jewellery. However, there was nothing Indian about her. She was as English as English could be. She was even called Mary England, though she had changed it now to Mary Gogoi. She had no desire ever to return to the land of her birth, and intended to spend the rest of what she hoped would be a long life right here at Wild Grass.

Hers was a sad story. Mary had spent many years abroad, mostly in the Middle East, where her husband was employed. She had been widowed a few years ago and retired to a country cottage in Oxfordshire. There she had hoped to live out her days near her family. England had changed, however, and her children couldn't be bothered with her. She felt lonely and out of place. But Mary England was of the old breed, with an unquenchable thirst for life. She put her affairs in order, and set out for India. Why India? I asked. She had always been stubborn and contrary, she told me: it was the one place her husband had always refused to take her. She had one contact in the country, on a tea estate in Assam, and she arrived there in 1993 when restrictions for foreign visitors were lifted. She had ended up at Wild Grass where, like Bhaiti, she had found a family. And, like Bhaiti, she felt she had finally arrived home.

Sometime during that long and noisy night, as the liquor flowed freely, Aditya and I apparently expressed a great desire to take an elephant ride around the sanctuary the following day. We should have known better. Very early the next morning, our heads spinning and our stomachs uneasy, we found ourselves lurching through the long dewy grass on top of one of the sanctuary's

domesticated tuskers in search of one of the planet's most endangered species – the Indian one-horned rhinoceros.

In the thirteenth century, Marco Polo came across this strange
creature and thought he had found the legendary unicorn. For
many years – until Kaziranga was closed to hunting in 1908 – it
was shot by sportsmen and poachers for pleasure and the supposedly aphrodisiacal qualities of its horn. Even then, a kilo of rhino
horn fetched around $12,000 at today's prices. But by the end of
the nineteenth century hardly any rhinoceros remained. In 1902,
Lady Curzon, the wife of the Viceroy, expressed a wish to see the
'three-toed, one-horned beast' that Marco Polo had thought was a
unicorn. There were only twelve left.

Today, Kaziranga, an area of about 430 square miles, is one of
the best protected wildlife sanctuaries in India. Highly trained anti-
poaching units are on twenty-four hour alert, armed with a
shoot-to-kill policy. It has been through their dedication and dili-
gence that rhino numbers have increased dramatically. But
poaching is still a constant threat. Today, rhino horn fetches
$40,000 a kilo. Until the rich, paunchy potentates of the Orient
realise that their impotency cannot be cured by a mashed-up tonic
of rhino's horns, this beautiful animal's future hangs in a delicate
balance.

Kaziranga also holds a great variety of other wildlife – wild buffalo, gaur, swamp deer, sambar, hog deer and wild boar. And
thousands of different species of bird. Due to our hangovers they
all passed us by in a blur that morning. But we did see rhinoceros –
in fact fourteen of them. Aditya created history in the annals of
wildlife photography. He took the first ever picture of a flying
rhino – the result of double exposure and extremely shaky hands.

Later that morning, we set off by car to Guwahati to sort out the
confusion of the boat to Bangladesh with my yacht broker Manju.
As we drove, I took the opportunity to study the large sheaf of

faxes that Ranesh had given to me at Wild Grass. I began to understand why Manju was exasperated. I realised I had some serious sucking-up to do.

The correspondence was endless, and it was all about Bangladesh. Back in England, I had asked people I knew at a major Indian tea company with plantations in Bangladesh if there was anyone they could recommend to act as a guide and translator for my journey through the country. They had arranged for a young planter called Shaamshuzzaman, or 'Shaams' for short, to accompany me. There were desperate letters from the company's office in Dhaka, asking when Mr Shand was coming and where Shaams was supposed to meet him. There were official Government letters welcoming Mr Shand to Bangladesh. There were letters from the National Tourist Organisation in Parjatan, who were excitedly awaiting Mr Shand's 'cultural' tour of their country. There were even messages from top brass in the military, from the Bangladesh Rifle Security Forces, the equivalent of the Indian Border Security Forces, identifying the bewildering labyrinth of checkpoints. They were on full alert, ready to escort Mr Shand at the border.

This, I realised, was all very well and kind, but amazingly no one, in a country that spent most of the year underwater, seemed able to find me a boat. Instead, all the letters ended on the same, absurd note: did Bhaiti hold a British passport? I could already see the complications. It was becoming a terrible muddle. There was only one person, I realised, who could sort it out, and he was snoring right next to me, fast asleep. It was going to take all my powers of persuasion. I nudged him.

'Wha-at?' croaked Aditya, irritably. 'I was just having a wonderful dream. A dream about going home.'

'What do you know about Bangladesh?' I asked, innocently.

'Nothing,' he replied grumpily. 'Don't want to, don't care, and don't want to go there – ever.'

I tried another tack. 'Apparently, it's a beautiful country,' I said.

'Beautiful rivers, beautiful people, stunning birdlife – great for photography.'

'Bollocks,' he said, 'Bangladesh represents three things to me: people, wind and water. Too many people, too much wind because they all talk so much, and too much water – most of the year the country's submerged.'

'Well,' I replied, indignantly, 'India doesn't exactly set an example on population. And all that water is due to you lot constantly chopping down the trees in the north.'

'Bollocks,' he said again, 'nothing to do with us. It's the Bhutanese and the Chinese in Tibet, they're the real villains. Decades of uncontrolled logging up there have denuded the slopes, so now the earth runs straight into the Brahmaputra. You've already seen the havoc the river wreaks in the monsoons in Assam. Bangladesh just gets the worst of it. Anyway,' he said, 'what's all this got to do with anything?' He stared at me in astonishment. The penny had finally dropped. 'You want *me* to come with you, don't you?'

Diplomacy had not worked. It was now a question of laying my cards on the table – the full house. I was going to have to rely on compassion.

'Look, Aditya,' I pleaded, 'I'm desperate.' I showed him the sheaves of correspondence. 'For a start, I can't get a boat, and secondly, it seems that my journey is going to be turned into a sort of cultural tour by the Government. And thirdly, what if I don't like Shaams? I'll end up discussing tea planting for two weeks. I'll be bored rigid. No fun.'

'Well, you've got Neeraj and Topguy,' he said.

'I can't take them into Bangladesh,' I said. 'They haven't got passports. Please . . . '

He sighed. 'Bloody hell. The things you get me into.' He mulled it over for a few minutes. 'Well, it means me flying back to Delhi, flying to Rajasthan for a day to do my shoot, then flying back to Delhi, going home to Gualiar, then back to Delhi, and then taking a plane to Dhaka. Doesn't give me much time. How, when and where am I ever going to meet you?'

'That's simple,' I said. 'Everything's arranged. The border crossing is at a place called Doikhawa. You can get in touch with Shaams and meet us there. The only thing that isn't arranged is a boat. All *you* have to do is try and find us one.'

'OK,' he said wearily. 'I'll come. But on two conditions.'

'And what are they?'

'First, I'm back in Delhi by the 25th. I've got work to do.'

That was no problem. I had to be back in *England* by the 25th. For Christmas.

'And secondly, I fly on British Airways, not Biman.'

'OK,' I said, 'fine. But why?'

'Air miles,' he replied.

At around 2 p.m. we reached Manju's house in Guwahati. We heard him before we saw him, shouting on the telephone through the open window of his first-floor office.

Manju Barua was the Fidel Castro of Assam. He was a great bear of a man with a tangle of knotted black beard that hung like a bib on his chest, and blazing black eyes that seemed to look into your very soul. When he spoke, he raised his silver-ringed hands in supplication, as if calming a great crowd after whipping them into a frenzy with his impassioned words. It was easy to be intimidated by him. But the bluster just camouflaged a very different man – gentle, honest, spiritual and modest. Manju could translate Sanskrit fluently, and he knew the habits and Latin names of every species of animal and bird that roamed or flitted across this lush state. He was a superb botanist, an authority on cricket, a talented traditional musician and a tremendous singer. His immense repertoire included every single song written by the Beatles, which he sang with great gusto in his bath at night. Most importantly, he loved elephants.

His tentacles were powerful and far-reaching, and although he would tell you he was just a humble travel agent who owned a small jungle camp, his office, which was unusually quiet today, was normally crammed with a wide spectrum of Assamese society from high-ranking Government officials and wildlife officers, to mahouts and musicians.

His office was as deceptive as his manner. Every inch of flat space, every chair and table was covered by piles of dusty documents and files. The bookcases that lined the walls seemed to teeter precariously as if at any moment they would explode like a volcano and burst in a flowing lava of eclectic literature.

But everything had its place. This was highly organised chaos. Still sitting in a pile of dusty boxes, which I had noticed on my last visit, was a sophisticated computer system. This had been supplied by an exasperated friend in a vain attempt to modernise communications, to replace Manju's battered and chipped old typewriter. Manju's answer had been perfectly logical. He had replied that he would modernise the communication systems by painting his typewriter. His one concession to modern technology was a fax, which was the only way he communicated in writing with the outside world. I had often seen his ingenious way of dealing with foreign travel agents trying to make a booking.

The telephone would ring, which he hated. 'Hello, hello, hello,' he would shout, holding it at least two feet away from his ear. 'Yes, this is Wild Grass. You're calling from where? Sweden? I can't hear you.' He could, of course, perfectly. 'Please send a fax. The number is – hello, hello, I can't hear you,' and he would slam down the telephone.

'God,' he shouted as we entered the room, 'finally my nemesis has arrived. You don't know *what* a bloody nuisance you've been, and—'

I interrupted him. 'Hear me out, hear me out,' I shouted, mimicking Manju's favourite phrase. 'Your worries are over. You can wash your hands of me. Aditya's going to meet me on the Bangladeshi border. And he's going to find a boat.'

'I'm not talking about boats,' he interrupted. 'I'm being badgered by calls from the Tourist Office, the Chief Secretary, and even the Chief Minister. They all think for some extraordinary reason that your river journey is going to help promote tourism in Assam. Now they want me to organise the logistics. As if I didn't have enough on my plate.'

I thought about it. It was a brilliant idea. For a tourist, or an adventurous tourist, I could think of nothing better. Day one: a little culture, a blessing at the great Mother Temple of Kamakhya. Then, aboard a refitted *Kailash* or some other suitably equipped, luxurious vessel to putter down the majestic waters of the Brahmaputra with its unfolding kaleidoscope of different water birds. A wonderful camp would be set up on the silent and empty sand *char*, and under a full moon, a fabulous dinner would be topped off by Topguy's lemon pie. Finally, bedtime to the sound of a thousand wings as the bar-headed geese migrated south overhead. Day two: for the spiritually or artistically minded, a visit to the Stepford Wives of Majuli. Days three and four: from the comforts of Wild Grass, two days wildlife-watching in Kaziranga Wildlife Sanctuary, with a guaranteed sighting of the rare one-horned Indian rhinoceros. And then a comfortable drive back by car to Guwahati.

'It's a brilliant idea, Manju,' I said. 'You'll make a fortune.'

'I'm a travel agent, Mark, not a marketing manager,' he reprimanded me. 'And talking of travel, Aditya, your flight's been cancelled today due to fog in Delhi. I've booked you on the next flight, tomorrow afternoon. Now, that means you've got a day and a night to kill and I don't want you in my hair causing me any more problems. What are you going to do?' He settled into his chair, rolled a cigarette, popped a pickled chilli into his mouth from a glass jar, and propped his feet on the desk.

I noticed a map hanging on the bookshelf. 'How far is Shillong?'
I asked.

'Shillong? About two hours' drive. Why?'

'Because,' I said, 'I want to find some women.'

'Now look here,' he said tersely. 'You're married. They've a certain reputation for promiscuity up there. It's the land where women
rule.'

'No, no, you don't understand. I'm looking for four very old
ladies called Million, Billion, Trillion and Snow White. A friend of
mine – Charles Allen, who lived in Assam as a young boy – asked
me to look them up. He named his chickens after them.'

Manju looked at Aditya. Aditya looked at Manju.

'What do you say, Aditya?' I asked. 'John Edwards gave me the
address of a Welsh friend of his who still lives in Shillong. He'll
help us track them down.'

'I'm on,' replied the Maratha. 'But there's something else we
should check out. They say the people there are haunted by a terrifying snake-spirit called U-Thlen. They blame it for everything,
every misfortune or illness. But the word is that U-Thlen can also
make you rich – in return for fresh human blood. Which you
obtain from a hired assassin, one of his disciples.' He paused, and
gave a sinister smile. 'Do you know anything about it, Manju?'

'Load of nonsense,' said Manju, helping himself to another dried
chilli. 'Right – I've got work to do.'

Racy ladies and hired assassins: it sounded like a very dangerous
mission. Bond would have approved, I thought, as Aditya and I set
off on the steep drive up to Shillong, the capital of Meghalaya, the
'land of the clouds', or the 'land where women reign supreme',
where steep hill ranges divided Assam from Bangladesh. On the
way, Aditya gave me a short history lesson on how the local
women's lib had come about.

The local Khasis, he told me, were originally a fearsome, warlike
tribe who enjoyed nothing better than swooping down from their

mountain strongholds to rape, pillage and plunder the more prosperous people in what is now Bangladesh. The women became fed
up with staying alone at home doing all the work while their men-
folk were permanently out fighting. An extraordinary deal was
struck. Not only would the women inherit all the property, but
they would pass their own surnames to their children. In a nutshell,
the women gained all the power: they looked after the family kitty
and they wore the trousers.

Today, this matrilineal society still exists, but not in quite such
harmony. The women say the men are 'good for nothing', 'just par-
asites'. And the men argue that they have been emasculated and
turned into 'breeding bulls' and 'babysitters'. A battle of the sexes
is in full swing.

From 1874 to 1972, Shillong was the capital of Assam, until
Meghalaya became a separate state, after an eighteen-year battle
for autonomy with Assam. It was the first of the north-eastern
regions to break away. As we climbed steeply through the rolling
hills, the wet mist and the pine trees, I could quite understand why
the British loved this area to which they flocked to escape the heat
of the plains.

It reminded them of home. They called it the 'Scotland of the
East'. It should have been called the 'Cardiff of the East'. It was the
Welsh, not the Scottish, who first came here in 1842, in the form of
zealous Methodist missionaries. They had certainly spread the
word of the good Lord. Today traditional Khasi society is rapidly
disappearing, having been replaced by Christian converts – 1.2
million of them.

The reputation of the women for promiscuity that Charles had
described also seemed to have taken a bit of a knock, as we
passed endless signs proclaiming the dangers of Aids. However,
one indication that traditions were still alive – just – came when
we passed one huge sign which read 'Don't have sex with
strangers.' Underneath some local wag had added 'Just fuck your

best friend'. Shillong was celebrating World Aids Day. It was also a dry day. Booze was banned.

We checked into a colonial hotel, a leftover from the Raj aptly called The Pinewood. In the gloomy wood-panelled dining room, decorated with Landseer sporting prints, we were served a very English dinner by old uniformed retainers who flitted around us like moths. After dinner, we retired like a couple of old planters to our splendid bedroom with its mahogany washstands and creaking brass beds. There, we settled down in a couple of armchairs in front of a blazing fire, with a bottle of Royal Stag whisky which the Maratha had magically conjured up. Before we turned in, I called John Edwards' Welsh friend. No doubt, I thought, some old buffer who had stayed on. We agreed to meet after breakfast the following morning.

The gloomy dining room was transformed the next day. Sun filtered through the windows, a coal fire burnt brightly in the grate, and a clock was ticking on the mantelpiece. A covey of jolly Khasi women wearing gay, pink poplin aprons waited expectantly. Aditya and I treated ourselves to a traditional English fry-up of eggs, bacon, sausages, toast, marmalade and fresh pineapple juice.

After breakfast, John's friend arrived. He was not quite what Aditya and I had imagined. We had expected a gruff old bounder, perhaps a retired planter wearing a pair of whipcord trousers and an old tweed jacket and carrying an early morning pink gin. He was wearing Levis, a cosy, homespun cardigan and a blue baseball cap, turned the wrong way round. He was not gruff at all, but quiet, extremely courteous, softly spoken, with a pious air about him. He apologised for being late. He had just returned from worship.

Worship, I thought. This could be tricky. How was I going to get on to the subjects of sex and sacrifice?

'Umm, sir,' I said, 'Aditya and I are looking for some women.'

His face paled beneath his blue baseball cap. 'Look here,' he said gravely. 'I'd just like to make one thing clear before you get any misconceptions about the reputation of this place. Shillong is not Bangkok.'

'No, no. Of course not. Goes without saying. It's just that a friend of ours who was here as a child asked us to look up four old ladies who he remembered were – how shall I put it? – er, very popular with the British troops.'

'Million, Billion, Trillion and Snow White,' barked Aditya diplomatically. 'Heard of them?'

He looked gobsmacked. 'I think,' he said, 'that was a little before my time.'

'Absolutely – of course,' I said. 'Goes without saying. But on another subject, Aditya has been telling me a bit of history. Meghalaya is apparently a matrilineal society. Women wearing the pants and holding the purse strings. Is that right? Obviously this doesn't affect you,' I imagined his wife to be a nice cosy Welsh memsahib, 'but I wonder how the men cope. They must feel a bit emasculated – no money, loads of housework, endless babysitting . . . ?'

'I'm married,' he said quietly, 'to a Khasi woman. We're Christians.'

Oops. I cringed. Over to Aditya, perhaps his subtle, Indian approach would unravel the other mystery.

'Look here, my friend,' Aditya barked. 'What's all this I hear about a snake spirit? U-Thlen or something? Has assassins to murder people and feed him human blood? I hear . . . '

There was a sudden crash. One of the jolly Khasi women in her gay, pink poplin uniform had dropped a plate of bangers. The room became dead silent. Even the clock stopped ticking.

The Welshman got to his feet. 'I think this conversation has gone far enough,' he said firmly. 'Why don't I show you a bit of the real Meghalaya? I think you'll like it. I'll take you gambling.'

He drove us to the middle of downtown Shillong. In a small soggy field, bordered by tall, sad pine trees on one side and the back of the National Bank on the other, was the Tier, or the Khasi Hills Archery Sports Institute of Shillong. It was cold and damp and filled with thousands of men. Our friend did not need to take us any farther to prove that Meghalaya was a matrilineal society. The Tier was obviously where the men came to escape from their household duties and spend whatever money their wives gave them in an old, traditional male pursuit – a spot of gambling.

Up until the 1960s, horse racing was big in Shillong, but now it had been replaced by archery. The Khasis are renowned all over India for their accuracy: most of India's Olympic archery team come from these hills.

Everybody was blind drunk on *kiat*, a fiery local brew made from distilled millet and rice. There were a few women. They were raking the money in, shovelling it into big, brown purses strapped to their waists, from the lines of drunken customers who lurched outside their booths. They certainly wore the trousers here as well; several times I witnessed totally inebriated men reel back from good solid right-handers.

Now, I had never gambled – it was not one of my vices. And neither am I able to add up, so this complicated game was way beyond my reach. I have the vaguest idea as to how the Tier works. You place a bet with roving bookies, their ears clamped to mobile phones, in contact with the big punters as far afield as Itanagar. Then teams of archers fire thousands of arrows in the space of three minutes at a small bamboo target about thirty metres away. Then the arrows are counted. Search me how, but somebody wins. Or loses – lots and lots of money. It's a legal operation run by the government of Meghalaya. They take 10 per cent. Gambling is banned in the other north-eastern states, but everybody plays it here – it's like the National Lottery. Crores of rupees, hundreds of thousands of pounds, change hands regularly, every day.

As far as I was concerned, the odds were just as bad as the National Lottery. By the end of the day, I had nothing left. I had been fleeced. Annoyingly, I noticed that Aditya's wallet was bulging. Clearly, the Maratha was a veteran gambler.

We thanked John's friend for his hospitality and apologised for our numerous faux pas. He told us we must return when we had more time. He would explain to us the mysteries and superstitions of the place. I doubt it, I thought. We needed a more liberal guide to get to the bottom of the strange and confusing state of Meghalaya.

'God bless you,' he shouted, as we waved to him from the car.

Something troubled me about his farewell. God made me think of missionaries, and missionaries made me think of Verrier Elwin, the champion of tribal rights. I realised that he had spent the last nine years of his life here, in the 1960s. I wondered what he'd make of it now, this once proud tribal society now almost suffocated by the slick and hypnotic banter of evangelism.

Aditya and I parted at Guwahati airport. 'See you at Doikhawa,' I said. 'Make sure you get a good boat, and be sure to stock it up well.'

'No problem,' he replied. 'Actually, I'm rather looking forward to visiting Bangladesh now. I'm going to bring an extra pair of binoculars.'

'Why?' I asked.

He chuckled. 'All that bird life you told me about.'

Manju's office was noisy and smoky and full of big men with long black-and-grey knotted beards. They were all old elephant men – retired wildlife rangers – their passion for these great animals etched on their faces as they swapped stories and discussed ancient elephant lore. I was flattered, and honoured, to find out that they had read my books. Compared to them, I was a mere novice. But, because I loved elephants, I found myself embraced by their warm camaraderie.

We discussed the works of the great old elephant experts, the elephant manuals of A. J. Milroy, who was largely responsible for establishing Kaziranga, and the writings of P. D. Stracey. Assam is where ancient elephant lore had its beginnings, as far back as the sixth century BC. The great sage Palakapya was the founder of elephant lore – or *gaja-shastra*, as it is known in Sanskrit. He was supposed to have had a supernatural origin, having been born from an elephant. He lived and wandered with the wild elephants, eating only the food they ate; he learnt all about the ailments that afflicted them and was reputed to be the author of a treatise on their medical conditions. Palakapya was said to have had his hermitage 'where the Lohitia flows towards the sea', at the confluence of the Lohit with the Brahmaputra.

One of the rangers told us a story. As he talked, his hands shook from grief, spilling the whisky from the glass he held. Near Kaziranga he used to admire a magnificent tusker. It was his favourite elephant: he called it the 'king of kings'. As the forests were cut down, the 'king of kings' became angry. He killed twelve people – exactly the right number for the wildlife law of this country to impose the death penalty on an elephant. For weeks the ranger tried to capture the elephant with *phandis*, or noosers. But the elephant was too clever. In the end, he himself had to shoot the great tusker. He made an arch where it fell, on which he wrote 'Here lies the king of kings.' Every year, he plays a football match in honour of the great animal and the winner's trophy is a magnificent silver elephant.

Next we drank a toast to Manju. Manju had recently forced the Government to give pensions to old, retired elephants, so that they could live out their last days looked after and well fed. He had cleverly pointed out that all Government servants received a pension on retirement. So why not elephants? After all, they were the most dependable and loyal of all Government servants.

And then they drank to my health. For the Assamese, to give an elephant freedom from work, to give it a wonderful home as I had for Tara, is the ultimate gift – the gift of life, or *hathi-daan* as it is known. Because of what I had done, they said, everything in my life would turn to gold.

It was late by the time I set off back to Wild Grass. Manju told me he had contacted the District Commissioner of Dhubri, the last Indian town before the border with Bangladesh, who would help with the crossing. He embraced me in a huge bear hug. 'Try and keep out of mischief,' he said with a chuckle, 'but cause as much as you can in Bangladesh.'

In the early hours of the morning, I reached Wild Grass. Everybody was in bed except Ranesh's servant. He showed me to the guest room and then, with awe in his voice, told me about Bhaiti.

'Sir,' he said, 'Bhaiti not dog, but god. Twenty-three times in two days.'

I climbed into bed. I was lonely – and jealous. Bhaiti and Sumo were sleeping with Ranesh. I must have fallen asleep because a scratching at my door awoke me. I climbed groggily out of bed and opened the door. A happy, shagged-out Bhaiti staggered in, with a look in his eyes as if to say, 'We are leaving tomorrow, aren't we?' and I fell asleep contentedly with the river dog snoring in my arms.

It felt good to be back on board the next day. I had missed my battered little tub. Everybody had recovered. The *Kailash* had been fully revictualled. We had fuel on board, provisions and, I noticed, as a familiar sweet-smelling smoke poured out of Gamma's cabin to mix with the early morning mist, a new supply of top-quality Wild Grass weed.

We started early that morning. Ranesh and Sumo waved us off from the ghat and Sumo howled as her river dog ran, rather than walked, the gangplank to his kennel beneath Gamma's feet. Because of time restraints and the complications of flying Bhaiti back from Bangladesh to India, Ranesh and I had hatched a plan for returning him to Wild Grass at the end of our trip. It was perfectly simple. Aditya and I would meet Ranesh at Tamabil, one of the few places you could cross the India–Bangladesh border by road. We arranged to meet on either 22 or 23 December. If we failed to arrive, Ranesh warned me, both Sumo and he would send the Indian Army after us.

The mist began to lift as we left the fringes of Kaziranga. Suddenly, a great bellow – a bellow of pain – echoed across the river. Quickly, I grabbed my binoculars and scanned the bank. It was an old tusker. I could see his long yellow tusks protruding from his gaunt, sunken face; his once magnificent body now just a mass of creases and folds like an old pair of trousers. He had come to die. I watched him bellow again in frustration as he dipped his head to feed on the soft reeds that grew by the river. Once this animal could consume five hundred kilos of rough fodder a day. Now, with his last molars almost worn away, he could only digest the softest of plants – the plants that grew by rivers. In a few days, or perhaps less, he would collapse. His body would be stripped by vultures and other scavengers, and the large skeleton would slowly sink into the soft mud to be carried away by the river – the treasury of elephant bones.

I was exhausted, as was Bhaiti, though for different reasons. We soon dozed off curled up together in the shade of the awning. Then, in the late afternoon as we approached the town of Tezpur, we were awoken by the sound of traffic. We were passing underneath Tezpur's Kalea Bhomora bridge, its name derived from a great general of the Ahom kingdom. Quickly, I grabbed my camera and shot an entire roll of film. A series of pictures of a bridge taken from below would not set the photographic world alight, but for me it was tremendously exciting. It had become a ritual – a very childish ritual. Bridges in India cannot be photographed by law, for some arcane security reason. I had spent the best part of thirty years amassing a huge collection of pictures of these forbidden structures, taken surreptitiously from every kind of transport, including an aeroplane and an elephant, but never a boat. This was a unique occasion.

Tezpur, the 'city of blood', derived its name from a mythical battle between two gods who fought furiously to win the hand of a beautiful princess called Usha. Another battle had nearly taken place here much more recently: a little farther north the Chinese army had finally stopped, turned round and returned home after invading India in 1962.

As we passed the ghat leading to the town, I stood to attention on the poop deck and saluted smartly.

Neeraj thought I had had too much sun. 'What are you doing, boss?' he asked in bewilderment, trying to offer me a mug of tea.

'I'm paying tribute to a very important Englishman who is buried here with his wife. Without him,' I said, and I pointed to the mug, 'we wouldn't be drinking that.'

The Englishman was Charles Alexander Bruce, commander of the first steam vessel on the Brahmaputra, the gunboat *Diana*. In 1825, this paddler of thirty tons set out from Calcutta on an epic two-month voyage of over a thousand miles entirely by river, right up to the Himalayan foothills barely sixty miles from the border with Tibet. It was the first successful voyage up the Brahmaputra.

Charles was the brother of Robert Bruce, who had discovered tea when he was given seeds by some Singpho tribal chieftains in 1823. After Robert died, Charles collected the plants his brother had grown and took them back downstream on the *Diana* to re-plant them at Chabua, near Sibsagar. Here, the first tea garden was established. In 1838 the steamer *Calcutta* puffed down the Brahmaputra with the first cargo of tea bound for Mincing Lane in London. Bruce had founded the great British tea empire.

We camped that evening on another empty *char*. While I bathed in the river's warm, calm waters, Bhaiti hunted for our dinner. He sat patiently, staring intently into a large pool, which was filled with little fish. Like a heron, he would suddenly plunge his head into the water, then re-emerge with his catch wriggling between his teeth. Later we walked together across the sand. In the moonlight we played games, chasing crabs, hide-and-seek, and tug-of-war with bits of old driftwood. Then, as we walked back to the boat, we disturbed hundreds of bar-headed geese and watched them erupt in a flurry of wings, like a great gathering of grey ghosts.

THIRTEEN

Just like the Siang, the son of Brahma had cast his spell on me. His waters worked like therapy, my troubles and worries washed away in the bubbling wake of the *Kailash*. It was quite wonderful. There was nothing to do at all, except sit back and enjoy it. A timeless passage – one day blending into another – water and sky, sky and water. It was the early mornings I loved the most, chilly and misty. I was always awoken by the same sound and the same smell as I lay cocooned and warm in my sleeping bag. It was the sound of a mantra being softly chanted, the rasp of a match, a sharp inhalation and then the sweet smell of ganja seeping through the old battered cabin to envelop me in pungent clouds. This was the signal. It was time to go. Gamma was flying.

Then the boat would come slowly to life, the crew flitting like ghosts through the mist. The sound of Laxman tinkering with the engine; the sudden splash as Vijay hurled a bucket over the side to collect the water for our tea; the scrape of wood on wood as Pandit pulled up the gang plank and the slap of wet rope on deck as he pulled up the anchor. Then, one long shrill blast of the bell would announce that Gamma was ready; a crunch of gears, an increasing thud of the engines as they built up power; and the *Kailash* slid off into the dawn.

As the sun began to filter through, the activity and sounds increased – the clatter of pots and pans from below in the galley and the hiss of the stove being lit, followed by the smell of breakfast as the magician in the kitchen plied his trade. Neeraj's head would pop up, followed by two strong cups of tea. We would sit together in companionable silence, making the most of the coolness of the morning before the sun broke through and evaporated the night's condensation, turning everything into a cauldron of molten, white light. Bhaiti would make one of his few appearances. He would come out from the cabin, yawning, settle down beside us and, like some grand sultan, wait for Topguy to appear from the galley with his shiny bowl heaped full of rice, dhal and vegetables. After wolfing it down he would amble back to join Gamma, and together they would 'dream' the river.

The river narrowed as we approached Guwahati, and we hit traffic for the first time – not much, but enough to make Gamma concentrate. We wove a passage through the slim canoes of the fishermen, and bobbed in the wake of the dangerously overcrowded *bhut-bhuthees* that ferried people back and forth across the river. As we passed the ghat, I hid below in the galley, convinced that at any moment a launch, carrying a furious Reeta, would sweep out to intercept us. I felt bad about not stopping to see her. After all, if it hadn't been for her I would never have met my river dog. But I knew what Bhaiti felt about Rani. More importantly, I knew what he felt about Sumo.

We passed Peacock Island, the dome of the Shiva temple Umananda peeping through the thick vegetation on its summit. Gamma signalled to Laxman to slow the engines. We had hit a traffic jam. Now an almost continuous flotilla of small boats crossed ahead of us, like a river train.

West of Guwahati we entered Lower Assam, where the river broadened considerably. The silt, no longer pushed by the huge pressure of the more powerful currents upstream, spread out in a vast sea of shifting sands, treacherous shoals and perilously shallow waters. The *Kailash* began to weave dangerously until suddenly I was thrown forward as we ground to a halt. We had hit a sandbank, but it was nothing to do with Gamma. Two new pilots had taken over: Neeraj at the wheel, and Bhaiti with his paws up on the ledge acting as lookout. They both looked extremely embarrassed. Fortunately, no damage was done and we were soon on our way again, after Pandit had poled us out into deep water.

To our right, to the north, the foothills of Bhutan receded into the distance. Manas National Park, another of India's game sanctuaries, nestles in there, harbouring the largest number of endangered species in India. But unlike Kaziranga, it is no longer well protected. This riverine reserve has become the jungle stronghold of the Bodos, another of Assam's terrorist organisations. There is a bounty for the army on every terrorist's head of about £7000. The real victims, however, are the wildlife, their skins, bones and fur traded for arms for the terrorist cause.

As the hills disappeared, so did the lushness of Assam, for soon the son of Brahma made a long winding left-hand bend towards the Bay of Bengal. Gone were the bamboo, the paddy, the palm trees, to be replaced by an endless mirage of sand, disappearing into infinity like a strange watery desert. But unlike a desert, it was not empty.

Hundreds of boats zig-zagged across the river, carrying goats, silk, pots and pans, rice and paddy, while giant bamboo rafts the size of two football fields hardly seemed to move at all as groups of men strained against the long poles. Little plumes of smoke drifted up into the still air from small rattan shelters that provided makeshift homes on these floating plateaux. A labyrinth of nets covered the river's surface, watched vigilantly by lines of white egrets, like sentries on parade. They would have to be very patient. Massive net fishing has deprived this gigantic river of most of its fish. Ironically, 80 per cent of Assam's fish is now imported from another state, Uttar Pradesh.

Amongst all this river bedlam, 'chicken catchers', as Aditya described the police, patrolled like wolves, stopping any boat on a whim and extracting a little 'douceur'. We had entered the district of Dhubri, once known as the Gretna Green of Assam, the first place across the border from East Bengal, where immigrants were legally placed under contract with their employers. Not any more. These people were all illegal immigrants from Bangladesh who had flooded over during the last thirty years.

Just before the sun dipped below the horizon, gilding the golden dome of the Guru Teg Bahadur Sahib, the largest Sikh temple in the north-east, we arrived at Dhubri, once a busy crossroads for steamer traffic connecting Calcutta and Dhaka with the cities of north-east India.

I liked Dhubri. Like all border towns, it had an air of transience. In 1883 Dhubri was made the headquarters of the Assam Mail Service, which established a daily 'single-handed' service between Dhubri and Dibrugarh served by a fleet of fast river steamers built in London and Glasgow and named after the tribal people of the north-east: the *Naga*, the *Garo*, the *Lushai*, the *Miri*, the *Duffla*, the *Sylu*, the *Kuki*, the *Abor* and the *Mikir*.

Although those days were long gone, Dhubri was still alive, jostling and full of intrigue. On the tree-lined promenade behind which lawns swept up to the old, crumbling British residences, sadhus peddled their wares – magic potions of monkey skulls, bones of rodents, claws of lizards, fangs of serpents, and little brown bottles filled with elixirs to cure all diseases. Barbers did a brisk trade. Their customers, with their heads held back and lath-ered necks exposed, risked their lives not only from the quick, deft strokes of the bloodstained cut-throat blades, but also unknowingly from the danger of infection from Aids. Shifty-eyed smugglers squatted in groups on their hunkers, wheeling and dealing, while busy bureaucrats strode self-importantly to their offices – to another day of doing nothing.

Through this bedlam, Neeraj and I made our way to the office of the most important person in Dhubri – the District Commissioner. Having dropped us off, Gamma had moored the *Kailash* on an empty spit of sand opposite the ghat. Neeraj and I were early. We waited outside the office, watching a procession of peons arrive for work, their positions in the hierarchy signified by the number of pens they carried in their top shirt pockets. The very junior ones carried one pen, the middle management three or four, and the *really* important senior management five or six *and* a small plastic briefcase. All of them looked down their noses disdainfully at Neeraj and me, dressed, I admit, not suitably for this hallowed hall of bureaucracy, in shorts, tee-shirts and *chappals*.

There was a sudden bustle of activity. Another peon, clearly the most important, sporting ten pens, two plastic briefcases and a bunch of keys, unlocked the door to the District Commissioner's office. Invisible behind a cordon of armed police, the District Commissioner was ushered into the office. We waited while Neeraj tried in vain to persuade the peons guarding the inner sanctum that we had an appointment. Eventually, he slipped one of them a fifty-rupee note. We waited several more minutes. Suddenly, the floodgates opened and a covey of obsequious peons rushed out, bowing and scraping, and ushered us into the large, quiet office. Neeraj, I noticed with pleasure, deftly retrieved the fifty-rupee note from the peon's pocket.

Sitting behind an empty desk reading a paperback edition of *Memoirs of a Geisha* was a small, handsome woman, dressed in a blood-red sari. She was the first female District Commissioner in India, Mrs Gayatri Baruah. She welcomed us warmly, and for the next half an hour questioned me excitedly about *Yes, Minister*, her favourite television programme. She asked me if the English Government was *really* like that. I told her it was *exactly* like that. She beamed happily and told me that the Indian Government was *exactly* like that as well. Nobody had *any* idea what anybody was doing.

Eventually, after a further long exposition on her favourite books and TV programmes, I managed to steer her towards a more pressing problem – my exit stamp out of India into Bangladesh at Doikhawa. No foreigner for many years had been allowed to enter Bangladesh from India via the Brahmaputra River. Two entire pages of my passport were filled with my unique permission, acquired in London from the Bangladeshi Embassy during my long paper journey: 'The holder is allowed to enter Bangladesh by the Brahmaputra River from India – *vide* Ministry of Home Affairs *vide* Ministry of Foreign Affairs . . . ' It was almost a short essay. I showed it to the District Commissioner. She rang a bell. A few minutes later the door opened and the man with real power entered the room: Dhubri's Superintendent of Police, the chief chicken catcher. Dhubri, I realised, being a border town, represented rich pickings, as was clear from the heavy, solid-gold watch on his wrist. In the company of the District Commissioner, the Superintendent was disarmingly polite and courteous. But underneath this façade, I sensed he resented a woman holding such a position of power. I did not like the cut of his jib at all. However, my passport was quickly chopped to register my arrival at Dhubri, and he assured me that he would personally alert the Border Security Forces at Doikhawa, who would give me my exit stamp out of India. Perhaps I had misjudged him, I thought.

Just as we were leaving, the District Commissioner asked me if I was going to visit Pratima.

'Pratima who?' I replied, bewildered.

'Pratima Pandey, of course,' she reminded me. 'You wrote about her in your last book. She's a friend of mine. She was in my office only yesterday.'

Pratima, I thought. How extraordinary. She was one of India's greatest folk singers – and the sister of my old friend Parbati Barua, the 'queen of the elephants'. 'Pratima lives in Dhubri?' I asked in amazement.

'No, no, no,' she said, 'in Gauripur, only a few miles from here. You have a bad memory, Mark. You've been there before.'

I could not believe it. Life had come full circle, and it was all to do with elephants. Three years ago Parbati had shown me around her ancestral home, during our elephant journey together across Bengal and Assam. To celebrate the end of our travels, Pratima and her musicians had met us on the banks of the River Sankosh. There, accompanied by her musicians, Pratima had sung the songs of Assam's great elephant lore, of the catching and training of wild elephants, the nomadic life of the mahouts and the lament and longing of loved ones left behind. I had never forgotten that day. Her extraordinary voice still haunted me three years on.

'Remember to take her a little something, Mark,' the District Commissioner reminded me.

'Thank you, madam,' I laughed. Pratima was fond of rum. She called it her 'magic'.

After stopping at a booze shop, Neeraj and I arrived by rickshaw in Gauripur. The house was perched on a small hill overlooking the town. It was the *only* hill in the entire district and had actually been built of mud by Parbati's and Pratima's grandfather eighty-five years ago. As we walked up it, the memories came flooding back. I showed Neeraj the great stone mausoleum in which lay the heart of Prabat Singh, Parbati's and Pratima's father's favourite elephant.

Although Parbati didn't live here anymore, the sisters had sepa-rate parts of the palace, which was called Matiabagh, or 'mud garden'. In many Indian princely families, feuds over inheritance and property are rife, and this was no exception. We approached the crumbling old mansion, surrounded by its ornate wrought-iron balustrade. I led Neeraj round the right side of the building into a tumbledown courtyard, the flagstones exploding with weeds, like the stuffing from an old sofa. It was criss-crossed by a washing line festooned with drying lunghis. An old retainer flitted out of the dark door like a moth. I asked if Pratima was there. He nodded and gestured me to wait. A few minutes later, a shuffling figure wearing a cheap cotton sari and rubber *chappels* walked out into the sunlight. I hardly recognised her. She had aged so much, although she still carried herself with dignity. Her worn and hand-some face was now a cobweb of lines. But her eyes hadn't changed. They were the colour of walnuts – sad, yet proud. I introduced her to Neeraj. He tried to touch her feet in respect but she waved him away, as if she felt she was not worthy of such obeisance.

'It's been a long time, Mark,' she said, clasping my hand. 'We've both got older.'

'Pratima,' I said, 'will you sing for Neeraj and me?'

She smiled – a sad smile. 'My voice is old and rusty. Anyway, how can I sing without my "magic"?'

I handed her the brown paper bag.

She smiled again. 'Ah, I see you haven't forgotten. I will sing for you, with my daughter. She sings like an angel. But first,' she said, 'I must give you both food. You have come a long way.'

A bunch of keys hung from a piece of string around her neck. She selected one, glancing at me in embarrassment. 'I'm reduced to this,' she said. 'I have to lock everything up. I trust no one. Everybody steals from me. Even my servants.'

Pratima opened the wooden door of the kitchen and produced some hard-boiled eggs, a loaf of bread and some tea, which she served us in chipped glasses. I asked for a spoon for the sugar. She glanced around as if to check that no one was looking, and then produced from the folds of her lunghi one beautiful silver spoon bearing the Gauripur coat of arms. It was painful to see. Over breakfast, I asked after Parbati. Momentarily, a slight tinge of regret clouded those proud eyes. She told me that they hardly ever saw one another.

It was only nine in the morning, but I could smell the liquor on her breath. She had already taken her 'magic'. Her daughter arrived, a pretty girl with dark eyes and full lips, her face framed in a swathe of long black hair. She was heavily pregnant with her second child and wore a flowing pink maternity gown. Pratima disappeared back into the kitchen for a moment, no doubt for a refill. When she returned, she was smiling.

'We will sing a duet for you,' she announced. 'I sang it when we met last time on the River Sankosh. It is a mahout song.'

The moment Pratima started to tap out a rhythm with a small brass bell against her knee, I recognised it immediately. I was transported back to that misty day amongst the elephants on the banks of the river. The song, like all the elephant songs of Gauripur, was poignant and evocative. It told of a beautiful young girl who falls in love with a mahout while he is capturing wild elephants in a nearby forest. But all mahouts are rogues, and he breaks her heart.

Two angels sang to us that morning in the tumbledown courtyard. Their voices complemented each other's perfectly. Not a note was dropped as Pratima sang first, her familiar low voice as soft as falling rain. Then her daughter joined in, soaring effortlessly to the higher notes; and then together their voices, like a bird caught by the wind, hovered for a moment and were swept gently away, echoing, fading into the old stones of the courtyard.

I sat transfixed, my whole body covered in goosebumps. Neeraj was weeping.

Pratima smiled quietly. 'It is nice my songs can still give pleasure.' She embraced her daughter. 'Now they will carry on giving pleasure.'

As she walked us out, she stopped and unlocked another door. It was her bedroom, bare except for an old mahogany bed, and a two-tiered table. She touched it reverently, almost as if it were a shrine. In a way it was: a shrine to her life. On the lower shelf, the stuffed heads of a tiger and leopard snarled at me. She had shot them with her father when she was just twelve years old. On the top shelf, on a shred of old scarlet Assamese silk, lay a collection of trophies awarded to her over the years for the gift of her golden voice.

But in pride of place was a framed manuscript, hanging on the wall above the table. It was the Padma Shri, the highest cultural award that the Government can bestow upon a civilian. When you receive the Padma Shri, you become a national treasure. But now this national treasure had been forgotten, discarded, to live almost like a beggar. I felt angry and sad. Although her daughter was undoubtedly talented and could continue Pratima's tradition, no one could replace this great diva. India should hear that golden voice again, before it was too late.

On our way back, Neeraj and I cadged a lift in a canoe to take us back to the *Kailash*. I could hear Bhaiti before I could see him. He was barking furiously. He had finally met his match – in the form of a group of very cheeky, very clever crows. They were every-where, perched insolently like stowaways all over the *Kailash*. They were even, much to Gamma's fury, helping themselves to his garden on top of the cabin.

Bhaiti shot around the boat like a whirlwind, chasing them off, but they would just regroup on the sand. He tried another tack. Slinking quietly down the wooden gangplank, employing his Tripuri Lushai hunting genes, he stalked them like a tiger, crawling across the sand on his belly. Then, he pounced. They rose effort-lessly in a silky black cloud of feathers, cawing impudently and settled back down a couple of metres away. Then they formed a circle around him. They were playing with him. Bhaiti became hysterical; he didn't know which way to turn. One crow, cheekier than the others, even pecked at his tail. Bhaiti howled in outrage. Eventually he slunk back to the boat and positioned himself on the gangplank. He wasn't going to give up. If he couldn't catch them, he was determined to keep them off the boat.

However, perhaps distracted by the crows, the insectocutor had been neglecting his duties. In the kitchen we found Topguy laid out, shaking violently underneath a blanket. The dark, damp galley had become a breeding ground for mosquitoes. I took his temperature. It was nearly 41 degrees Celsius. I was pretty sure he had malaria. He needed medical attention quickly. I had no option but to leave him here, in Dhubri, at a hotel. Neeraj would pick him up on the way back after dropping me at the border.

Topguy was crestfallen. He implored me to change my mind, insisting that he would recover. He desperately wanted to finish the journey. He felt he was letting me down. Topguy had never let me down. But I would be letting him down if I allowed him to continue with us. We gathered his belongings and returned to the ghat in a canoe. I telephoned the District Commissioner. She recommended a good hotel and arranged for her doctor to meet us there.

The hotel was clean and his room was light and airy with a television and a view over the city. Neeraj instructed the staff to look after Topguy like a brother. The doctor soon arrived: he diagnosed a strain of viral fever, possibly pneumonia. Topguy needed rest – lots of it. In the meantime, the doctor would check on him every day until Neeraj returned.

I couldn't have imagined a worse situation in which to say goodbye to my friend. I hugged his shivering body and wished him well. We were both moved by the emotion. I could see the tears in his eyes through the tears in mine.

The crew had built a big fire on the sand spit. It was our last evening in India, and our last night all together, for tomorrow Bhaiti and I would bid the others farewell at Doikhawa, at the border with Bangladesh. But it wasn't the same without Topguy, and neither was the cooking; even though Neeraj did his best as stand-in chef. We lay around the fire, drinking rum and puffing on Gamma's *chillum*, listening to the sounds of India rolling across the water from the ghat; the hymns of worship in the Sikh temple; the laughter of a wedding party; the shouts of the *paan* sellers; the shrill bells of the rickshaws, and the occasional phut, phut, phut as the *bhut-bhuthees* slid past us in the gloom.

As the sky darkened the great dome of the temple was lit up like some fairytale castle. Thousands of birds screeched and squabbled as they fought for a space to roost in the giant peepul trees. An hour later, almost shocking after all that noise, there was silence, just occasionally broken by croaking bullfrogs and the gentle lapping of the river.

The mist was unusually thick when we set off early the next morning. Although Gamma could 'dream' a passage through almost anything, it had been a long time since he had been this far down the river and it had changed dramatically over the years. It was dangerously shallow now and we soon became grounded. Laxman slammed the engine into a lower gear and tried to force us off the sandbank by using more power. If anything, it made the situation worse, digging us in deeper. While we all manned the poles, Pandit dived under the water to check the rudder and found it hanging by just one screw, the sheer force of the collision having ripped it from its cowlings.

We decided to wait until the fog cleared. We could hardly see each other. It was eerie sitting there, the tendrils of mist curling around us like the spirits of drowned *majhi*. An hour later the sun blazed through, bathing us in its warm morning light. We heaved the *Kailash* into deeper water and Pandit secured the rudder. The river was huge here. There was no sign of land. We proceeded in fits and starts with Pandit standing on the prow, poling us off each time we grounded. Gamma just couldn't find the river's path.

Suddenly, a sinuous black shape broke the surface just in front of us and then quickly disappeared. A few seconds later it emerged again, chirping. It was a dolphin – one of the rare freshwater Brahmaputra dolphins that have been almost wiped out by net fishing. He was showing us the way. We followed our friendly guide as he arched in and out of the water, until we eventually hit a deep channel. Then, as if saluting us the dolphin soared clean out of the water, flipped on its side, chirped again and went on its way.

Gamma signalled to Laxman to cut the engines. Climbing on to the top of the cabin, he picked a bunch of marigolds and fashioned them into a garland. He placed it in a little wicker basket, lit some incense sticks and, leaning over the side of the boat, pushed the offering out across the water to give thanks to his river guide.

The river had by now divided into a labyrinth of channels, lined by long, high sandbanks. All of them were dead ends. We were lost again. Gamma decided to backtrack. Almost immediately, Neeraj spotted a small flag – an Indian flag – fluttering just above the rise of a bank on our left. Doikhawa! It must be Doikhawa – the Indian side of the border post. Aditya couldn't be far away.

Gamma moored the *Kailash*. Neeraj and I sprinted up the bank to find a little Border Security Force outpost – a neat sandy compound across which a volleyball net was strung, surrounded by small thatched huts. We were stopped by a bewildered and suspicious soldier. He was armed. Neeraj and I peered down the barrel of an automatic rifle. Hastily, we raised our hands. Neeraj explained our situation. The soldier gestured with his rifle for us to follow him. We entered the compound where Neeraj soon befriended the corporal. It turned out that they were both from the same part of the country.

But pleasure at this discovery soon gave way to disappointment at another. We quickly found out this was not in fact Doikhawa. Doikhawa was farther down the river, and the corporal couldn't

give us permission to carry on until his commanding officer arrived
back from patrol. The corporal was most hospitable, bringing us
biscuits and tea, while we waited in the shade of his boss's quarters.
I knew this man was trouble the moment I set eyes on him as he
strutted in like a turkey. He was a non-commissioned officer – a
Sikh, with a chip on each shoulder as big as his oversized epaulettes –
and he spoke good English.

'What are you doing here, sir?' he demanded.

I explained our situation, patiently at first, but I could feel the
anger rising. Neeraj felt it too, and patted my arm to calm me
down.

'You cannot go to Doikhawa. No boats can go to Doikhawa.
No boats are allowed.'

I had to get to Doikhawa. It was now the seventh. Aditya would
be waiting with the Bangladesh Rifles to welcome us. Impatiently
I shoved my passport under his nose. 'You see, sir,' I hissed, 'it says
I'm allowed to enter Bangladesh by the Brahmaputra, from India.'

He inspected it briefly, scornfully. 'That is from Bangladesh
authorities, not from India.'

'I have got permission,' I said through clenched teeth, '*from*
India. From the Superintendent of Police in Dhubri. He told me he
would alert the Border Security Forces at Doikhawa of my arrival.'

'This is not Doikhawa,' he snapped. 'No one has alerted us, sir.
Anyway, who is going to stamp your passport – your exit visa?'

'You . . . ' I bit my tongue. 'You are, sir.'

He drew himself up. 'We are not immigration, we are soldiers.
We do not issue exit visas. The only place you can leave India is at
Mankachar. Even there you will have trouble. It is closed border.
To get there, you must take boat to Halidaygunge, two miles from
here on left bank of river.' He flipped his hand dismissively. 'Then
you take road to Mankachar.'

I leapt out of my seat. 'Now, listen here,' I shouted. What was
this crap about a 'road'? I was going by river. I had permission to

bloody well go by river, and this idiot was trying to stop me. 'I am not going to Mank . . . whatever the hell the bloody place is called. I am going to Doikhawa.'

'You are not, sir,' he replied. 'If you do not give me your word now that you will go to Mankachar, we will impound your boat.'

I stood for a moment, shaking with fury, and then slumped back into the chair. Of course it was not the officer's fault, I realised. It was the chief chicken catcher in Dhubri, the Superintendent of Police who had buggered it all up for me. He had not bothered to alert anybody about our arrival at Doikhawa. He must have known all along that I would have to go to Mankachar. His arrogance had cut out one of the most important parts of the journey – my unique, seamless passage by boat from India into Bangladesh.

Abruptly I stood up. 'Let's go, Neeraj. Let's get out of here. We're wasting our time.'

'Do you give me your word, sir, that you will not go to Doikhawa?'

I nodded, turned on my heel and returned to the boat.

Neeraj tried to calm me down. But I was raging. All I could think of was that policeman in Dhubri. The anger lasted for the hour it took us to reach Halidaygunge. It was such a bad ending to a wonderful trip. Gamma and the boys felt it as well: they had been as excited as me to end the journey by river, and disappointment was etched on all their faces. I hugged them one by one – these loyal, splendid *majhi*. Not only had they been wonderful friends, they had shown me the true magic of the river. I would never forget them. They all fussed over Bhaiti. Gamma had made him a little collar of marigolds from his cabin garden. He tied it around Bhaiti's neck.

I turned disconsolately to Neeraj. 'Well, my old friend,' I said, embracing him. 'Looks like this is it. I can't ever thank—'

'I'm coming with you,' he interrupted me.

'Coming with me!' I exclaimed in bewilderment. 'How? You haven't got a passport.'

'Mark,' he said, 'I *have* passport. And I think it better I come with you. You are like bomb. Bomb will explode soon. There will be more trouble. I can help. When meeting Aditya, I return.'

I wasn't going to argue. In fact, I breathed a sigh of relief. The truth was I needed Neeraj more than ever now. I was pretty sure that there would be more problems just ahead at the border. So, his offer gratefully accepted, Neeraj arranged to meet Gamma back in Dhubri in a few days. Then Bhaiti, he and I stood on the bank, watching the battered little *Kailash* puff up the river until it was engulfed by the haze.

In Halidaygunge, Neeraj commandeered a beaten-up old Ambassador taxi. I noticed the number plate. It started with an M – M for Meghalaya. But I'd thought we were in Assam. I couldn't bloody well believe it. We were going in circles. Where the fuck were we? I found out an hour later, after a road journey from hell, when we arrived in Mankachar. Mankachar was plunged in darkness. Because of the fury of the past monsoons, it had been without power for the last three and a half months.

No power meant no lines; no lines meant no communication. We were stuck. Neeraj was having to think for me now. I was in a daze.

Neeraj's desperate cry disturbed my state of fugue. 'Mark! Mark!' he yelled. 'Quick, quick! Bring Leki! Bring Leki!'

'Leki?' I said, looking round in astonishment. I thought Neeraj had gone mad. Who the hell was Leki? As far as I knew, I didn't know anybody called Leki. 'Who the fuck is Leki?' I yelled back.

'Leki,' he yelled. 'Leki, Leki. Trekking stick. In car! Bring fast! Bhaiti's in trouble.'

'Bhaiti's in trouble', magic words that demanded immediate action. I ripped open the boot of the car, grabbed the Lekis and rushed round the back of a dark building to find a furious dog fight in full flow – flying fur, snarling, flashing teeth. Bhaiti and Neeraj were outnumbered. They were being attacked from all sides by a street gang of mangy mongrels. Bhaiti had sunk his teeth into the neck of one of them, while another hung on to his flank. Neeraj grabbed the mongrel by the legs and flung it into the gutter. I threw a Leki to Neeraj and waded in. It didn't take long once the curs felt the sting of tempered steel. Each time I struck, I thought of the Superintendent of Police in Dhubri. It was a good feeling.

Once the dogs had been chased off, I checked Bhaiti. Apart from a missing patch of fur on his left flank he was undamaged, but I quickly put the chain on him. His days of freedom were numbered. We were about to enter the land of dog haters. Inevitably, a huge crowd had gathered. Neeraj asked for directions to the border. Mankachar had nothing to offer. The sooner we got out, the better. For the first time in my life I was actually happy to be leaving Mother India.

After a confusing drive through dark and squalid backstreets, we arrived at a small concrete house surrounded by a bamboo fence – the Immigration Office of Mankachar. It was closed but we could see the flicker of a candle through the window. We banged on the door. A small, balding man wearing a white shirt, a yellow and grey sleeveless cardigan decorated with a tribal motif, smart blue trousers and *chappels* opened it. He gaped at us. We smiled at him.

'Good evening, sir,' I said. 'We've come to get our passports stamped. We want to go to Bangladesh. You are the Immigration Officer?'

'Yes, yes, yes,' he said, looking very puzzled. 'I am Chief Immigration Officer of Mankachar, but I've never stamped passport – not in all my seven years here. Nobody crosses here. It is closed border. But please come in,' he said courteously.

I noticed his hands were trembling with excitement. The Chief Immigration Officer of Mankachar had just met his first clients.

Mankachar, he told me, had once been a regular crossing point for trade between India and Bangladesh. But due to the massive exodus of Bangladeshis fleeing their country, and smuggling, India had closed the border many years ago. I knew well from newspaper reports that tensions between Bangladesh and India over immigration ran high, particularly along this stretch bordering the Indian states of Assam and Meghalaya. Today, although precise figures are impossible to calculate, they say as many as 150,000 Bangladeshis cross illegally into India each year. It is a bitter endless feud, and the soldiers regularly shoot people who stray near the border.

Over innumerable cups of tea, Neeraj explained about our journey. I produced my documentation – the letters from the Bangladeshi authorities welcoming me to their country – and wearily described our problems with the border security forces blocking my river passage. For a moment, the Chief was silent, as if pondering a huge decision. He took a deep breath, got up, stood on a chair and pulled down an old, thick ledger from the top of a cupboard. He blew the dust off it and placed it reverently on his desk.

'This, sir, is immigration book. I must fill up with all your details. Please give me moment. I have not done filling in before.'

He twisted the cap off a fountain pen, his hands shaking even more. 'Now, sir,' he said excitedly, 'please start from beginning.'

It took an hour for him to transcribe in his beautiful handwriting my entire family history, starting with the names, places and dates of birth of my paternal great-grandfather, grandfather, and my father. And then the names, places and dates of birth of my maternal great-grandfather, grandfather, and my mother. Then he wanted to know the names and dates and places of birth of my sisters. Then my wife's good name, her father's good name, and finally my good name, date and place of birth, occupation, and date of entry into India. It took him two minutes to fill in Neeraj's form. He finally laid down his pen. He had filled up two pages of the ledger.

'Well, sir,' he said happily. 'That is all fully correct.'

'Excuse me, sir,' I said. 'What about my dog?'

'Ah,' he said. 'Your dog is not my department. That is Department for Custom and Excise.'

'Well,' I asked, 'can we go there?'

'No, no, sir. My friend, Chief Officer of Custom and Excise, Mankachar is in full bed rest. First thing tomorrow morning, we will go. But,' he whispered conspiratorially, leaning towards me, 'I can hurry procedure up by stamping passport now, with tomorrow's date.' He beamed with pleasure, delighted by his ingenuity.

This took another half an hour as he could not find the passport stamp. He eventually located it on top of another cupboard, blew more dust off it, dabbed it into an ink tray and with a great flourish stamped my passport. He laughed uproariously, 'Ha, ha, ha, ha. You have left India, but you are still here.' Tears were running down his face. 'Now,' he said, wiping the tears from his eyes, 'we must go to Zero Point.'

'Zero Point,' I asked. 'What's that?'

Clearly this was a big adventure for the Chief. 'Zero Point,' he said in awe, 'is where you leave India and enter Bangladesh. We must meet with Border Security Forces to alert them to full and complete crossing tomorrow.' Now this sounded exciting. Another Bond-like mission.

We piled into the taxi and set off down a narrow potholed road, hemmed in tightly on both sides by small bamboo houses. The road, if you could call it a road, came to an end and turned into a sandy track. To my left, I could make out the shape of a tall barbed-wire fence.

'Zero Point,' the Chief whispered excitedly, and told the driver to stop the car.

Our driver did not seem to understand. He simply drove on, without any lights. For a man of some years, the Chief moved quickly. He whacked the driver hard over the back of the head, causing him to slam on the brakes, and then scrambled frantically out of the car and yelled into the dark night.

'No shoot! No shoot! No shoot! Please no shoot. Chief Immigration Officer,' he yelled even louder. 'No shoot!'

In the silence I heard the familiar sound of automatic weapons being cocked, and then we were illuminated by a blinding search-light. Neeraj threw himself on to the floor of the car. I grabbed Bhaiti, wrenched open the door and threw myself into the sand. There I lay on top of Bhaiti, covering my head with my hands. It only took a few seconds but it seemed like an hour. Cautiously, I raised my head to find a heavily sweating Chief Immigration Officer surrounded by a group of heavily armed soldiers. They shouldered their rifles reluctantly.

We had been lucky. It would have been the last straw to have been shot dead trying to leave, not enter India, at Mankachar, a closed border. The Chief soon organised everything with the Border Security Forces. We arranged to meet early the next morning at Zero Point before crossing into Bangladesh, and dropped him back at his office.

'Please be here 5.00 a.m. precisely,' he said. 'My friend, Chief Officer of Custom and Excise, Mankachar will return from temple by then. Goodnight, sir.'

'Goodnight, sir,' I said, 'and thank you.' Thank you for *every-thing*.

Our next problem was where to spend that 'good' night. Back in our taxi Neeraj suddenly did something totally out of character. The driver received his second whack over the head that evening. Then Neeraj grabbed him from behind, pulled him out of the driving seat, climbed into it and took over.

'What the hell are you doing?' I asked.

'I'm driving,' Neeraj said.

I wasn't going to argue with that. 'But where are we going?'

'To police station.'

'Police station!' I yelled, 'I'm not going anywhere near chicken catchers. They've already buggered up my journey enough. They'll bugger it up even more. Forget it.'

'Please to be calm, Mark. I will organise all.'

Twenty minutes later, we pulled up outside the Police Headquarters of Mankachar. I refused to come in and sat sulking with Bhaiti in the back of the car. Neeraj soon returned, grinning, accompanied by a policeman who was hastily tucking his tunic into his trousers.

'Everything full and total control,' Neeraj said. 'I am speaking to District Commissioner in Dhubri. She's on line. She wants you.'

Still in a rage, and ignoring the policeman, I marched into the office and picked up the radio receiver. Annoyingly, it was one of those press-button jobs, like a walkie-talkie. I pushed the button. 'Hello, hello, hello. Hello, madam,' I said. I released the button.

'Hello, Mark,' a soft voice crackled down the receiver. 'There's something very important I have to tell you.'

I pushed the button. 'You can say that again, madam. My whole trip has been . . . ' The line started to crackle. 'Hello, madam. Hello, madam.' I released the button.

'Yes, Mark,' she answered. 'As I was saying, you must send it to me immediately.'

I pushed the button. 'Send what, madam?' I released the button.

'Your address, Mark, your address in London. I will be coming soon. I would like very much to meet you there.'

I couldn't believe it. I pushed the button. 'Madam,' I said firmly, 'I hardly think it's the time to talk about your visit to England when I haven't even got out of your country. Anyway,' I shouted, 'I want to make an official complaint . . . ' The line started crackling again. I released the button.

'Oh, how *lovely*, Mark,' she said. 'You live in the *country*. I've never been to the English country. I hear it's lovely.'

I sighed. I was getting nowhere. I pushed the button again. 'Yes, it is lovely, madam,' I said. 'I'll send you my address and thank you for all your help. Goodbye.'

'Goodbye, Mark,' she trilled. 'See you in England.'

I had to laugh. The whole thing was just too surreal. 'Where are we sleeping?' I asked Neeraj.

'At Circuit House,' he said. 'Driver can fuck off now. Chicken catchers do the needful,' he smiled. 'District Commissioner's orders.'

Grudgingly I shook the policeman's hand. While Neeraj went off to make arrangements for the next day with the police, I was shown to the Circuit House. There was only one bedroom, with three beds in it. One of the beds was occupied – but not for long. A dishevelled-looking man wearing a lunghi leapt out and pumped my hand enthusiastically. He was a magistrate. He had been posted down here for the last three and a half months. I could see he wanted to talk, a lot. My bed beckoned me enticingly from the other side of the room.

The magistrate slumped down in a chair and opened a bottle of rum. 'You know,' he said, 'you know what I do? I work from six to nine each day. Then I come back, shit-tired. Then I get shit-drunk. You want to get shit-drunk with me?'

Desperately, I looked for a way out. It was Bhaiti, as usual, who came to my rescue. In the darkness of the bedroom, he had found prey, a rat. He chased it relentlessly around the room, finally executing it neatly right under the magistrate's chair. Now completely shit-drunk, the magistrate lurched to his feet and scrambled quickly to the safety of his bed. The old caretaker arrived, asking if I would like some food. I held up the savaged rodent by its tail and gave it to the old man.

'Thank you,' I said, 'but I've already eaten.'

*

A posse of police jeeps with sirens wailing carried us swiftly to the Chief's office the next morning. We were bang on time. 5.00 a.m.

'Good morning, sir,' I said. 'Is your friend from Customs and Excise here?'

'No, sir,' he replied. 'He is in bathroom.'

'Oh,' I said.

We waited half an hour.

'Er,' I enquired politely, 'is he going to be a long time in the bathroom?'

'Oh, no, sir,' he replied. 'He's not in bathroom. He has gone temple. Very religious man. Brahmin.'

'Oh,' I said.

We waited another half an hour. He finally arrived. The Chief Officer of Customs and Excise was almost an exact replica of the Chief Officer of Immigration. They could have been twins. He was extremely excited. He pumped my hand vigorously. We walked to his office, next door. He settled back behind his desk and took out another ledger. His office was covered with posters advertising auctions of recently seized contraband – 250 kilos of rice, 150 kilos of apples, 22 crates containing 241 oranges each, and other such exciting goodies.

'Now,' he announced formally, 'will you be having anything to declare? A gift?'

'One gift,' I said. 'A dog.'

'Ah, dog,' he said, rubbing his hands together. 'Who gifted dog?'

'A friend,' I said. 'A friend in India.'

'Mmmm,' he mumbled. He wrote something on a page in my passport, and stamped it. 'You are cleared, Mr Shand,' he said, handing it back to me. 'Please be enjoying your journey.'

'Thank you,' I replied. I studied the page of my passport. It was interesting reading. 'Reported in L-C-O MCR on 09.12.98 at 7.30 hours for his departure to B/desh along with E/Dog, Small size.'

'Sir,' I asked, 'What exactly is an E/Dog, Small size? Do you mean a small English dog?'

'No, sir.'

'Well, is it a small European dog?'

'No, sir.'

'Well, what is it then?' I asked, bewildered.

'It is alsatian dog, sir,' he replied, 'Small size.'

This was confusing. 'But,' I argued, 'he's not an alsatian dog. He's an Assamese dog. Why don't you change your entry in my passport to A/Dog, Small size. Then he can both be Assamese and alsatian dog.' It seemed to me a very logical solution.

'No, sir,' he said firmly. 'He's alsatian-type dog – E/Dog, Small size.'

I realised I was getting nowhere. I was now officially the proud owner of one alsatian-type dog – E/Dog, Small size.

Everybody piled in the jeeps. We followed the same route as the night before and soon arrived at the place where we had nearly been shot – Zero Point. To my left, through the tall barbed-wire fence I looked into Bangladesh – a flat caramel carpet of fields, in which hundreds of people were working. In the distance, I could make out a small village.

We screeched to a halt opposite a large wooden gate: the entry point to Bangladesh. Opposite the gate was a heavily fortified compound, with sandbags shaded by mango trees. A table had been laid out with biscuits, oranges and tea. We chatted to the soldiers.

At exactly 8.41 a.m. the Border Security Force guards opened the gate. A strip of land about a hundred metres wide and demarcated by red flags stretched out before us. This was no man's land. We bid farewell to the two Chiefs and to the soldiers. The soldiers saluted us. We stepped into no man's land. Immediately, the gate was closed behind us. Carrying our rucksacks, we stumbled across a little furrowed field until we reached a line of blue flags. This was the border. We stepped over. At long last, though unfortunately not by river, we had entered the 'land of Bangla'.

Bangladesh is a country that over the centuries has evoked mixed reactions among its visitors. In antiquity it was known as 'golden Bengal'. The Moghuls called it the 'paradise of nations'. Fa Xien, a Chinese Buddhist pilgrim who visited Bangladesh in the fifth century, was impressed 'by its great structures and the prosperity of the land'. Marco Polo called it 'a land populated by wretched idolaters with a peculiar language'. A fourteenth-century Moroccan visitor from Tangier, Ibn Battuta, called it, 'a hell crammed with blessings'. And in the seventeenth century when Saheedf Beg had been nominated Viceroy of Bangla, he exclaimed, 'Ah . . . your Majesty could find no better place to kill me than Bangla.'

Bhaiti formed his own impressions very quickly. He sniffed the little blue flags suspiciously, stepped over them, and like a good, loyal Hindu dog cocked his leg in the land of Bangla.

FOURTEEN

'Well, Neeraj,' I said, shaking him by the hand, 'welcome to Bangladesh.'

'Well, Mark,' Neeraj said, shaking me by the hand, 'welcome to Bangladesh.'

We collapsed in laughter. We had finally made it, but just where we were was quite a different matter. A crowd of curious onlookers surrounded us – more than a crowd in fact, a great, jostling, gaping throng. We looked at them. They looked at us. Neeraj opened the batting. The floodgates opened as they all started talking at the same time, waving their arms around in different directions.

'What are they saying?' I asked Neeraj.

'People say go Rowmari. Twenty kilometres from here. Nearest important place. Bangladesh Rifles are there.'

'Ask them if they know where Doikhawa is.' A hundred and fifty heads nodded. It was difficult to ascertain if this was a yes or a no. One or two pointed vaguely in various directions.

'OK,' I said to Neeraj, 'we'll head for Rowmari. Maybe the

Bangladesh Rifles will know something about us. They might even know where Aditya is.'

For a few rupees, three young boys shouldered our rucksacks. We set off like a little army along the top of the nullahs, criss-crossing the dusty fields. As we walked along, I began to take stock of my surroundings. The terrible destruction caused by the monsoons on this unfortunate land was pitifully evident. Every square centimetre of ground was being tilled and turned by groups of emaciated men, their shoulders stooped in despair as they tried to eke a living and provide food to feed their families from the crumbling, dusty soil. There was no laughter, not even from the children. They gazed at me, their big, brown eyes filled with sadness, their bellies distended from malnutrition and famine. Even the cattle and the goats were muzzled to stop them eating the crop. Bangladesh, in just a few miles, had touched me with its despair. I did not feel easy being here amongst all this misery – a foreigner from a land that had never known the meaning of hunger. I wanted to get on the river fast, and get to the sea. I felt like a ghoul – a ghoul with a dog.

Still, the ghoul with the dog gave these poor people something else to think about for the moment, something to take their minds off their misery. At every little village, Neeraj and I gathered more troops until we soon commanded a large army. But in the end, I am ashamed to say, I lost my patience. There were just too many of them, pushing up against me, gawping, shouting, chattering – particularly one garrulous young man, a chemistry student, who, of course, wanted to practise his English. Neeraj invented the perfect ploy. I was wearing very dark sunglasses. Neeraj told the crowd that I was blind and that Bhaiti was my guide dog. It worked like a dream, for although this astounding news actually gathered more people as it spread like wildfire through the villages, they respectfully kept their distance and left me and Bhaiti in relative peace.

A couple of hours later, after crossing two small rivers in canoes, we arrived at Rowmari. In the monsoons, the town had been totally submerged. I could see the water marks clearly, high up on the buildings.

Our porters guided us to the Bangladesh Rifles headquarters. They weren't helpful. I did not blame them. They had more important things on their minds than the journey of an Englishman and a dog. Infuriatingly, however, we did discover that they had in fact received a signal to expect me at Doikhawa, where a detachment had been waiting for me for two days. I asked where Doikhawa was. Twenty-five miles upstream, they said, on the right bank of the river. I couldn't believe it.

Neeraj suddenly arrived with a policeman. Unlike Dhubri, Rowmari's Chief of Police was polite, courteous and helpful. If it hadn't been for him, I would never have found Aditya. He escorted us to his office where he fed us, took away our passports, which were returned in half an hour stamped by both Customs and Immigration, and gave me the use of his private loo where I managed to clean up a little. He was not even put out when Bhaiti, having finished his own lunch, forgot his manners and climbed up on to the desk to help himself to the Chief of Police's. We waited and waited as he patiently dialled and redialled, effectively blocking the only communication out of Rowmari, attempting to get through to Kurigram, the District Headquarters, to try and locate Aditya. After an hour, he got a connection and left an urgent message for the District Commissioner to call him back. Half an hour later, the telephone rang. The policeman picked it up, listened for a moment, and handed it to me.

'Where the hell have you got to?' Aditya roared down the line. 'I've been waiting for two days for you. So has everybody at Doikhawa. There was a big welcoming committee for you.'

The red mist descended on me again. 'Bastard,' I shouted.

'What!' he bellowed back angrily.

'Sorry. I didn't mean you,' I yelled quickly. I explained to him what had happened in Dhubri. 'Where are you, by the way?'

'In Kurigram,' he shouted. The line was hissing and crackling. I could hardly hear him. 'But we're leaving now for Chilmari.'

'Have you got a boat?' I yelled.

'Yes, yes, yes,' he yelled back impatiently.

'Fully stocked? All supplies aboard?'

'Yeah, yeah, yeah,' he yelled back, 'Don't worry. Full control here.'

'Where the hell's Chilmari?' I yelled back again.

'Dunno!' he shouted. 'Ask the chicken catcher. Can't be far. I'll meet you at the . . . ' The line went dead.

Chilmari, we found out, was almost exactly opposite Rowmari, on the other side of the river. We could reach it by country boat, a local ferry – if we hurried. The Chief of Police checked his watch. The ferry was leaving in half an hour. Fuel, like everything, was in desperately short supply around here. I will never forget that policeman's kindness as he ferried Neeraj, Bhaiti, me and all our baggage in two journeys to the ghat on the back of his motorbike. We just made it in time. The ferry was jam-packed. Neeraj, who had arrived first, managed to find us a little space on top of the deck, which soon widened as Bhaiti stepped on board. I waved goodbye to the policeman. I did not even know his name.

If I thought the Brahmaputra was big, it paled in comparison with the Jamuna, the Bangladeshi name for the river. There was absolutely nothing to see, except a sea whose banks have shifted constantly over the centuries. As far back as 1809 Major James Rennell, the 'father of Indian geography', had completely given up trying to trace them as they had undergone such changes. Even in the last twenty years, the Jamuna has completely eroded its banks nine miles inland. Chilmari was in danger of disappearing altogether. It was, I knew, a town famous for good brass utensils, bell metal plates, and cups for cooking and eating. Excellent, I thought. Aditya could restock the boat's galley here. And the name Chilmari meant the 'place of eagles' – *chils* – named by the

Moghul sportsmen who slew them in great abundance. They had obviously done a good job. Unlike India, there were no birds of any kind around here. I think birds feared for their lives in these desperate parts.

I struck up a conversation with one of my fellow passengers, a sweet old man who spoke perfect English. He lived in a coastal town farther down the river. He had come to help out his family who had suffered badly during the monsoons. I asked him about the floods.

He spread his hands in despair. 'These were the worst floods I can remember,' he said. 'And our people are used to floods. Each year they come. But this year it was as if Allah was angry. Ninety per cent of my country flooded. Sixteen million people homeless. Thousands died. Even our capital, Dhaka, was affected. Our aeroplanes could not take off or land.' He sighed, spreading his hands. 'But we do not blame the river. It is our destiny. The river is in our blood. It rules us. It has its own will and power. It cannot be placated. It does not see. It does not hear. It does what it wants.' He looked out for a moment at the river that does what it wants, and then back to me. His eyes, I noticed, were angry. 'It is the Government we blame. They do nothing for us here. We get no relief. We sit on top of our homes and watch our children, our families die in front of us from disease, like my granddaughter, and my son this year. If medical relief had come, they would be alive today.' He looked away again. The sun was setting – a huge, orange, flaming orb sinking silently into the river. He unrolled a small mat and placed a white cap on his head. 'Please excuse me, sir, it is time for my prayer.' He prostrated himself towards the west, towards Mecca, across the river that had taken his family, calling out to a greater power.

We reached Chilmari in the early evening. It had a big ghat with several large boats moored along the bank. I noticed a familiar figure standing like an admiral, his hands behind his back on the prow of a sleek metal launch. I waved frantically. He waved back. I knew it – Aditya never let me down. What a boat! We would finish this journey in style.

Hauling myself up on to the deck, I slapped the Maratha's hand. 'Aditya,' I said, 'you're a genius! Look at this boat!' I gazed around me in wonder, taking in the bridge, its roof bristling with all sorts of exciting antennae. The deck shook as the powerful engines rumbled. 'We'll be in the Bay of Bengal in a jiffy. Fantastic!'

'What *are* you talking about?' he said.

'The boat – you're a genius. How did you wangle this one?'

He sighed. 'This is not our boat, Mark. This is a government boat. Ours is there,' he pointed farther up the bank.

'Where?' I asked. All I could see was a line of long, slim canoes with rounded cabriolet tops made from bamboo matting.

'That one – the one in the middle. It's a little cramped, but it's a good boat.'

'Jesus!' I said, 'We're travelling in *that*?'

'What did you expect?' he replied irritably. 'This is Bangladesh, not San Tropez.'

I looked longingly as the smart crew swarmed around in preparation for departure. 'Christ,' I said. 'Who the hell is that?' I had suddenly noticed a Danny La Rue lookalike with bouffant hair, dyed bright orange, staring at me intently through a pair of pink-framed dark glasses.

'Ah,' Aditya said, grabbing me by the shoulders and pulling me farther along the boat. 'Let me explain quickly, so you get the drift. That is the manager of the Bangladesh National Tourism Organisation. You were right, my friend,' he continued. 'Our journey was in danger of turning into a kind of promotional jolly for Bangladeshi tourism. As you see, he is not cut out for this kind of lark. He nearly shat himself up on the border. I really put him through the mill. It's taken a lot of Maratha diplomacy, but now he's dying to get the hell out of here. Just meet him, thank him, and,' he added, 'be sure to say how sorry you are that he's leaving. That's all.'

Danny La Rue reminded me of one of those large colourful fish that hang around coral reefs – the ones with those rubbery, grey lips.

He spoke in a plummy English accent, enunciating precisely each vowel. 'It is an honour – a great honour – to meet you, Mr Shand,' he said, grasping my hand in a sticky fin. He handed me a card. 'Welcome to Bangladesh.'

'Thank you. It is an honour to meet you as well,' I said obsequiously. 'I hear you've been a great help to my friend, Aditya. It sounds like you've had quite an adventure.'

'Oh, Mr Shand,' he exclaimed, patting his bright orange bouffant hair. 'It was nothing. It was only my duty as senior representative of my country's tourism.'

'Well, I hear you're leaving us. What a pity. It would have been wonderful to travel with such an exper—'

Aditya nudged me, whispering urgently through clenched teeth. 'Don't overdo it. The bugger might stay.'

But there was no way he was going to stay. He was longing to go back to the comforts of Dhaka. 'Well, Mr Shand,' he announced, 'I think you're in safe hands now. The dangerous part is over. Mr Aditya has been most kind to relieve me of my duties.' He coughed delicately, covering me in a slime of little bubbles. 'I'm having most awful congestion of chest.'

'Well, you go and relax,' I said. 'Thank you for all your help, and,' I lied, 'I'll contact you when we reach Dhaka.'

'Bone veyoge, Mr Shand and Mr Aditya,' he replied.

'Bon voyage,' I replied. We watched him squeeze his large body into the front seat of the Landcruiser. Aditya and I made our way along the top of the bank to our little boat. 'By the way,' I said, 'where's Shaams?'

Aditya pointed to a small figure standing on top of the roof next to Neeraj. Neeraj was not tall, but compared to Shaams, he was a giant. Shaams was snapping orders at the crew in quick, staccato sentences.

'What's he like?' I asked.

He laughed. 'Shaams is OK. He does everything by the book. Like clockwork. He's always checking lists, and he wants to know exactly how much everything costs. He's a typical tea planter. He's full of bravado, but I'm not sure it'll last too long. I don't think he quite knows what he's got himself into. He's used to quite a sheltered life.'

I knew what he meant. I had been a regular visitor to the tea estates of Goodricke's in India, the sister company of Duncan's in Bangladesh where Shaams worked as an assistant manager. The companies' concern for the welfare of their employees – from managers to tea-pluckers – was legendary.

The moment I met Shaams, I knew I had found *the* candidate for my cupboard full of extremely useless travelling accessories. Shaams was gadget man. He wore one of those Japanese watches which told the time in a hundred different countries, combining stopwatch, calculator and musical alarm.

He introduced himself in a curious way. 'I'm Shaams,' he said, shaking me firmly by the hand. 'And this is Magi.' Magi was black, heavy and long. Magi was a torch – a Maglite. He thumped it up and down in his hand. 'Magi,' he said, 'is good for blinding and beating. I'm beating many people with Magi. Magi will be useful on this trip. There are many robbers on the rivers.'

'Well, Shaams,' I said. 'Let me introduce you to a friend of *mine*.' I pulled out one of my Leki Trekkies from my rucksack, extended it to its full length and thumped it up and down in my hand. 'This is Leki, Shaams. I don't beat people. I beat dogs with Leki. But only dogs that attack my dog.'

His sharp little eyes glittered excitedly. His little black moustache twitched nervously. 'How much cost?' he demanded.

'I don't know,' I said. 'Probably about fifty quid.'

'What fifty quid?'

'A quid is one English pound, Shaams.'

He quickly made a calculation on his wristwatch. He whistled. 'Exactly 4100 takas. Magi only 2350 takas.' He eyed the Leki with longing. Shaams was a funny little guy. He was cocky, aggressive and full of energy. He just could not sit still.

We had a crew of four *majhi*: Mukram, whose father owned the boat, Zahir, his brother, Shahalam, and Sukumuddin. They were totally different from the *Kailash* gang. They were downtrodden, desperate. They all had sad eyes.

The boat was their lifeline. It was used for fishing and for transporting goods like jute, hay, wood, in fact anything that would feed their families. It was a typical country boat, about six metres long, its hull hewn from one piece of solid timber, and decked throughout with bamboo. Inside it was low – one had to stoop – and divided into three compartments, opening out on to a long pointed prow.

The design of these slim, elegant boats has not changed for centuries, except for one ingenious addition that has recently revolutionised river transport in Bangladesh – the engine. But this was no ordinary piece of machinery. It was a tubewell pump engine that had been converted for river use to avoid paying the heavy import tariff imposed on boat engines made overseas. There is no import duty on tubewell engines. They are cheap and easy to run. Ours was Chinese and made by a familiar company, Dong Fen. It seemed that I was wedded for life to these contraptions: a grumbling, puffing engine that had once powered my house in Bali; one that had not so long ago powered me up the steep Tibetan plateau; and now another that was going to power me down the river.

With a deafening roar, Dong Fen exploded into life and we moved farther down the ghat for the night to avoid the noise and the relentless mosquitoes. Bhaiti soon found his place – in my sleeping bag under the prow. I asked Aditya what had happened on the border.

He laughed. 'I'll tell you later over a drink. It's quite a story. I found it pretty grim up there. I've never seen such poverty – such devastation. Those poor people.' He sighed. 'Somehow doing this journey makes me feel . . . makes me feel like a . . . '

'A ghoul?' I suggested.

'Yeah. That's the word. A ghoul. It's got to you as well? The sooner we get down this river, the better.'

'At this rate, it won't take long,' I replied. We were fairly clipping along. 'Out of interest, what's the boat costing?'

'It's so cheap,' he said, 'it's embarrassing.'

Shaams interrupted. 'Exactly 1034 takas per day,' he said, after a quick calculation on his wristwatch.

'What's that in pounds?'

He tapped the calculator again. 'Twelve quid. Aditya bad bargainer. Expensive.'

Aditya and I looked at each other in astonishment. We somehow doubted that Shaams had *ever* experienced the real Bangladesh.

We reached a quiet place on the ghat and moored the boat for the night.

Neeraj, Bhaiti and I settled down on top of the bamboo roof. It was chilly – the sky studded with stars like chips of ice. I was hungry and looking forward to dinner. It was not what I expected. Our supplies consisted of two large bottles of Black Label scotch, four cartons of Benson & Hedges cigarettes, two crates of Tiger beer, twelve cases of Duncan's mineral water and three tins of Fox's glacier mints – fruit flavoured. There was no food and nothing to eat or drink from, no plates and no mugs.

I looked at the pile in amazement. 'You call this stocking up?'

'I most certainly do,' Aditya replied indignantly. 'All the essential – the *really* essential items – are here. Here,' he said, 'have a fruity Fox's glacier mint. They're delicious.'

I was gobsmacked. 'But what about the food – the proper food? And what are the crew going to eat?'

'It's all arranged,' Aditya replied dismissively. 'They've got a little rice on board – enough for them. After we cross the river back to Rowmari tomorrow to drop Neeraj, we're stopping at Mukram's village a little farther downstream. He's going to pick up some plates and things, and we can get some grub there. It won't hurt you to starve for a night. Anyway,' he added, 'I didn't have time. It was a choice between Danny La Rue and starvation.'

He had made the right decision. 'But what are we going to drink from?' I asked, eyeing the Black Label longingly.

'Improvisation, my friend.' He grabbed Bhaiti's shiny metal bowl and filled it half with scotch and half with mineral water.

'What about Bhaiti?' I asked. 'What's he going to eat?'

'He can drink as well,' Aditya said. 'He's a river dog.'

Bhaiti didn't starve that night. The faithful Neeraj managed to steal a little rice from the crew, which Bhaiti ate from a banana leaf, while we used his bowl.

After several rounds of bowls, Shaams announced he was tired. He disappeared below and crashed out.

Aditya filled up the bowl again, and handed it to Neeraj. 'Now,' he whispered, 'let me tell you what happened on the border.'

It was a typical Maratha story of carefully planned logistics, diplomacy and ingenuity. It had as well, he pointed out to me with relish, a frisson of danger. He was operating in enemy territory. Shaams had met him at Dhaka airport. He was dressed in typical tea planter's gear – shirt, shorts, long socks and trainers. He was carrying a small bag containing a lunghi, a toothbrush, toothpaste and some shaving equipment. And Magi. Shaams had clearly never left a tea garden. At a market Aditya equipped him with a towel, some blankets and a waterproof. Next stop was the hotel. The Maratha decided to test Sham's ingenuity and inclination. He sent him on a mission to find refreshments, in a land where liquor is forbidden. Shaams passed with flying colours on both counts, soon returning with two bottles of Queen Anne whisky, camouflaged in polythene bags. That night, as the Maratha described it, he 'loosened' Shaams up a little.

The next morning they picked up the second member of the Bangladeshi team – Danny La Rue. The Maratha realised immediately that Danny had to go. Using all his diplomacy, he suggested that perhaps this kind of journey would not be suitable for such an important executive from the Bangladesh Tourist Corporation. However, Danny had his orders. In fact, he was rather put out by Aditya's suggestion. Aditya decided to bide his time. Danny quickly changed into a suitable adventure outfit – a two-piece grey safari suit – and packed a large suitcase. They then climbed into a Landcruiser and drove the eight and a half hours north to Kurigram – a journey not without incident. In the most densely populated country in the world, driving is hazardous. The driver managed to claim not one, but two victims. Both survived. They were seen picking themselves up off the road and limping into the darkness. However, Shaams, a veteran of Bangladeshi roads, ordered the driver to drive on immediately. If they stopped, they would be lynched.

They stayed the night at the Circuit House in Kurigram. The next morning they met with the District Commissioner, who had been fully briefed on my imminent arrival. Accompanied by a small squad of the Bangladesh Rifles, they walked six kilometres across the sandy, dried-up riverbed to where a launch was waiting to take them upriver to Doikhawa. Danny was ill-equipped for such a journey. His feet turned to a mass of blisters and his face soon resembled his hair – streaked by orange swathes of hair dye.

The launch took them to Doikhawa, a sandy spit where a line of stone pillars, a hundred metres long, demarcated Bangladesh from India. The Bangladesh Rifles had set up a reception committee under an awning. Four or five chairs surrounded a little table covered with a pretty tablecloth. A splendid tea was laid out. After tea the Bangladesh Rifles hoisted a blue flag – a signal to the Indian Border Security Force that a meeting was necessary. The moment the flag was raised, the Indians, whom Aditya could see clearly, disappeared.

They waited. Nothing happened. The commander suggested Aditya send a note. Aditya wrote an explanatory note in English. One of a group of small boys, who act as couriers, took it across. An hour later, the boy returned with another note. All it said was 'Thank you.' The Indian commander did not understand English.

What to do? Aditya suggested that he walk across with his arms in the air, holding up his passport. The Bangladesh Rifles became very anxious. Relations were tense here. Aditya could get fired on. Aditya did not want to be shot, particularly by soldiers from his own country. Another solution was hatched. The Bangladesh Rifles commander would write a note himself. He knew the English alphabet. He wrote the note in Hindi but in Roman script. The boy dutifully took the chit back across. A few minutes later, history was made. For the first time ever, the Bangladesh Rifles and the Indian Border Security Force, sworn enemies, crossed no man's land and sat down and had tea with one another. The Maratha had become a diplomat.

The Indians knew nothing of my arrival. Nobody had informed them. Aditya requested that if I did turn up they alert the Bangladesh Rifles, who would in turn alert him in Kurigram. Aditya would wait there until noon the following day. The enemies who had become friends shook hands warmly, and then went back to being enemies.

At about 11 a.m. the next day, the District Commissioner in Kurigram received an urgent message from the Chief of Police in Rowmari that Mr Shand had arrived. Aditya went to the ghat and hired the boat to take them all down to Chilmari, much to Danny's alarm. He clearly wanted to return in the comfort of the jeep, but he could not lose face. During the journey to Chilmari, Danny was terrified even though they were accompanied by a soldier. At every moment, he thought they were going to be attacked by robbers. He was also cold and hungry, and was suffering from hypertension and a congested chest. Aditya worked on him relentlessly.

When they reached Chilmari, Danny was putty in Aditya's hands. He asked Aditya if Mr Shand would be upset if he did not accompany us on the rest of the journey. Aditya told Danny that Mr Shand would certainly not expect a senior executive from the Bangladesh National Tourism Organisation to accompany him on such a journey. He would think Danny had already done quite enough, and had much more important things to attend to in Dhaka. Danny was so overcome with gratitude that he embraced Aditya, smearing his face with orange hair dye.

I filled up Bhaiti's bowl with a Patiala 'peg' – four parts scotch, no parts water, named after the Maharaja of Patiala for the infamously strong whiskies that were served in his palace.

'I would like to make a toast,' I said, raising the brimming bowl, 'to my three brave Indian friends who have acted far and beyond the call of duty, infiltrating enemy lines in extreme and dangerous conditions.' I felt like pinning a medal on all of them. '*Jaimata*, Aditya! *Jaimata*, Neeraj! *Jaimata*, Bhaiti!' I raised Bhaiti's bowl, took a long swallow and handed it to Neeraj.

'*Jaimata*,' Neeraj shouted, handing the bowl to Aditya.

'*Jaimata*,' Aditya growled, putting it in front of Bhaiti.

'Woof,' Bhaiti barked.

I offered around the last tin of Fox's fruity glacier mints. There was one left – the green one, nobody's favourite. They both declined.

'No, no, you must take it,' I said, 'I insist. You deserve it.' I watched Neeraj saw it in half, relishing the tickle of paper against my skin of the most delicious Fox's fruity glacier mint, the strawberry one, that I had secreted in the folds of my lunghi. 'By the way,' I said, 'has the boat got a name?'

'Not yet,' Aditya said. 'We've got to give it one. Why don't we name it after Shaams?' he suggested. 'After all, it's a Bangladeshi boat.'

We all thought, in silence.

'I've got it,' Aditya said suddenly. 'Let's call it the *Koyel*. The koyel is the national bird of Bangladesh, the magpie robin. It's aggressive, chirpy, noisy and always poking its beak into other people's business. What do you say?'

'To the *Koyel*,' we shouted, emptying Bhaiti's bowl.

Aditya had made a good choice, I thought later as I tried to wrestle my sleeping bag away from Bhaiti. In the old days the magpie robin, because of its aggression, had been trained to fight by the country people of Bangla.

It took us most of the next morning to cross the Jamuna from the right to the left bank – from Chilmari to Rowmari. We had to fight the current. Rowmari was a little farther north than Chilmari. At the ghat, Aditya and I hugged Neeraj. I presented him with one of my Leki Trekkies.

'No, no, sir! Er, boss! Er, Mark.' He grinned. 'All Lekis will be needful in this country.'

'Okay,' I said. 'Send my blessings to Topguy and the *majhi*, and see you soon.'

He bent down and hugged Bhaiti. Bhaiti gave him a special lick – a lick under the chin, one reserved only for the people he really loved.

Neeraj shouldered his rucksack and climbed on to the bank. 'May Bolenath be with you,' he shouted, steepling his hands.

'Bholay Shankar,' Aditya and I shouted. He started to climb up the bank.

'Neeraj,' I called.

'Sir? Er, boss? Er, Mark?'

'Try not to get shot.'

We headed due south. In the early afternoon we picked up speed as if the river had gained momentum, pushing us even faster over a surface that had now become choppy, muddled, a labyrinth of whirling currents. We had reached a confluence where the Tista meets the Jamuna. In the monsoons, the Tista thunders down from its fountainhead on the border of Nepal and Sikim, crossing the exposed slopes of the Himalayan foothills, gathering soil and silt, adding to the estimated 150 million tons that the Jamuna brings down from the north each year.

I felt like a spider in an emptying bath being swept towards the plughole, the plughole of the Bay of Bengal. Bangladesh is a huge drain into which the whole subcontinent dumps its waste. But the rivers bring life and forgiveness to this plughole of a country. Water *is* Bangladesh. Ten per cent of the people live in boats. Up to 50 per cent depend on the sea and rivers for their livelihoods, and everybody depends on the rain and floods for food.

We were travelling on the cusp of two seasons: *seet*, from the beginning of November when the flowers start to bloom and the dew is heavy, and *basanto*, when the mornings are misty, the days are warm and the nights are crisp and chilly. These two seasons follow *hemanto*, which begins at the end of the rains in September and finishes in November. It is this season that raises Bangladesh from its watery grave to once again become a land – an ever-changing land. A new country emerges in the shapes of islands, peninsulas, and, most importantly, the *chars*, those rich deposits of soil and silt that give life back to people, on which they can plant and harvest, maybe for just a few months, but enough time to fill the bellies of their families.

This year was different. As in so many areas in the world, weather patterns are changing, due, the experts say, to deforestation and global warming. Seasons are becoming something of the past, all blending into one. In Bangladesh so much rain had fallen that all the great rivers flooded simultaneously, turning the country into a virtual sea.

If I had made this journey at the same time last year, I would, as I stopped at Mukram's little village, have seen the people vibrant and happy. The flowers would have been blooming. The golden jute would have been harvested, lying in bundles like the silken tresses of some medieval princess's hair, waiting to be taken to market. The villages would have been buzzing with the sounds of country fairs. The children would be laughing – diving, splashing and playing in the shallows of the riverbanks. But not this year – the year of the worst floods in centuries. There was no laughter. No planting, or harvesting of jute. The people were still in shock after three months, wearily picking through the debris of their lives. And they were angry, just as the old man told me on the ferry – not with the river, but with the Government. The hundreds of stories which Shaams translated were horrifying, each more terrible than the last.

For three months these people had sat on their makeshift homes watching helplessly as the river became a sea – a sea bloated with corpses. The corpses of unknown families and of their own fami-lies, the corpses of leopard, deer and elephants from the jungles of Assam – all this roared past them in a deluge of death. Then came the diseases – the cholera, the typhoid and all the rest, quickly draining the essential fluids from the bodies of these already des-perately sick people. There was no medical relief. The Government did almost nothing for three months. A couple of supply ships arrived with a little wheat, rice and biscuits. A family of fifteen was given only nine kilos of rice. A dignified old woman, rich by village standards a few months ago, told us that she would die a beggar.

There was no press coverage. The disaster was embargoed by the opposition party who controlled these areas, desperate to play down the devastation and avoid the bad publicity. An angry old man told us that in the 1970s the President, Sheikh Mujibur Rahman, had eaten well. Now his daughter the Prime Minister, Sheikh Hasina Wajed, ate well too. 'While they eat,' he said, 'we starve.'

These people had nothing – yet they gave to us willingly. Mukrum's mother supplied pots and pans, and mugs. We bought a little coarse rice and dhal. But there were no vegetables. We purchased firewood, the splintered remains of the people's houses. Mukram's mother washed the prow of the *Koyel* with river water, blessing it and her sons for a safe journey. The crew were very nervous. Piracy and murder were rife around here.

The river widened and deepened as we passed squat white tugs pulling barges filled with railway carriages on their way to the ghat at Bahadurabad, a big railway depot connecting with Dhaka. Near the ghat, the Jamuna sweeps imperiously past another river – a river that gave birth to her. It is the old Brahmaputra, now just a silt-laden canal that meanders slowly east of Dhaka to join with the Padma, south of the capital. Until 1797, this was the main course of the Brahmaputra, but massive flooding, which killed a third of the population, caused it to change course and it became the great artery that splits the country in two.

We weaved in and out of thousands of little canoes, each carrying a lone fisherman. They stood like bronze statues, waiting for a bite on their long lines, or movement in their nets. The crew called out desperately, '*Mach*?! *Mach*?! *Mach*?! Fish, fish?!' They would turn slowly, spreading their hands in despair, their hooks and their nets empty. Bangladeshis live on fish. It seemed that even the very essence of their country, that oily protein, had mysteriously disappeared from the waters.

Later in the evening, little dhows danced in and out of the mist like fireflies, their bows lit up with hurricane lamps, dragging nets in their wake – empty nets. At a little ghat, we managed to buy a few small bony fish from a fly-infested stall. They were not fresh, but they were food.

The crew cooked them on a little fire made from rotting bamboo from the *Koyel*'s deck. They offered them to us. Aditya and I declined. They needed it more than we did. Shaams quickly joined the crew to share the meal. The journey was beginning to take its toll on the chirpy little tea planter. He was becoming morose, complaining of hunger and pains in his legs.

The crew were horrified when I fed Bhaiti a little of our dhal and rice first. It was beyond their comprehension. I could understand their reaction. Dogs were not a priority around here. The rice was coarse and stank, but washed down with plenty of whisky it didn't taste too bad.

In the early hours of the morning, we were awoken by Bhaiti. He was standing on the riverbank, his hackles up, barking furiously. In a confused jumble of legs, arms, sleeping bags, a flying Leki and a heavy Magi, Aditya, Shaams and I leapt up on to the shore. Shaams switched on Magi, its powerful beam just illuminating a group of figures slipping swiftly away. We could hear the slap of their bare feet on the sand. The crew were terrified. The youngest, Shahalam, was up to his waist in the water, preferring to take his chances with the river.

Aditya and I sat down and praised our faithful guard dog. Shaams danced up and down like an angry ferret, waving Magi and yelling a fusillade of insults at the fleeing robbers. 'Seora bacha!' he yelled. 'Haram zada! Tor mayere chudi! Torpachay bamshbibo!' When he calmed down, I asked for a translation. Shaams had not held back. Sons of pigs, bastards, he had called them, telling them that he would fuck their mothers and shove bamboo up their arseholes. We had been lucky – because of Bhaiti. From now on, the crew treated the Tripuri hunting dog from the Lushai Hills of Assam with the utmost respect.

The horror that these wretched people had suffered during the monsoon months on the upper river was really brought home to

Aditya and me late one night, as we walked Bhaiti across an empty sand *char*. Like Mukram's village, every other little makeshift settlement we had visited on our way down the Jamuna had revealed the same tragic story. But nothing had prepared us for what we found that night. It was the final nail in the coffin.

Bhaiti had run off into the cold evening mists. We heard him barking in the distance. A few minutes later, he returned, wagging his tail happily. He was carrying something – a dog's ultimate treasure – a bone. He dropped it at my feet, looking at me expectantly, as if he wanted me to throw it and start a game. I picked it up. It was bleached white and felt cool in my hand. It was a little bone. It looked like the femur of a child. We followed Bhaiti across the powdery sand.

Bhaiti started digging furiously and we watched appalled as he uncovered first a skull, and then a rib cage and finally a whole array of splintered shards. He had found a macabre ossuary, the remains of villagers swept away by the river during the monsoons. Here they had rested, rotting in a watery grave until the river subsided. The sun and a scavenger had completed the task. I grabbed Bhaiti roughly and threw him behind me in anger. He looked hurt and bewildered as he sprawled in the sand. How was he to know? To a dog, a bone is a bone. I picked him up and stroked him gently.

Aditya dug a hole in the sand. Carefully we replaced the remains and marked them with a tangle of driftwood. It was not much, but it was the best we could do. I wondered how many others lay beneath my feet, their human remains mixed with the bones of animals washed down from the jungles of Assam.

The next day, it was a graveyard of a different kind that caused the *Koyel* to lurch and weave, and then, like a surfboard, pick herself up and surge across the swells of the river. Here the most holy river in India, the Ganges, the mother of all rivers, joins with the Jamuna, or the Brahmaputra, the father of all rivers, bringing down not only the silt of India but its ashes: the ashes of the

millions of Hindus who have been cremated over the centuries on
its sacred banks. Together they flow as the Padma, the 'lotus
flower' spreading its petals towards the ocean.

We were now nearing Dhaka, a city that owed its position and
prosperity to the Ganges. In the sixteenth century, the Ganges
changed its course and headed east, transforming Dhaka into a
main commercial and trade centre by linking it with the rest of
Moghul India and – through the Bay of Bengal – the rest of the
world.

Crossing the river to Aricha, a busy steamer and train terminal
on the left bank of the Padma, we hit traffic. Tugs plied up and
down, puffing out great plumes of smoke, darkening the clear blue
sky. Passenger ferries packed to the gills steered dangerously close,
their horns blowing imperiously, warning the little *Koyel* to move
out of their way. Flotillas of wooden dhows laden with wood,
goats, chickens and cattle floated impotently, their scraps of sail
billowing occasionally in a breath of wind.

On the banks, garish hoardings advertising Coca-Cola, cars and
washing machines towered over a flowing lava of pastel, as women
poured down the ghat to bathe and collect water in large metal
pots elegantly balanced on their heads. Mango and orange
orchards surrounded concrete houses, their roofs exploding with
clusters of antennae. And the constant, tinny sound of pop music
echoed out across the water.

The *Koyel* veered suddenly, avoiding the bloated corpse of a
dead cow, its body covered in a black gloss of wings as the crows
squabbled in a feeding frenzy. Bhaiti had slunk out from his home
beneath the prow to join us on deck. He rushed up and down the
boat, barking in frustration at his old enemies. Insectocutor was
back in action – a whirling, snapping ball of brown fur – executing
the thousands of flies that had descended on the *Koyel* from the
banks of the river.

Trouble loomed as we hooked a net, invisible below the surface

of the river, attached to bobbing little plastic bottles that littered
the surface of the river. We found ourselves surrounded by angry
fishermen in canoes, who threatened us with drawn knives. Shaams
rose to the occasion by pretending to be a policeman. He yelled at
them, hurling a tirade of insults, informing them he was going to
board their boats and ram not bamboo but Magi up their arses.
They dispersed quickly. Although uncontrollable, net fishing is illegal. This method of non-selective catching has almost wiped out
the fish of the river, by taking not only mature fish but babies, the
breeders of the future. Through the evening mist an armada of
dholias, the broad, beautiful, high-prowed wooden cargo boats
that have plied these rivers for centuries approached us – in ones,
twos, threes – and then in lines of fifty roped together. Like ghost
ships, they glided silently by, the fluttering of a hurricane lamp at
the stern briefly illuminating the pilots, the only proof that they
were manned at all. Then, as they passed, the thunder of their
engines echoed back across the river.

It was our last night on the *Koyel*, and our last night of peace.
Tomorrow we would hit the bedlam of Dhaka. There we would
say goodbye to the boat and her crew. From Dhaka we would take
alternative transport to tackle the Meghna: the largest river isthmus
in the world and the gateway to the sea, the end of our journey in
the Bay of Bengal.

It was foggy and cold the next morning when we turned left up a
small canal to join the Dhaleshwari, the busy feeder that connects
Dhaka with the Padma and the sea. Bhaiti, Aditya and I huddled
together on the prow, watching the early morning bathers in the
shallows, ducking, soaping and ducking, and then relaxing for a
moment, floating in the gentle current. The wail of the muezzin
echoed tinnily across the river, calling them to prayer.

We joined the Dhaleshwari. Like a magician lifting his cape
the mist dissipated, revealing a riotous streamer of colour, noise,

movement and madness. The capital's main feeder had woken up. There was not a moment to lose.

Old and new jostled for space in many different craft. Dhows, piraguas, *oolaks*, *dholias*, and *pulwars*, powered by sail, oars and pole and driven by converted engines, mixed with gaily painted ferries, tugs, steamers, trawlers and tankers. They carried cargoes of jute and mud, hay and rice, goats and buffaloes, bricks and bamboo, cooking pots and coconuts, trucks, cars and oil. It was like a time warp – nothing essential in all this rivery bedlam had really changed for centuries. Ever since the advent of Islam, Dhaka, the 'city of the kings', has revelled in its significance as the hub of trade. Routes gradually opened up by land along the Grand Trunk Road as far as Afghanistan, by sea from the Bay of Bengal east to Burma, Java and China, west to the Arab countries and beyond to the Mediterranean. And it became the great crossroads for sailing ships carrying rice, jute, silk and ivory from the Indian subcontinent, tea from China, and spices from the Moluccas. As the great Moghul empire flourished vessels arrived from Persia and Turkey, bringing priceless carpets, jewels, delicate coloured glass, the great Muslim teachers and the Sufi mystics.

As I sat on the prow of the *Koyel* watching the scene unfolding in front of me, I reflected that John Masefield could have found inspiration here for his evocative poem 'Cargoes':

> *Quinquireme of Nineveh from distant Ophir,*
> *Rowing home to haven in sunny Palestine,*
> *With a cargo of ivory,*
> *And apes and peacocks,*
> *Sandalwood, cedarwood, and sweet white wine.*
>
> *Stately Spanish galleon coming from the Isthmus,*
> *Dipping through the Tropics by the palm-green shores,*
> *With a cargo of diamonds,*

Emeralds, amethysts,
Topazes, and cinnamon, and gold moidores.

Dirty British coaster, with a salt-caked smoke stack,
Butting through the Channel in the mad March days,
With a cargo of Tyne coal,
Road-rail, pig lead,
Firewood, iron-ware and cheap tin trays.

With no disrespect to the poet, the scene moved me to add a stanza of my own.

Brave Bangla country boat with a long bamboo prow,
Weaving down the river through the thick winter fog,
With a cargo of whisky, cigarettes and sweeties,
A Hindoo, an Englishman and an Indian river dog.

There was a pecking order on the river as we followed the flotilla inland. It was like being on a busy motorway, with no central reservation. By law the incoming boats should keep to the left, and the outgoing boats to the right. But the river knew no laws and there was the added confusion of crossing traffic. Being a small, humble country boat, we tucked in for safety behind a *dholia* piled twelve metres high with straw. The pilot steered it ingeniously, sitting on top of the haystack, his foot attached to a long rudder. Behind us, belching smoke, a small iron ferry followed, so laden down with a cargo of mud that it was only an inch from the waterline.

Zahir got bored by the slow-moving queue. He tried to overtake the haystack, pulling in quickly as a ferry painted like a mosque powered by with horns blaring. We pulled up at a lay-by, where a line of tiny boats with domed bamboo awnings sat bobbing gently in the shallows. They looked like floating dog kennels. I was excited, for the inhabitants of these kennels were the Bahdi, the river gypsies, who for centuries have traded herbal medicines and the pink freshwater pearls found in the molluscs in the river's silt.

References to these 'teardrops of nature' can be found in the ancient Indian Vedic texts, fifteen hundred years before the birth of Christ. Alexander the Great and Julius Caesar were bewitched by these rosy gems. I wanted to buy some pearls to make necklaces for my wife and daughter.

Shaams and I managed to squeeze into one of the gypsy boats. The interior was neat and simple, just a sleeping mat and shelves full of pots and pans. A wooden chest took most of the space – no doubt, I thought, the repository of their treasure. I was to be disappointed. It opened to reveal only cheap little plastic trays full of modern cosmetics. The Bahdis' days are numbered. Occasionally they sell the pink pearls – small ones for around two pounds, bigger ones for five or six – but they hardly bother any more. Cheap cosmetics are a much more lucrative business and the molluscs are fast disappearing, mashed up to make lime.

We rejoined the waterway, whipping out quickly between a small open ferry filled with white-capped pilgrims on their way to a mosque, and a slow-moving country boat carrying sheaves of golden jute stalks. Teetering precariously on the crumbling banks of the river stood a tumbledown *rajbari*, its faded façade glistening wet with morning dew. These palatial little palaces were once the homes of the rich Hindu *zamindars*, or landlords, who were influenced by European tastes – a strange mishmash of Victorian, Georgian and neo-Renaissance architecture.

As we neared Dhaka, the bedlam increased. Shipwreckers swarmed like ants, ripping apart the rusty bones of retired sea-going vessels. At a boatyard, sections of brightly painted wooden boats in reds, greens and yellows, lay in the sun, waiting to be pieced together like blocks of Lego. A cricket team, dressed in whites, practised near a brick foundry, its chimney belching out a filthy black fog that mixed with the exhausts of the boats,

darkening the sky in a brown smog. A river kite wheeled patiently
above in the air, biding its time, and then flashing down between
two boats to extract a mid-morning snack. Groups of little boys,
on seeing a white face, hurled themselves into the water to risk
their lives to swim towards us among the river traffic. They hung
on to the sides of the *Koyel* asking for money. I doled out handfuls
of coins. Their little brown faces lit up with pleasure as they dived
back in, wriggling towards the safety of the banks. Other, larger
creatures swam even more gracefully around us – freshwater dolphins. There were lots of them, arching out of the water just in
front of our prow. These clever, adaptable mammals had finally
found a safe haven, however polluted, from the nets of the open
river. They had become scavengers.

The river narrowed as we joined the Buriganga, which flows to
the south of the old city of Dhaka. Floating restaurants now occupied the river banks, keel to stern, adding a certain air of grandeur
to the madness. On one, the *Mary Anderson*, white-coated waiters
served lunch to Bangladeshi businessmen entertaining their foreign clients under green, blue and red umbrellas. The Ganga Pura
bridge loomed just ahead. A huge hoarding advertised the wonders
of Femenol – low-dose birth-control pills – obviously not much in
demand in a city with an exploding population of nearly twelve
million. Zahir shut down the engine as we approached the river
terminal at Sadarghat. He wanted to bid us farewell in midstream
here rather than at the terminal itself, so he could slip in and out
quickly to avoid damaging the little wooden *Koyel* against the steel
hulls of the hundreds of ferries that steamed to and from the ghat.
We packed our gear for a quick getaway and bid farewell to the
crew, wishing them a safe journey back north.

Zahir waited patiently and then surged forward between the
departure of one ferry and the arrival of another. The *Koyel*
stopped gently against the rusty old pier. Thousands of people
descended on us as we climbed ashore. I started to wave goodbye

but the boat was already gone, back into the endless flotilla. I
turned around, straight into the embrace of a mad woman. She
cackled insanely and squeezed me tight, pressing her hideous, blistered face against mine. Forcibly, I extracted myself, and then
Bhaiti from a display of fly-infested dates that he had pounced on
for a spot of insectocution.

We were swept by a multitude of porters towards our transport – gaudily bejewelled, extravagantly tasselled, psychedelically
painted three-wheelers – the infamous rickshaws of Bangladesh.
Dhaka is the rickshaw capital of the world, with an estimated fleet
of six hundred thousand plying their trade and causing immense
bicycle jams. We hired three. With Bhaiti and me in one, Shaams
and Aditya in another, and our baggage in the third, we set off and
joined the river of bicycles that flowed like an iridescent ribbon
through the streets of Dhaka.

I didn't take to Dhaka with its population of twelve million,
swollen each year by the influx of desperate people fleeing the
countryside. It is fast turning into one of the biggest cities in the
world, and it is already the most polluted. A filthy, lethal cocktail
of lead, unburned carbons, construction dust and auto fumes hung
like a permanent black storm cloud over the place. I found I could
not breathe at all, let alone smoke. Forget the therapists, hypnotists
and the nicotine patches, all of which I had tried unsuccessfully. A
couple of hours in a rickshaw was all it took.

Fortunately Bhaiti and I were hermetically sealed, for the brief
time we stayed there, in the luxurious air-conditioned apartment
reserved for executives at the headquarters of Duncan's Tea.
There I started smoking again, read the papers and watched the
cricket on television, and Bhaiti and I were waited on hand and
foot by the resident Jeeves while Aditya and Shaams set off to
find a boat.

I also received a fax from Neeraj. It was alarming reading.

Dear Mark,
<u>About crossing border</u>

After leaving you in Bangladesh, I went to police station and met the inspector who had helped us when we were at Rowmari earlier when we had reached there from India. It was almost getting dark but somehow I along with inspector travelled on motorbike as quick as possible to cover the uneven route with a view to crossing to Mankachar at the earliest.

When we reached visibility was poor. The friendly inspector told me about the disturbance there in the village because of killing of three smugglers by the security guards day before while they were trying to sneak into Bangladesh not caring to respond to the repeated warnings by the security guards.

I was advised by the inspector not to take risk but I was obliged to take decision before the nightfall to move further towards the border flagline that is the entry gate which was about 1400 yards away from me. My life was at stake. The inspector could not go beyond that as it was limit for him.

I thank him for all the help he rendered to me. I shall never forget these moments. Now it was for me to decide further course of action before it was too dark. I paused for a while. I remembered Bolenath with my whole heart and started moving forward towards the entry gate holding my passpost in my one hand and heavy duffel bag in other. There was no one insight nearby.

After I had walked a few yards I heard the sound of firecrackers. It was difficult to distinguish between sound of a bullet fire and a cracker.

I started shouting holding my passport in a raised hand that look, I am Indian. I heard the sound of bullet from a distance but immediately there after there was total silence and no sound of any kind. In a while I realized that I was near the entry gate. But here much to my horror I was suddenly attacked by the dogs.

I do not know whether they were from India or Bangla side but they were furious ones. I wished for Leki to drive them away, then suddenly I heard sound of selfloading rifle. I was accosted and asked as to what I was doing. I told that I was trying to whisk away the dogs. I was asked to stay where I was. I told that I was Indian holding a valid passport.

I was told that it was not the time to cross the border. But the guard told me that he would have to take permission from his seniors. I requested him to allow me to be on the other side. He at last accepted my request and allowed me to cross the border. I heaved a great sigh of relief when I was in India. Those were always unforgettable moments which made me to cover the whole episode in 10 minutes which would have otherwise taken 40 long minutes. It was my undaunted courage which saved me from bad situation.

I reached to the waiting *Kailash* ahead. Never ending memories with me. Thanks for every thing my friend. This is the end of this episode when I was left behind.

May Bolenath be with you for rest of journey. Neeraj.

In the evening I took Bhaiti for 'walkies', armed with a newspaper which I had fashioned into a pooper-scooper. We sneaked outside on to the little roof garden surrounded by beautiful climbing plants, reserved for senior executives. We only hit the streets once, to change money. The currency office was just across the road. It took us an hour, not because the money changers were inefficient, but the traffic was so heavy that Bhaiti and I could not get across.

While I had been relaxing, Aditya and Shaams had been less fortunate. They had spent most of their time back at the river ghat trying to find a boat, bartering with the union bosses, the rogues who control the river traffic. They returned just as we were settling down to a TV lunch of ice-cold beer, fish and chips and ice cream for me, and steak and rice for Bhaiti, served on trays by Thomas. The cricket had just started.

Aditya was irritable and hot. 'Right, you two, move your arses. Pack up. We're leaving. I've found a boat.'

'What kind of boat?' I asked vaguely, my eyes glued to the screen as Sachin Tendulkar despatched the first three balls to the boundary.

'You'll find out when you get there,' he snapped.

We avoided the hellish, choking rickshaw ride to the ghat. We travelled in style in an air-conditioned Landcruiser. On our way, we stocked up with essential supplies – mineral water, cigarettes, whisky, beer and, of course, a few tins of Fox's fruity glacier mints. We fought through the crowds at the ghat, avoiding the date seller and the mad woman. A long line of ferries bashed against one another, like hungry pigs jostling at a trough.

'Where's the boat?' I asked Aditya.

'There,' he replied.

'Where?' I asked.

'There – are you blind?' He pointed at one of the large ferries.

I gulped. Aditya really had hired me the *Titanic*. It was called the *Tanvir*. 'Have you gone mad?' I exclaimed in astonishment. 'There's only three of us, and a dog. There must be room for . . . '

Aditya interrupted me. 'Officially four hundred but usually they jam in about seven hundred.'

'Well, er – I mean, couldn't you have found something smaller?'

'Bloody hell,' he exclaimed. 'Are you ever satisfied? A week ago, you were complaining about the *Koyel*. Anyway, I couldn't find a smaller boat.'

'Well,' I said, 'I feel a bit embarrassed. I mean, look at that boat.' I pointed at the ferry that was moored next door to ours.

People were packed in like sardines, fanning themselves with newspapers. A young woman leant over the side and vomited into the water.

'Oh,' he said, his voice edged with sarcasm, 'it's compassion now, is it? Since when have you turned into Mother Theresa? Look at it like this,' he explained patiently. 'Your money will benefit somebody. It'll fill the bellies of some family. The crew, for instance – there are twelve of them. And the captain.'

I was not too sure that the captain needed money to fill his belly. He was dressed in an immaculate white shirt, a silk paisley cravat, and a peacock-blue lunghi, and he carried a smart leather briefcase which would not have looked out of place in the shop window of Hermès. I hoped it was filled with charts. In the waters of Bangladesh some five ferries sink each year, killing on average about a hundred people. And as an additional hazard, we were just on the cusp of the cyclone season.

Bhaiti and I settled down in the comfort of the first-class accommodation – *only* fifty-eight comfortable spongy red seats fringed by lacy antimacassars. The cabin smelt of vomit, sweat and diesel. There was a sign above the entrance: 'Almighty God, Allah, save me from all danger.' And, in large capital letters underneath, 'THIS COMPARTMENT IS TWO TIMES PRICE OF ONE BELOW.' I checked that one out. It was as big as a bowling alley – 342 empty hard wooden seats.

The river took on a different perspective from the high prow of the *Tanvir* as we ploughed down the Buriganga river. Now I could fully appreciate Zahir's driving skills as country boats like the *Koyel* swarmed across our prow like rats leaving a sinking ship. We hit the Dhaleshwari again and were soon engulfed in the filthy fumes of the brick factories that lined the banks. But this pollution was the by-product of an industry that plays a vital role for the people of Bangladesh. Astonishing though it seems, there is virtually no natural stone in the country – just one small quarry. What stone there ever was has long been buried beneath hundreds and hundreds of feet of silt. Bangladesh is built on silt. Its bricks are made from a laterite clay found just beneath the earth's surface. The clay is mixed with a red stain and carbon, while the chippings are ground up and made into a type of concrete.

After crossing the Tropic of Capricorn, we rejoined the Padma and late in the evening berthed in the busy steamer and railway depot of Chandpur. It looked like Dante's inferno, lit up like a concentration camp. A constant spew of humanity poured in and out of the vessels. People shouted, horns and sirens blared, and whistles blew. The air made you gasp from the pervading smell of petrol and diesel that turned the water of the harbour black and shiny, like ink. Thousands of people lay sleeping on the ghat, laid out like corpses swathed in their blankets.

We moored alongside an old navy frigate, covered ourselves in mosquito repellent and tried to sleep. Bhaiti was out of sorts, his nose hot, his fur sticky. He refused to eat and curled up miserably on one of the seats. It was a long, noisy night. Sleep was intermittent. A deafening siren and a blinding white searchlight that lit up the *Tanvir* like a fireworks display announced the arrival of the *ghazi*, one of the huge paddle steamers known locally as the 'rockets', as it swept imperiously into the harbour, dwarfing our four-hundred-seater ferry. It was not the only interruption. Our arrival in Chandpur had coincided with the anniversary of Bangladesh's War of Liberation. On 16 December 1971, the Pakistani Army had surrendered after a short but bloody conflict. East Pakistan ceased to exist and the People's Republic of Bangladesh was born, establishing the 139th country in the world. All night long, tannoys blared out replays of those bloody days – stirring victory speeches mixed with the sounds of war, of falling bombs and the rattle of machine guns.

We slipped out early the next morning. We were finally on the Meghna. The trinity was at last complete. Finally, the three rivers –

the Jamuna, the Padma and the Meghna – had merged to form the largest river delta in the world, an area the size of the Netherlands and Belgium combined. And Bhaiti had recovered, the clean fresh air clearing his little head. He was alert, excited, his beautiful Assamese eyes bright and happy. I could see he sensed too the anticipation that I was feeling, the feeling that descends when one is near the end of a long journey.

We headed due south towards the island of Bhola, in reality just an enormous *char* situated in the middle of the isthmus created over the centuries by the turning of the tides. From there we hoped to pick up a sea-going boat to take us out into the Bay of Bengal. My journey would only end there, when I reached the sea – when I tasted the salt. As we weaved our way through the canals the countryside became lush and fertile, rich with rice fields, banana plantations and tall palm trees that swayed gracefully, as if waving us on our way.

The bird life returned. The Maratha sat up on deck, his binoculars glued to his eyes, twitching, catching iridescent flashes of blue and red as kingfishers flitted from the banks.

We left the *Tanvir* at Bhola and spent the night at the Circuit House. It was empty except for an ancient chowkidar. There was no electricity – Bhola's power was supplied by generator. But it had broken down. No doubt it was made by Dong Fen. We dined on duck curry, spicy popadoms, dhal and rice, cooked by the chowkidar on a fire on the lawn of the Circuit House. The next morning, we left early by motor rickshaw to the sea port of Doulatkhan.

Ironically it was a policeman again who came to our rescue in Doulatkhan. While Aditya and I waited at the police station, Shaams had gone to the little estuary to find us a boat. He returned empty-handed. The seafaring folk of Bangladesh, descendants of those crafty Arab traders, were more than a match for the bargaining skills of an up-country tea planter.

The policeman was known as Pandit because he was an authority on films. In fact, he was an obsessive movie buff. When the film
Gandhi had come out, he had queued for thirty-six weeks before
getting in. His favourites were the naughty ones, the ones with the
bubbly south Indian girls – unscissored, as he called them. His
record was twenty-three unscissored videos in one day. But there
was one film that stood way above the rest – *Last Tango in Paris*.
He had watched every performance while it was showing. He
described it as 'full daring, and full unscissored'.

Pandit had more success striking a deal with the sea folk. They
would drop us at Chittagong, Bangladesh's biggest port situated on
the long spit of the country that stretches south, bordering Burma.
Our new boat was fifteen metres long, deep-keeled for sea passage,
and built in Chittagong from *chapla* wood. It was a brave, jolly
little craft. It reminded me of a pirate boat. Its sweeping prow was
decorated with a crescent moon and stars of shiny beaten metal. It
was called *Oh God*.

The galley, the crew's quarters and the convenience were at the
back. Our captain and owner Ahmed had his cabin amidships in a
dark little harem covered with fat, embroidered pillows. The light
was soft and diffused, filtering through the coloured glass windows shaped like Moghul arches. By the time we had bought our
provisions it was too late to set sail, Ahmed told us, so we slept the
night there, on a square of open iron decking, surrounded by a filigree of metal fretwork designed like peacocks' tails. Overhead,
little multi-coloured flags criss-crossed the deck, attached to
bamboo poles.

Ahmed was jolly, irreverent and very fat. He wrapped his head
in an old towel to protect it from the sun. His fingers were always
firmly stuck up his arse, trying to extract the folds of his lunghi
from the rolls of his flesh. He was a real sea dog and captain of a
crew of seven.

We caught the noon tide the next day and chugged slowly up the little estuary into the Shahbazpur channel, waving goodbye to hundreds of children running alongside on the bank. Setting a south-easterly course, we joined a procession of vessels – cargo boats, tankers, and hundreds of little fishing dhows, their scraps of sail ballooning as the fresh wind sent them skimming across the choppy waters. The sky was indigo blue. Gulls and terns followed us, screeching in our wake.

As we rounded the northern tip of Hatiya Island, the water began to change colour, from muddy brown to muddy blue. I threw a bucket overboard and tasted the water – not even a tinge of salt.

Later in the afternoon, the wind got up, pushing formations of grey wispy clouds across the sky. I shivered nervously, remembering a previous experience on a boat when I had been shipwrecked by a hurricane off the Solomon Islands. The Bay of Bengal is the world's most infamous area for cyclones. People still talk about the cyclone of 1970 in which 500,000 people died. And the one of 1991 which, although much more violent, killed only 200,000 people, thanks to storm shelters – the long rectangular concrete bunkers that lined the shores of Hatiya.

The clouds began to melt away, dispelling my fears, and *Oh God* cut through a sea the colour of freshly spilled blood. Ahmed stopped the engines and we drifted up a small deep channel between a labyrinth of emerging islets. I argued with Ahmed. I wanted to move on, to sail into the night towards the sea that seemed to be trying to elude me. I was running out of time. Ranesh was waiting for me and Bhaiti. But Ahmed wouldn't risk it: the passage by night was far too treacherous in these ever-changing waters.

The rich new soil of the *chars* was a haven for the watery waders, and flocks of sandpipers, greenshanks and Indian skimmers patrolled the shallows. Overhead, sea eagles soared in the thermals. After supper, Aditya, Bhaiti and I climbed up on to the metal deck. We lay back in our sleeping bags, listening to the wind tugging at the flags overhead and to a chorus of snores from Ahmed and Shaams in the harem below. Aditya soon joined in with the chorus. Bhaiti and I crept quietly off the deck and made our way to the prow. We curled up together in my sleeping bag and eventually, lulled by the soft rocking of the boat, fell asleep.

By 9 a.m. the following day, everybody was fed up with me. We had been heading south since the early hours of the morning, and were now passing the southern tip of Sandwip Island. Every hour, I had chucked a bucket over the side. Every hour, I had tasted muddy water. Where was the bloody sea?

'If we go on much longer,' Aditya exclaimed in exasperation, 'we'll hit the Antarctic. We've nearly passed Chittagong. For Christ's sake, Mark, this is the sea.'

'It's not,' I replied stubbornly. 'It doesn't taste of salt.' I had to find salt. Salt meant sea. Sea meant the end of my journey. Only then would I accept I had succeeded. But where was it? On a map, I was in the Bay of Bengal. The Bay of Bengal is a sea. It could not be that hard to find. The beginning of my journey had been difficult enough. Every time I had tried to cross a border, it had been chaos. Surely the ending wouldn't be as muddied and frustrating as all the rest. Perhaps the river went on forever.

Aditya sighed, and went over to appease the crew. But they did not have long to wait. A few minutes later, I yelled at Ahmed to stop the boat. The water in my bucket was salty! I had reached the sea! It tasted like champagne. A swift current ran close to a muddy bank, just visible beneath the water line. I climbed over the side of the boat. Ahmed warned me to be careful. The bottom was soft – quicksand. He had seen many a man sucked under in seconds. There was no seabed here – no stones.

But Ahmed was wrong. There was one stone – a magical stone that I had carried all this way wrapped in a handkerchief, just for this moment. I had plucked it from a tiny glacial stream high on the roof of the world where the river was born, and brought it here to the Bay of Bengal, where the river ended its long journey in old age. It was like a gift from a child to a respected elder. I waded out, feeling the cool, silky silt beginning to tug at my legs. I reached into my pocket and unfolded the handkerchief and took out the smooth round pebble. Then I turned towards the north – towards Tibet. I threw the stone and watched it arc through the air, and then drop, barely denting the surface, as insignificant as a falling raindrop, but a symbol of final reunion.

I waded carefully back to the boat. It was time for Bhaiti and me to pay our last obeisance to the river. A reluctant river dog was lowered into my arms. I looked at Bhaiti. He looked at me, those cool, hypnotic eyes clouded with resignation.

'I'm sorry, little brother,' I said, 'but I promise you, this is the *last* time.'

He sighed. I held his nose. I held my nose. Together we ducked below the surface of the sea.

EPILOGUE

I reached home in time for Christmas. The last twenty-four hours had passed in a blur and it was only on the long flight back that I was able to gather my thoughts.

After *Oh God* had dropped us at Chittagong we had driven all the way to the north-east of Bangladesh, to Shumsernugger tea garden, where we said goodbye to Shaams.

By noon the next day, Aditya, Bhaiti and I had reached the Bangladesh–India border at Tamabil, nestling in the shadow of the Jaintia Hills. The border itself was demarcated by two black-and-white-striped poles separating fifty metres of tarmac – no man's land. Ranesh was waiting, waving to us from India. I waved back. Fortunately in this part of the world, animals do not need passports. If I could get Bhaiti to enter India without me, I thought, I would avoid the inevitable bureaucracy. And I hate long drawn-out farewells.

I knelt down and took off Bhaiti's lead. Then I hugged him tightly. He stared at me with those cool, hypnotic eyes and then, I could have sworn, he winked at me.

'Catch you later, little brother.' I said. 'Be good. Ranesh,' I shouted, 'call Bhaiti! Call him!'

'Bhaiti!' Ranesh shouted. 'Come, come, come! Bhaiti, come!'

The little Tripuri hound from the Lushai Hills of Assam looked at me questioningly and then walked slowly under the pole towards India. He kept pausing and turning back towards me.

'Come, come!' Ranesh shouted. 'Come Bhaiti!'

Halfway across, Bhaiti stopped. He looked at Ranesh. Then he looked at me. The dog that once was from nowhere, was nowhere again – in no man's land.

'Come, come Bhaiti!' Ranesh shouted.

Bhaiti sat down and scratched. He was thinking. He zapped a passing fly. Then, his mind made up, he trotted back into Bangladesh, back to me. As far as Bhaiti was concerned, we were going to finish this journey together.

Two hours later, I walked slowly back across the border from India into Bangladesh, dangling an empty lead. I pulled on it out of habit. This time, it didn't pull back. My passport was now full. It read: 'Exited Bangladesh with E/Dog, Small size. Entered India with E/Dog, Small size. Exited India without E/Dog, Small size. Entered Bangladesh without E/Dog, Small size.'

As I struggled to get comfortable in the cramped confines of my seat, I already missed him. But I knew that soon we would be reunited on the roof of the world, to face the river once again. We were going to have a ball, however hard the journey. With the courage and the companionship that my little river dog had given me, I felt I could take on anything.

But then in January I received disturbing news. The Chinese had closed the entire Tsangpo Gorge area in Tibet, where the river plunges through the deepest valley in the world before crossing into India. Foreigners were banned for what the officials called 'environmental reasons'. The river in Tibet was up to its old manipulative tricks again.

However, I drew my own conclusions. When I had been making my way down the India–Bangladesh section of the Brahmaputra, two American explorers had led an expedition, accompanied by a film crew, into the Tsangpo Gorges. They rapelled down into the last unexplored section of the gorges and made a remarkable discovery. It was the 'romance of geography' that had puzzled explorers for centuries. They had found a waterfall – if not of Niagaran or Victorian proportions, still a waterfall twenty-five metres high. Aptly, they had named it 'Hidden Falls'.

Unfortunately the Americans had upstaged a Chinese scientific expedition that was also searching for the waterfall just a few miles farther upstream. Both claimed to have found it first. The television network that was backing the explorers launched a massive publicity campaign and effectively claimed the prize.

I did not care who had found it first. I applauded both expeditions. A discovery of that magnitude is a truly remarkable achievement, but for a mere traveller like me it had a terrible consequence. It meant I couldn't return to Tibet to complete my journey. They had put an end to my twenty-year dream.

Still, I did not give up. I tried every trick in the trade. I pulled every string in the book. I wrote countless pleading letters to important people. And countless more were written on my behalf. But my pleas fell on deaf ears. There was nothing I could do except wait. I am still waiting, and hoping to complete the last great Asian adventure.

A year later, I returned to India. I went back to my river and my river dog. On the banks of the Brahmaputra I was received with all the affection of a long-lost elder brother. Bhaiti had aged. White flecks now streaked his russet coat and the once coal-black hairs on the tip of his tail. He had picked up a few more scars. His training on the streets of Guwahati had served him well. But age had not dulled the power of those cool, hypnotic eyes, and his breath, as he licked me softly underneath my chin, was as sweet as the day I first met him.

With fraternal pride, I met Bhaiti's growing family, an unruly pack of little hunting hounds, fussed over by their doting mother, Sumo. For the few days I was at Wild Grass, like old river dogs, Bhaiti and I were inseparable.

I made a decision then. Whether or not I ever managed to reach the Tsangpo Gorges, I would not be taking Bhaiti with me. The once homeless dog was well and truly home. His travelling days were over.

But what of mine?

A few days later, after returning to England, I received a telephone call.

'Mark,' a familiar voice echoed in my ear. 'It's Charles. Charles Allen. Now, do you remember I told you about that penis park? Well . . . '

BIBLIOGRAPHY

I have referred to some of these books in the text and they have all provided helpful background information.

Charles Allen, *A Mountain in Tibet: The Search for Mount Kailash and the Sources of the Great Rivers of India*, 1982

Charles Allen, *The Search for Shangri-La – A Journey into Tibetan History*, 1999

Joan Allen, *'Missy Baba' to 'Burra Mem': The Life of a Planter's Daughter in Northern India 1913–1970*, 1998

K. M. Ameer, *Rain and River*, 1991

F. M. Bailey, *China-Tibet-Assam: A Journey*, 1945

F. M. Bailey, *No Passport to Tibet*, 1956

F. M. Bailey with Henry Treise Morshead, *Reports on an Exploration on the North-East Frontier*, 1913

B. N. Dutta Barua, *The Red River and the Blue Hill*, 1954

K. L. Barua Bahadur, *The Early History of Kamarupa*, 1933

Henry T. Bernstein, *Steamboat on the Ganges*, 1960

Gabrielle Bertrand, *Secret Lands Where Women Reign*, 1958

B. N. Bordoloi, G. C. Sharmah Thakur, M. C. Saikia, *Tribes of Assam*, Part I, 1987

B. N. Bordoloi and G. C. Sharmah Thakur, *Tribes of Assam*, Part II, 1988

B. N. Bordoloi, *Tribes of Assam*, Part III, 1991

Sir Sidney Gerald Burrard, *Explorations on the Tsangpo in 1880–84 by Explorer Kinthup*, 1911

Major C. Chambers (ed.), *Indian Notes about Dogs, Their Diseases and Treatment*, 1881

Major C. Chambers (ed.), *The Care and Treatment of Dogs in India*, 1933

S. P. Chamoli, *Rafting Down the Mystic Brahmaputra*, 1992

Victor Chan, *Tibet Handbook: A Pilgrimage Guide*, 1994

J. N. Chowdhury, *A Comparative Study of Adi Religion*, 1971

J. N. Chowdhury, *Arunachal Panorama*, 1979

J. N. Chowdhury, *Ki Khun KHASI – KHARA (The Khasi People)*, 1996

Ronald Cardew Duncan, *Toma from Tibet and Other Dog Stories*, 1950

Dr P. C. Dutta and Dr D. K. Duarah (ed.), *Aspects of Customary Laws of Arunachal Pradesh*, 1997

Emily Eden, *Up the Country: Letters from India*, 1930

Verrier Elwin, *The Art of the North-East Frontier*, 1959

Verrier Elwin, *India's North-East Frontier in the Nineteenth Century*, 1959

Verrier Elwin, *Leaves from the Jungle*, 1936

Verrier Elwin, *Myths of the North-East Frontier of India*, 1958

Verrier Elwin, *A Philosophy for NEFA*, 1957

Verrier Elwin, *The Tribal World of Verrier Elwin (an autobiography)*, 1964

Abu 'L-Fazl, *Ain-I-Akbari*, translated by H. Blochmann, 1873

Miriam Fields-Babineau, *Dog Training: BASICS*, 1997

Filippo de Filippi, *An Account of Tibet – The Travels of Ippolito Desideri of Pistoia, 1712–1721*, 1932

Richard D. Fisher, *Earth's Mystical Grand Canyons*, 1995

Sir Edward Gait, *A History of Assam*, 1905

U. N. Gohain, *Assam Under the Ahoms*, 1942

Lhama Anagarika Govinda, *The Way of the White Clouds*, 1962

P. J. Griffiths, *A History of the Joint Steamer Companies*, 1979

Lieutenant-General P. R. T. Gurdon, *The Khasis*, 1914

Angus Hamilton, *In Abor Jungles*, 1912

Heinrich Harrer, *Seven Years in Tibet*, 1953

Right Reverend Reginald Heber, Lord Bishop of Calcutta, *Narrative of a Journey through the Upper Provinces of India*, 1828

Sven Hedin, *Trans-Himalaya*, 1910

Sven Hedin, *Southern Tibet: Discoveries in former times compared with my own researches in 1906–1908*, 1917

Joseph Dalton Hooker, *Himalayan Journals*, 1854

Peter Hopkirk, *Trespassers on the Roof of the World*, 1986

Peter Hopkirk, *The Great Game: On Secret Service in High Asia*, 1990

K. M. Sharmul Huda (ed.), *Trade and Industrial Guide*, 1979

W. W. Hunter, *Statistical Account of Assam*, 1879

W. W. Hunter, *Statistical Account of Bengal*, 1876

Frank Jackson (ed.), *The Mammoth Book of Dogs: A Collection of Stories, Verse and Prose*, 1998

Major Ditaram Johri, *Where India, China and Burma Meet*, 1933

Bami Karta Katakati and Punya Prasad Duara, *The Mother Goddess Kāmākhyā*, 1948

Ekai Kawaguchi, *Three Years in Tibet*, 1909

Captain F. Kingdom Ward, *The Riddle of the Tsangpo Gorges*, 1926

Captain F. Kingdom Ward, *Himalayan Enchantment: An Anthology*, edited by John Whitehead, 1990

Captain F. Kingdom Ward, *Assam Adventure*, 1941

John Lockwood Kipling, *Beast and Man in India: A Popular Sketch of Indian Animals*, 1904

A. Henry Savage Landor, *In the Forbidden Land*, 1898

Lonely Planet Publications, *Bangladesh*, 2000

Lonely Planet Publications, *India*, 1999

J. W. McCrindle, *Ancient India as Described by Megasthenes and Arrian*, Calcutta, 1926

A. Mackenzie, *The North-East Frontier of India*, 1979

John M'Cosh, *Topography of Assam*, 1837

Trilok Chandra Majupuria and D. P. Joshi, *Religious and Useful Plants of Nepal and India*, 1988

Geoffrey Masson and Susan McCarthy, *When Elephants Weep: The Emotional Life of Animals*, 1994

Ian Morshead, *The Life and Murder of Henry Morshead*, 1982

P. T. Nair, *Tribes of Arunachal Pradesh*, 1985

James J. Novak, *Bangladesh: Reflections on the Water*, 1993

N. N. Osik, *British Relations with the Adis*, 1992

N. N. Osik, *A Brief History of Arunachal Pradesh*, 1996

Swami Pranavananda, *Exploration in Tibet*, 1955

Swami Pranavananda, *Kailash-Manasarovar*, 1949

Indra Singh Rawat, *Indian Explorers of the 19th Century*, 1973

Captain C. G. Rawling, *The Great Plateau*, 1905

R. Reid, *History of the Frontiers Bordering on Assam*, 1942

James Rennell, *Memoirs of a Map of Hindoostan and the Moghul Empire*, 1788

The Rough Guides, *India*, 1999

Sylva Simsowa, *Tibetan and Related Dog Breeds: A Guide to Their History*, 1979

Smith, Elder & Co., *Report of a Committee for Establishing the Rivers in the East Indies by Steam Boats*, 1839

W. V. Soman, *The Indian Dog*, 1963

R. A. Stein, *Tibetan Civilisation*, 1972

P. D. Stracey, *Elephant Gold*, 1963

Arthur Swinson, *Beyond the Frontiers: The Bibliography of Colonel F. M. Bailey*, 1971

Elizabeth Marshall Thomas, *The Hidden Life of Dogs*, 1993

Giuseppe Tucci, *Santi A Briganti nel Tibet Ignoto*, 1937

Annabel Walker, *Aurel Stein: A Pioneer of the Silk Road*, 1997

David Warrell and Sarah Anderson, *The Royal Geographical Society (with the Institute of British Geographers): Expedition Medicine*, 1998

W. Kenneth Warren, *Tea Tales Of Assam*, 1975

Thomas Webber, *In the Forests of Upper India*, 1902

Colonel Henry Yule and A. C. Burnell, *Hobson-Jobson*, 1903

Gazetteers

Arunachal Pradesh District Gazetteers, Subansiri, S. Dutta Choudhury, 1991

Statistical Abstract of Arunachal Pradesh, 1988

Arunachal Pradesh District Gazetteers, East Siang and West Siang Districts, S. Dutta Choudhury, Government of Arunachal Pradesh, 1994

Gazetteer of India, Arunachal Pradesh, Lohit District, S. Dutta Choudhury, Government of Arunachal Pradesh, 1978

Gazetteer of India, Assam State, Lakhimpur District, Government of Assam, Guwahati, 1976

Gazetteer of India, Assam State, Goalpara District, 1979

Assam District Gazetteers, volume XIII, Lakhimpur, B. C. Allen, Calcutta, 1905

Assam District Gazetteers, volume VII, Sibsagar, B. C. Allen, Calcutta, 1906

Assam District Gazetteers, Sibsagar District, Government of Assam, Shillong, 1967

East Pakistan Gazetteers, Government of East Pakistan, S. N. H. Rizvi, Dacca, 1969

East Pakistan District Gazetteers, Chittagong, 1970

Bangladesh District Gazetteers, Noakhali, Bangladesh Government Press, Dacca, 1977

Bangladesh District Gazetteers, Rangpur, Government of the People's Republic of Bangladesh, 1977

Bangladesh District Gazetteers, Comilla, 1977